AVID

READER

PRESS

Abundance

Ezra Klein
and Derek Thompson

Avid Reader Press

New York   Amsterdam/Antwerp   London
Toronto   Sydney/Melbourne   New Delhi

AVID READER PRESS
An Imprint of Simon & Schuster, LLC
1230 Avenue of the Americas
New York, NY 10020

First Avid Reader Press hardcover edition March 2025

AVID READER PRESS and colophon are trademarks of Simon & Schuster, LLC

Interior design by Ruth Lee-Mui

Manufactured in the United States of America

5   7   9   10   8   6   4

Library of Congress Control Number: 2024951721

ISBN 978-1-6680-2348-8
ISBN 978-1-6680-2350-1 (ebook)

EK: To Annie, Moses, and Kieran: My abundance

DT: To Laura and Isla

Contents

Authors' Note

SOME OF THE DETAILS AND LANGUAGE IN THIS BOOK APPEARED previously in columns, articles, newsletters, and conversations written and produced for the *New York Times* and the *Atlantic*.

Abundance

Introduction
Beyond Scarcity

YOU OPEN YOUR EYES AT DAWN AND TURN IN THE COOL BEDSHEETS. *A few feet above your head, affixed to the top of the roof, a layer of solar panels blinks in the morning sun. Their power mixes with electricity pulled from several clean energy sources—towering wind turbines to the east, small nuclear power plants to the north, deep geothermal wells to the south. Forty years ago, your parents cooled their bedrooms with joules dredged out of coal mines and oil pits. They mined rocks and burned them, coating their lungs in the by-products. They encased their world—your world—in a chemical heat trap. Today, that seems barbaric. You live in a cocoon of energy so clean it barely leaves a carbon trace and so cheap you can scarcely find it on your monthly bill.*

The year is 2050.

You walk to the kitchen to turn on the sink. Water from the ocean pours out of the faucet. It's fresh and clear, piped from a desalination plant. These facilities use microbial membranes to squeeze out the ocean salt. Today, they provide more than half of the country's fresh used water. Previously overtaxed rivers, such as the Colorado, have surged back now that we don't rely on them to irrigate our farms and fill our coffee mugs. In Phoenix and Las Vegas, previously parched cities are erupting in green foliage.

You open the refrigerator. In the fruit and vegetable drawer are apples, tomatoes, and an eggplant, shipped from the nearest farm, mere miles away. These crops don't grow horizontally, across fields. They grow vertically on tiered shelves inside a tall greenhouse. Banks of LED lights deliver the photons the plants need in precisely timed increments. These skyscraper farms spare countless acres for forests and parks. As for the chicken and beef, much of it comes from cellular meat facilities, which grow animal cells to make chicken breasts and rib eye steaks—no live animals needed, which means no confinement and slaughter. Once prohibitively expensive, cultivated meat scaled with the help of plentiful electricity. When your parents were young, nearly 25 percent of all global land was used to raise livestock for human consumption. That is unimaginable now. Much of that land has rewilded.

Out the window and across the street, an autonomous drone is dropping off the latest shipment of star pills. Several years ago, daily medications that reduced overeating, cured addiction, and slowed cellular aging were considered miracle drugs for the rich, especially when we discovered that key molecules were best synthesized in the zero-gravity conditions of space. But these days, automated factories thrum in low orbit. Cheap rocketry conveys the medicine down to earth, where it's saved millions of lives and billions of healthy years.

Outside, the air is clean and humming with the purr of electric machines all around you. Electric cars and trucks glide down the road, quiet as a light breeze and mostly self-driving. Children and adult commuters follow on electric bikes and scooters, some person-ally owned and some belonging to subscription networks run by the city. Another last-mile delivery drone descends from canopy level, pauses over a neighbor's yard like a hummingbird, and drops off a package. These e-bots now deliver a sizable chunk of online orders, reducing the drudgery of much human delivery work.

Your micro-earpiece pings: a voice text from a friend and his family, on their way to the airport for another weekend vacation. Across the economy, the combination of artificial intelligence, labor rights, and economic reforms have reduced poverty and shortened the workweek. Thanks to higher productivity from AI, most people can complete what used to be a full week of work in a few days, which has expanded the number of holidays, long weekends, and vaca-tions. Less work has not meant less pay. AI is built on the collective knowledge of humanity, and so its profits are shared. Your friends are flying from New York to London. The trip will take them just over two hours. Modern jetliners now routinely reach Mach 2—twice the speed of sound—using a mix of traditional and green synthetic fuels that release far less carbon into the air.

The world has changed. Not just the virtual world, that dance of pixels on our screens. The physical world, too: its houses, its energy, its infrastructure, its medicines, its hard tech. How different this era is from the opening decades of the twenty-first century, which un-spooled a string of braided crises. A housing crisis. A financial crisis. A pandemic. A climate crisis. Political crises. For years, we accepted homelessness and poverty and untreated disease and declining life expectancy. For years, we knew what we needed to build to alleviate the scarcities so many faced and create the opportunities so many wanted, and we simply didn't build it. For years, we failed to in-vent and implement technology that would make the world cleaner, healthier, and richer. For years, we constrained our ability to solve the most important problems.

Why?

Scarcity Is a Choice

This book is dedicated to a simple idea: to have the future we want, we need to build and invent more of what we need. That's it. That's the thesis.

It reads, even to us, as too simple. And yet, the story of America in the twenty-first century is the story of chosen scarcities. Recognizing that these scarcities are chosen—that we could choose otherwise—is thrilling. Confronting the reasons we choose otherwise is maddening.

We say that we want to save the planet from climate change. But in practice, many Americans are dead set against the clean energy revolution, with even liberal states shutting down zero-carbon nuclear plants and protesting solar power projects. We say that housing is a human right. But our richest cities have made it excruciatingly difficult to build new homes. We say we want better health care, better medicine, and more cures for terrible diseases. But we tolerate a system of research, funding, and regulation that pulls scientists away from their most promising work, denying millions of people the discoveries that might extend or improve their lives.

Sometimes these blockages reflect differences of beliefs or interests. A thousand square acres of solar panels can be a godsend to the city they power and a blight to the community they abut. A seven-story affordable apartment building in San Francisco means homes for those who would otherwise live hours from their work even as it blocks views and clogs parking for those who lived there before.

Other times, our crises reflect the overhang of the past into the present. One generation's solutions can become the next generation's problems. After World War II, an explosion of housing and infrastructure enriched the country. But without regulations for clean air and water, the era's builders despoiled the environment. In response, the US passed a slew of environmental regulations. But these well-meaning laws to protect nature in the twentieth century now block the clean energy projects needed in the twenty-first. Laws meant to ensure that government considers the consequences of its actions have made it too difficult for government to act consequentially. Institutional renewal is a labor that every generation faces anew.

But some of this reflects a kind of ideological conspiracy at the heart of our politics. We are attached to a story of American decline that is centered around ideological disagreement. That makes it easy to miss pathologies rooted in ideological collusion. Over the course of the twentieth century, America developed a right that fought the government and a left that hobbled it. Debates over the size of government obscured the diminishing capacity of government. An abundance of consumer goods distracted us from a scarcity of homes and energy and infrastructure and scientific breakthroughs. A counterforce is emerging, but it is young yet.

The Supply-Side Mistake

At the heart of economics is supply and demand. Supply is how much there is of something. Demand is how much of that thing people want. Economies balance when supply and demand meet and derange when they part. Too much demand chasing too little supply causes shortages, price increases, and rationing. Too much supply pooling around too little demand brings gluts, layoffs, and depressions. Supply and demand are linked. At least, they are in the real world. In our politics, they have been cleaved. Democrats and Republicans divvied them up.

The words "supply side" are coded as right-wing. They summon memories of the curve that the conservative economist Arthur Laffer jotted on a napkin in the 1970s, showing that when taxes are too high, economies slow and revenues, paradoxically, fall.[1] This led, in part, to decades of Republican promises that cutting taxes on the rich would encourage the nation's dispirited John Galts to work smarter and harder, leading economies to boom and revenues to rise.

Tax cuts are a useful tool, and it is true that high taxes can discourage work. But the idea that tax cuts routinely lead to higher revenues is, as George H. W. Bush said, "voodoo economics." It has been tried. It has failed. It has been tried again. It has failed again. These failures, and the Republican Party's dogged refusal to stop trying the same thing and expecting a different result, made it vaguely disreputable to worry about the supply side of the economy. It's as if the nonsense of phrenology made it sordid for doctors to treat disorders of the brain.

But the conservative agenda did something else, too: it cast production as a function of unfettered markets. Supply-side economics was about getting the government out of the private sector's way. Cutting taxes so people would work more. Cutting regulations so companies would produce more. But what of the places where society needed a supply of something that the market could not, or would not, provide on its own?

This is where you might have expected Democrats to step in. But Democrats, cowed by the Reagan revolution and frightened of being seen as socialists, largely confined themselves to working on the demand side of the ledger. When Americans in 1978 heard that "government cannot solve our problems, it can't set our goals, it cannot define our vision," the words didn't come from Ronald Reagan. They came from President Jimmy Carter, a Democrat, in his State of the Union address.[2] This was a preview of things to come. In 1996, the next Democratic president, Bill Clinton, announced that "the era of big government is over."[3] The notion that the US government cannot solve America's problems was not unilaterally produced by Reagan and the GOP. It was coproduced by both parties and reinforced by their leaders.

Progressivism's promises and policies, for decades, were built around giving people money, or money-like vouchers, to go out and buy something that the market was producing but that the poor could not afford. The Affordable Care Act subsidizes insurance that people can use to pay for health care. Food stamps give people money for food. Housing vouchers give them money for rent. Pell Grants give them money for college. Tax credits for child care give people money to buy child care. Social Security gives them money for retirement. The minimum wage and the earned-income tax credit give them more money for anything they want.

These are important policies, and we support them. But while Democrats focused on giving consumers money to buy what they needed, they paid less attention to the supply of the goods and services they wanted everyone to have. Countless taxpayer dollars were spent on health insurance, housing vouchers, and infrastructure without an equally energetic focus—sometimes without any focus at all—on what all that money was actually buying and building.

This reflected a faith in the market that was, in its way, no less touching than that offered by Republicans. It assumed that so long as enough money was dangled in front of it, the private sector could and would achieve social goals. It revealed a disinterest in the workings of government. Regulations were assumed to be wise. Policies were assumed to be effective. Cries that government was stifling production or innovation typically fell on deaf ears. A blind spot emerged. Political movements consider solutions where they know to look for problems. Democrats learned to look for opportunities to subsidize. They gave little thought to the difficulties of production.

The problem is that if you subsidize demand for something that is scarce, you'll raise prices or force rationing.[4] Too much money chasing too few homes means windfall profits for homeowners and an affordability crisis for buyers. Too much money chasing too few doctors means long wait times or pricey appointments. This leads to the standard Republican riposte: *Just don't subsidize demand*. Keep the government out of it. Let the market work its magic. That's fine for goods where access is not a matter of justice. If virtual-reality headsets are expensive, well, so be it. It is not a public policy problem if most households cannot afford a VR headset. But that cannot be said for housing and education and medicine. Society cares about access to these goods and services, as well it should. Democrats and Republicans passed policies into law that, collectively, spend trillions of dollars helping people afford them. But giving people a subsidy for a good whose supply is choked is like building a ladder to try to reach an elevator that is racing ever upward.

The results of that mistake are everywhere. In 1950, the median home price was 2.2 times the average annual income; by 2020, it was 6 times the average annual income.[5] Between 1999 and 2023, the average premium for employer-based family health insurance rose from \$5,791 to \$23,968—an increase of more than 300 percent—and the worker contribution to that premium more than quadrupled.[6] In 1970, the average annual cost of tuition and fees was \$394 at public colleges and \$1,706 at private colleges. In 2023, it was \$11,310 at public colleges for in-state students and \$41,740 at private colleges.[7] Child care for an infant and a four-year-old costs, on average, \$36,008 in Massachusetts, \$28,420 in California, and \$28,338 in Minnesota.[8]

An uncanny economy has emerged in which a secure, middle-class lifestyle receded for many, but the material trappings of middle-class success became affordable to most. In the 1960s, it was possible to attend a four-year college debt-free but impossible to purchase a flat-screen television. By the 2020s, the reality was close to the reverse.

We papered over the affordability crisis[9] with low prices for consumer goods, soaring asset values that kept richer Americans happy, and mountains of debt: housing debt and student-loan debt and medical debt that kept the working class semi-afloat. This makes some sense of the last few decades of our economic debates: a crisis of housing debt, a huge new program to subsidize health insurance costs, debates about making college free and forgiving student loans, endless rounds of tax cuts, proposal after proposal for the government to pay for child care and preschool, a bubble in crypto that attracted so many investors in part because it seemed like a rocket ship into wealth that anyone could ride.

But then came inflation. For years, the central problem in the American economy was demand. We both reported on the financial crisis, and every conversation with Obama administration economists was about how to persuade employers to hire and consumers to spend. The 2009 stimulus was too small, and while we avoided a second Great Depression, we sank into an achingly slow recovery. Democrats carried those lessons into the COVID pandemic. They met the crisis with overwhelming fiscal force, joining with the Trump administration to pass the $2.2 trillion CARES Act and then adding the $1.9 trillion American Rescue Plan Act and the trillion-dollar infrastructure bill on top. Democrats made clear that they preferred the risks of a hot economy, like inflation, to the threat of mass joblessness.

They succeeded. But solving the crisis of the pandemic economy created a new crisis for the post-pandemic economy: too much demand. Supply chains that had been battered by the pandemic and Russia's invasion of Ukraine began to break. Inflation returned with a vengeance. The conversations we had with the Biden administration's economists were different from the conversations with the Obama administration's economists, even when they were the same people. They needed companies to make more goods and make them faster. They needed more chips so there could be more cars and computers. They needed ports to clear more shipments and Pfizer to make more antiviral pills and shipping companies to hire more truckers and schools to upgrade their ventilation systems. They needed more supply and, if they could not get that, less demand.

"If car prices are too high right now, there are two solutions," Biden said. "You increase the supply of cars by making more of them, or you reduce demand for cars by making Americans poorer. That's the choice."[10]

By 2024, the surge in prices had slowed. Inflation, as economists measure it, had eased. But the broader affordability crisis that predated the bout of inflation persisted. The fear that we did not or would not have enough of what we needed settled heavily on politics.

Policymakers began to rethink globalization, warning that we could not depend on critical exports from China if conflict or crisis came between our nations. Governors and mayors focused their attention on housing supply as homeless encampments spread across their streets. The Inflation Reduction Act began the work of building the green infrastructure necessary to migrate our economy to clean energy. The CHIPS and Science Act dangled tens of billions of dollars to restart semiconductor manufacturing in America. Whether these policies will work remains to be seen. That these policies represent a break with recent decades of American politics is undeniable.

Politics is not just about the problems we have. It's about the problems we see. The supply problem has lurked for years, but it has not been the core of our politics. That is changing. A new theory of supply is emerging—and with it, a new way of thinking about politics, economics, and growth.

Society Is Not a Pie

Perhaps you've heard the cliché that the economy is a pie we must grow rather than slice. It is hard to know where to begin with what this image gets wrong, because it gets almost nothing right. If you somehow grew a blueberry pie, you'd get more blueberry pie. But economic growth is not an addition of sameness. The difference between an economy that grows and an economy that stagnates is *change*. When you grow an economy, you hasten a future that is different. The more growth there is, the more radically the future diverges from the past. We have settled on a metaphor for growth that erases its most important characteristic.

Dig within the equations that power modern economics and

you'll find that growth comes from one of a few places. An economy can grow because it adds more people. It can grow because it adds more land or natural resources. But once those avenues are exhausted, it needs to do more with what it has. People need to think up new ideas. Factories need to innovate new processes. These new ideas and new processes must be encoded into new technologies. All this is grouped under the sterile label of productivity: How much more can we produce with the same number of people and resources? When productivity surges, what we get is not more of what we had, but new things we never imagined.

Imagine going to sleep in 1875 in New York City and waking up thirty years later. As you shut your eyes, there is no electric lighting, Coca-Cola, basketball, or aspirin. There are no cars or "sneakers." The tallest building in Manhattan is a church. When you wake up in 1905, the city has been remade with towering steel-skeleton buildings called "skyscrapers." The streets are filled with novelty: automobiles powered by new internal combustion engines, people riding bicycles in rubber-soled shoes—all recent innovations. The Sears catalog, the cardboard box, and aspirin are new arrivals. People have enjoyed their first sip of Coca-Cola and their first bite of what we now call an American hamburger. The Wright brothers have flown the first airplane. When you passed into slumber, nobody had taken a picture with a Kodak camera or used a machine that made motion pictures, or bought a device to play recorded music. By 1905, we have the first commercial versions of all three—the simple box camera, the cinematograph, and the phonograph.

Now imagine dozing off for another thirty-year nap between 1990 and 2020. You would wonder at the dazzling ingenuity that we funneled into our smartphones and computers. But the physical world would feel much the same. This is reflected in the productivity statistics, which record a slowing of change as the twentieth century wore on. This is not just a problem for our economy. It is a crisis for our politics. The nostalgia that permeates so much of today's right and no small part of today's left is no accident. We have lost the faith in the future that once powered our optimism. We fight instead over what we have, or what we had.

Our era features too little utopian thinking, but one worthy exception is Aaron Bastani's *Fully Automated Luxury Communism*, a leftist tract that puts the technologies in development right now—artificial intelligence, renewable energy, asteroid mining, plant- and cell-based meats, and gene editing—at the center of a post-work, post-scarcity vision.[11] "What if everything could change?" he asks. "What if, more than simply meeting the great challenges of our time—from climate change to inequality and ageing—we went far beyond them, putting today's problems behind us like we did before with large predators and, for the most part, illness? What if, rather than having no sense of a different future, we decided history hadn't actually begun?"[12]

It is routine in politics to imagine a just present and work backward to the social insurance programs that would get us there. It is equally important to imagine a just—even a delightful—future and work backward to the technological advances that would hasten its arrival. Bastani's vision is bracing because it insists that those of us who believe in a fairer, gentler, more sustainable world have a stake in bringing forward the technologies that will make that world possible. That is a political question as much as a technological one: those same technologies could become accelerators of inequality and despair if they're not embedded in just policies and institutions. What Bastani sees is that the world we want requires more than redistribution. We aspire to more than parceling out the present.

New technologies create new possibilities and allow us to solve once-impossible problems. In a world where many of the countries with the largest greenhouse gas emissions are middle-income nations, like China and India,[13] the only way for humanity to limit climate change while fighting poverty is to invent our way to clean energy that is plentiful and cheap and then spend enough to deploy it. The only reason we have even the barest hope of avoiding catastrophic warming is that the cost of solar power has fallen by 89 percent and onshore wind costs by almost 70 percent in ten years.[14] California's decision to ban the sale of new gas-powered cars after 2035[15] would be unthinkable without the rapid advances in battery technology.

Much that we need for the world we want we already know how to build. But much that we need for the world we want still needs to be invented and improved. Green hydrogen and cement. Nuclear fusion. Treatments for the terminal cancers that overwhelm today's therapies and the shadowy autoimmune diseases that baffle today's doctors. AI that molds itself to the needs of children who learn and think differently. Markets will, we hope, proffer some of these advances. But not nearly enough of them. The market cannot, on its own, distinguish between the riches that flow from burning coal and the wealth that is created by bettering battery storage. Government can. The market will not, on its own, fund the risky technologies whose payoff is social rather than economic. Government must.

But let us not be naïve. It is childish to declare government the problem. It is just as childish to declare government the solution. Government can be either the problem or the solution, and it is often both. By some counts, nuclear power is safer than wind and cleaner than solar. It is inarguably safer than burning coal and petrol. And yet the US—facing a crisis of global warming—has almost stopped building nuclear power reactors and plants entirely. Between 1973 and 2024, the country started and finished only three new nuclear reactors. And it has shut down more nuclear plants than it's opened in most of our lifetimes.[16] That is not a failure of the private market to responsibly bear risk but of the federal government to properly weigh risk.

To take technology seriously as a force for change is to take it seriously as infused with values and, yes, politics. The relationship is bidirectional. It is not just that the politics we have will affect the technologies we develop. The technologies we develop will shape the politics we come to have. A world where renewable energy is plentiful and cheap permits a politics that is different than a world where it is scarce and pricey. A world where modular construction has brought down the cost of building opens different possibilities for state and local budgets.

In 1985, the great technology critic Neil Postman wrote, "to be unaware that a technology comes equipped with a program for social change, to maintain that technology is neutral, to make the assumption that technology is always a friend to culture is, at this late hour, stupidity plain and simple."[17] The corollary is also true: to have no program to harness technology in service of social change is its own form of blindness.

Too often, the right sees only the imagined glories of the past, and the left sees only the injustices of the present. Our sympathies there lie with the left, but that is not a debate we can settle. What is often missing from both sides is a clearly articulated vision of the future and how it differs from the present. This book is a sketch of, and argument for, one such vision.

A Liberalism That Builds

We are both liberals in the American tradition. The problems we seek to solve are mostly problems that exist within the zone of liberal concern. We worry over climate change and health inequality. We want more affordable housing and higher median wages. We want children to breathe cleaner air and commuters to move easily on mass transit systems. We have many disagreements with the modern American right. But we focus, in this book, on the pathologies of the broad left.

One reason for that is we don't see ourselves as effective messengers to the right. There are people seeking complementary reforms in that coalition, such as James Pethokoukis, author of *The Conservative Futurist*; the economist Tyler Cowen, who has called for a "State Capacity Libertarianism";[18] and the array of policy experts organized in the Niskanen Center. We wish them well.

But we focus on the left for larger reasons. This book is motivated in no small part by our belief that we need to decarbonize the global economy to head off the threat of climate change. To the extent that the right simply does not believe this—and in America, at least, it does not—it strikes us as naïve to describe the policies that would help Republicans build green infrastructure faster. It is folly to expect a coalition that does not share our goals to do the work to achieve them. It is more interesting to ask, as we will, why it is often easier to build renewable energy in red states than in blue states despite Republican opposition to the cause of climate change.

Then there is the anger any liberal should feel when looking at the states and cities liberals govern. One of us was born in California and lived there throughout much of the writing of this book. California's most populous cities are run by Democrats.[19] Every statewide elected official in California is a Democrat.[20] Both chambers of the legislature are run by Democrats. And California is a land of wonders. It leads the world in technology. It creates the culture that much of the world consumes. It is astonishingly, breathtakingly beautiful. If it were its own country, it would have the fifth-largest GDP in the world.

Liberals should be able to say: *Vote for us, and we will govern the country the way we govern California!* Instead, conservatives are able to say: *Vote for them, and they will govern the country the way they govern California!* California has spent decades trying and failing to build high-speed rail. It has the worst homelessness problem in the country. It has the worst housing affordability problem in the country. It trails only Hawaii and Massachusetts in its cost of living.[21] As a result, it is losing hundreds of thousands of people every year to Texas and Arizona.[22] What has gone wrong?

California's problems are often distinct in their severity but not in their structure. The same dynamics are present in other blue states and cities. In this era of rising right-wing populism, there is pressure among liberals to focus only on the sins of the MAGA right. But this misses the contribution that liberal governance made to the rise of Trumpism. In their book *Presidents, Populism, and the Crisis of Democracy*, the political scientists William Howell and Terry Moe write that "populists don't just feed on socioeconomic discontent. They feed on ineffective government—and their great appeal is that they claim to replace it with a government that is effective through their own autocratic power."[23]

In the 2024 election, Donald Trump won by shifting almost every part of America to the right. But the signal Democrats should fear most is that the shift was largest in blue states and blue cities—the places where voters were most exposed to the day-to-day realities of liberal governance. Nearly every county in California moved toward Trump,[24] with Los Angeles County shifting eleven points toward the GOP. In and around the "Blue Wall" states, Philadelphia County shifted four points right, Wayne County (Detroit) shifted nine points right, and Cook County (Chicago) shifted eight points right. In the New York City metro area, New York County (Manhattan) shifted nine points right, Kings County (Brooklyn) shifted twelve points right, Queens County shifted twenty-one points right, and Bronx County shifted twenty-two points right.[25]

Voting is a cheap way to express anger. Moving is expensive. But residents of blue states and cities are doing that, too. In 2023, California lost 342,000 more residents than it gained; in Illinois, the net loss was 115,000; in New York, 284,000.[26] In the American political system, to lose people is to lose political power. If current trends hold, the 2030 census will shift the Electoral College sharply to the right; even adding Michigan, Pennsylvania, and Wisconsin to the states Harris won won't be enough for Democrats to win future presidential elections.[27]

The problem is not just political. Young families are leaving large urban metros so quickly that several counties—including those encompassing Manhattan, Brooklyn, Chicago, Los Angeles, and San Francisco—are on pace to lose 50 percent of their under-five childhood population in the next twenty years.[28] Democrats cannot simultaneously claim to be the party of middle-class families while presiding over the parts of the country that they are leaving.

A good way to marginalize the most dangerous political movements is to prove the success of your own. If liberals do not want Americans to turn to the false promise of strongmen, they need to offer the fruits of effective government. Redistribution is important. But it is not enough.

The Abundant Society

There is a word that describes the future we want: abundance. We imagine a future not of less but of more. We do not subscribe to the seductive ideologies of scarcity. We will not get more or better jobs by closing our gates to immigrants. We will not turn back climate change by persuading the world to starve itself of growth. It is not merely that these visions are unrealistic. It is that they are counterproductive. They will not achieve the futures they seek. They will do more harm than good.

The abundance we envision is not indiscriminate. It is not an omnidirectional moreness. We take inspiration from *People of Plenty*, the historian David M. Potter's brilliant 1954 book on how abundance shaped American thought and culture. "If abundance is to be properly understood, it must not be visualized in terms of a storehouse of fixed and universally recognizable assets, reposing on shelves until humanity, by a process of removal, strips all the shelves bare." Abundance, he said, is "a physical and cultural factor, involving the interplay between man, himself a geological force, and nature."[29]

The kind of abundance we seek differs from the kind of abundance our generation has seen. Potter wrote of the way America was being "reoriented to convert the producer's culture into a consumer's culture," and the rupture deepened in the decades that followed.[30] American policy has been focused on enacting what the historian Lizabeth Cohen calls "A Consumers' Republic."[31] It has been remarkably successful. Catastrophically successful. We have a startling abundance of the goods that fill a house and a shortage of what's needed to build a good life. We call for a correction. We are interested in production more than consumption. We believe what we can build is more important than what we can buy.

Abundance, as we define it, is a state. It is the state in which there is enough of what we need to create lives better than what we have had. And so we are focused on the building blocks of the future. Housing. Transportation. Energy. Health. And we are focused on the institutions and the people that must build and invent that future.

Let's begin.

1

Grow

"GO WEST, YOUNG MAN, GO WEST. THERE IS HEALTH IN THE COUNTRY, and room away from our crowds of idlers and imbeciles."

It is not clear if Horace Greeley, the newspaper editor and liberal presidential candidate, ever uttered the advice so famously attributed to him. What is clear is that he never followed it. Greeley was born in 1811 to a poor family in rural Amherst, New Hampshire.[1] He did not seek his fortune in the vast expanse of the American West. He made his way to New York City in 1831. It was there, in the teeming center of urban American life, that he built his wealth and his name, founding the *New-York Tribune*, winning election to Congress, and losing the presidency to Ulysses S. Grant.

The tension between Greeley's life and his legacy echoes that of the country he loved. Americans have long lionized the frontier. But our futures have largely been made in our cities. That we preferred the romance of the West to the math of the tenements is no new fact. "We often forget that the country as a whole offered abundance in the form of fuel resources, mineral resources, bumper crops, industrial capacity, and the like, and provided the city as a locus for the transformation of this abundance into mobility," Potter reminded his readers in *People of Plenty*. "More Americans have changed their status by moving to the city than have done so by moving to the frontier."[2]

But this is not the story America told itself. The western expanse lingered in our mind as the true guarantor of our prosperity. Its settlement inflicted a kind of psychic trauma. Europe had cities, too. What America had was open—often stolen—land. Without that, wouldn't we, too, fall into stagnation? The fear held well into the twentieth century, emerging as a partial explanation for the Great Depression. Senator Lewis Schwellenbach, a New Dealer who would serve as President Harry Truman's secretary of labor, warned that "so long as we had an undeveloped West—new lands— new resources—new opportunities—we had no cause to worry."[3] But those days were over. Alvin Hansen, an influential economist, offered a more sophisticated version of this view. "We are more or less through the heavy task of equipping the continent with giant capital expenditures," he said.[4] The Depression, in this telling, heralded a new normal: a mature America could not expect the torrid growth of an expanding America.

But economies are not bounded by land. Ideas, and the technologies and companies and products they power, draw the outer borders of growth. The land that matters most is the land that aids in the fiery creation of the new. That land is in the heart of our cities, not at the edge of our settlements. And that land reveals the problem America faces now. A young family can still follow Horace Greeley's advice and find a cheap home in the rural West. What they typically cannot do is follow Horace Greeley's example and build a life in Manhattan, where the median home now sells for $1.1 million. Or in San Francisco, where the median home sells for $1.3 million. Or in Los Angeles, where the asking price hovers around $1 million. Or in Seattle, where the median home is over $900,000. Or in Boston, where it's $830,000.

Housing follows the laws of supply and demand. When supply is thick and demand is light, prices fall. The average home in Cleveland sells for about $115,000. When supply is tight and demand is hot, prices rise. That is the story of the pricey, blue cities listed above. America used to be adept at building homes. In 1950, the US Census Bureau reported that America had added 8.5 million units in the previous decade, even with the interruption of a world war. "This is the greatest numerical growth on record," the authors announced.[5] But in the late 1970s, home construction started to fall behind the pace of population growth. New permits per capita declined in the 1980s and again in the 1990s. After the Great Recession, the housing market crashed, and home construction in the 2010s was obliterated. Today, the average number of dwellings per thousand people in the developed world is about 470, according to the OECD (Organisation for Economic Co-operation and Development). France and Italy have nearly 600. Japan and Germany have about 500. The US has only about 425.[6] Where did all the houses go? The answer is that they were never built at all.

The result is a housing crisis of staggering proportions. Almost 30 percent of American adults are "house poor"—spending 30 percent or more of their income on housing.[7] But that understates the problem. Housing costs are highest in the superstar cities that now drive the economy. Millions endure multi-hour commutes, or far worse jobs, in order to live in a far-flung city where they can afford a home. These choices are missed in raw estimates of affordability, but they are a drag on the economy and an anchor on people's lives.[8]

To immerse yourself in analyses of American housing is to drown in data. But sometimes a number stands out. Here is one: The economist Ed Glaeser calculates that, prior to the 1980s, wages in New York City were unusually high even after correcting for the local cost of living.[9] The city had its problems, but most people would make more money by moving there. But that flipped. By the year 2000, moving to New York meant, for most people, taking an effective pay cut. That's not because paychecks have shrunk but because housing costs have risen. People now pay to live there; they aren't paid to live there.

"If New York City is a business, it isn't Wal-Mart, it isn't trying to be the lowest-priced product in the market," Michael Bloomberg, then mayor of New York City, said in 2003. "It's a high-end product, maybe even a luxury product."[10] New York was once where you went to make your fortune; it is now where you go to spend it.

Comments like Bloomberg's are common: if you cannot afford to live in the city, don't. Every so often, social media will convulse over some urbanite claiming they can't afford a middle-class lifestyle on $450,000 a year or some similarly princely sum. A common retort, even among self-styled progressives, is that they opted out of a middle-class lifestyle the moment they opted into an apartment on the Upper West Side. They chose to spend their money on an unattainable luxury, no different than if they'd purchased a speedboat or begun collecting pricey art.

Too many have bought into a perverse inversion of what the city should be. Cities are where wealth is created, not just where it is displayed. They are meant to be escalators into the middle class, not penthouses for the upper class. But through bad policy and worse politics, we are doing in the twenty-first century what we so feared in the nineteenth: we are closing the American frontier.

Why Cities Matter Now More Than Ever

A capsule history of the past few centuries of transportation and communication technology might simply say this: we fought distance, and we won. In 1800, it took a month and a half to travel from New York City to Chicago. In 1830, it took three weeks. In 1850, it took two days. Today, a flight takes two to three hours. The telegraph and the telephone and email and teleconferencing made further mockery of space. It is now faster to FaceTime family across the continent than to rouse a neighbor across the street.

What are cities, at their most elemental? "Cities are the absence of physical space between people and companies," writes Ed Glaeser in *Triumph of the City*. They are the ancient answer to the difficulties of distance. But technology eroded their obvious advantages. Cities should have languished. They have, so often, been expected to languish. But they have stubbornly refused to accept their fate. Instead, they thrived, attaining a centrality in modernity they didn't possess even in antiquity. This, Glaeser writes, is "the central paradox of the modern metropolis—proximity has become ever more valuable as the cost of connecting across long distances has fallen."[11]

In *The New Geography of Jobs*, Enrico Moretti, an economist at the University of California at Berkeley, explains why. A century ago, the American economy produced primarily physical goods.

Now we make ideas and services. Some of those are encoded into physical goods, but even then, production often happens elsewhere. The iPhone made Apple, based in Cupertino, California, into the most valuable company in the world even though two-thirds of the phones are assembled in Foxconn factories in Shenzhen, China.[12] Microsoft and Alphabet mostly sell bits of intangible code. Tesla's value lies in the software and battery advances that have taken electric vehicles from the automotive equivalent of granola to the sleek, fast cars of the future.

We do not trade in the fallacious belief that manufacturing and innovation are distant domains. Taiwan started out manufacturing commodity semiconductor chips that Intel cared little about. Over time, its lead in production allowed it to develop advanced chips that American companies cannot yet replicate and that American policymakers fear falling into Chinese hands. America lost its primacy in semiconductor innovation because much is learned in the making of things—a theme to which we'll return. The economic frontier is where new discoveries allow for the making of new things that can be sold to ever more people.

The rising returns to innovation are a result of the same technological forces that should have decimated the city. As distance collapsed, markets expanded. It was once difficult to expand your business to another region. Shipping was costly, and communication was challenging. That gave local producers a modest advantage. The factory nearby might not be best, but it was close, and that often made its products cheaper. Today it is routine for many businesses to sell across state lines and national borders. Goods that can be produced anywhere can also be purchased anywhere. Omnipresence is yet easier for digital products, where all that's needed is a download or the quick flash of an advertisement across a browser screen. Less than half of Apple's revenue comes from North America.[13] Slightly more than half of Alphabet's revenue is international.[14] The same holds for Tesla.[15]

Cities are engines of creativity because we create in community. We are spurred by competition. We need to find the colleagues and the friends and the competitors and the antagonists who unlock our genius and add their own. "Americans who live in metropolitan areas with more than a million residents are, on average, more than 50 percent more productive than Americans who live in smaller metropolitan areas," Glaeser writes. "These relationships are the same even when we take into account the education, experience, and industry of workers. They're even the same if we take individual workers' IQs into account."[16]

This is not a dumb gift of density. Jamming a mass of people into a chosen place will not allow you to re-create what other groups of people have achieved elsewhere, as the Soviet Union found out again and again. Cities are not interchangeable. What each offers is a specific gift of the ecosystems of people and practice it has nurtured. Once deep communities of interest and industry form, they are difficult to dislodge, and they prove nearly impossible to replicate.

New York leads the world in finance. San Francisco and Silicon Valley lead the world in technology. New York has tried hard to take Silicon Valley's crown. But if you look for multibillion-dollar technology companies in New York, you will find few of them. Where New York City has seen technological success is where code serves finance: Bloomberg is a multibillion-dollar technology business built around providing data to financial firms. Banks like Goldman Sachs and JPMorgan Chase now employ thousands of software engineers.[17] The same is true, in reverse, in San Francisco. There are successful banks and investment firms, but they mostly serve technology companies.

The result is that even global businesses are rooted in local phenomena. Take the rise of generative AI companies. Outside China, the industry is concentrated within a few square miles along the California coast. OpenAI is not far from Anthropic, which is a quick drive to Google, which is located near Meta. The sole exception is DeepMind, which is based in London, but sold itself to Google in part because it needed the computing expertise their Silicon Valley–based engineers provided.

Why doesn't Toronto or Atlanta or New York or Barcelona or Los Angeles or Berlin have a major entrant in the industry? Why not build your AI behemoth in Maui or Bali? These companies are feeding digital data to algorithms running on off-site server farms. In theory, this arrangement should be possible anywhere. In practice, the frontier of ideas is best breached by people who know each other well and work with each other closely and who move between different companies with different cultures and specialties smoothly. Those much-mocked Bay Area parties where young AI engineers gather in group houses to ingest psychedelics and contemplate the singularity matter.

"Companies appear to locate in absolutely the worst places," Moretti writes. "They pick very expensive areas—the Bostons, San Franciscos, and New Yorks of the world. With sky-high wages and office rents, these are among the costliest places in America to operate a business. We would expect these cities to be unattractive for firms, especially those that compete globally."[18] But they're not. It's the firms that locate outside these cities that struggle. The money you save in rent doesn't make up for the talent and knowledge that dissipate over distance.

Walmart is famously frugal, maintaining its headquarters in Bentonville, Arkansas, and insisting top executives locate there, too. But when it wanted to enter into e-commerce, it didn't pile software engineers into a new wing of its headquarters. "Instead it chose Brisbane, California, just 7 miles from downtown San Francisco, one of the most expensive labor markets in the world," Moretti notes.[19]

Walmart saw what many tech executives see. If you want the best software products, you need to locate amid the best software engineers. Those engineers aren't cheap to hire. But if a few dozen or a few hundred of them can build you an e-commerce platform that you will use for millions or billions in sales, it'd be foolish to locate elsewhere. Walmart now trails only Amazon in annual online sales.

Some thought that the dislocations of the pandemic, combined with the rise of videoconferencing, would finally sever the link between place and innovation. It's undeniable that white-collar employees are more likely to work remotely, and some have used this opportunity to move to smaller and cheaper cities while clocking in for firms based many miles away. But America's superstar cities still draw many of the country's most talented workers. While remote and hybrid work have stabilized at a much higher level than before COVID, it is notable that in August 2023, the videoconferencing company Zoom announced that they were demanding employees be in the office at least a few days each week. Eric Yuan, Zoom's CEO, explained that it was too hard to build trust without nearness. "Trust is a foundation for everything. Without trust, we will be slow."[20]

Zoom was no outlier. Amazon and Meta and JPMorgan Chase and Alphabet and Tesla and Pfizer and almost every other major company one could name had, by mid-2023, announced a plan for employees to return to the office for at least a few days a week. Remote work is a powerful force. But the centripetal power of the city is stronger. "To defeat the human need for face-to-face contact, our technological marvels would need to defeat millions of years of human evolution that has made us into machines for learning from the people next to us," Glaeser writes."[21]

This resolves the paradox of the metropolis: We vanquished distance for shipping and sales. But innovation thrives amid closeness. Which is to say: it thrives in cities. And because it thrives in cities, so does much else. It's in missing how much else that we made a terrible mistake.

The Great Divergence

Cities play two roles. They are engines of innovation and engines of mobility. High housing costs have blunted their role in innovation, but only modestly. The richest firms and most productive workers can still afford to locate in expensive zip codes. But high housing costs wreak havoc on the city's offering of opportunity. Think of it as the firefighter test. Could a firefighter serving a city afford to live in that city? If not, then not only is that firefighter going to be forced into a longer commute or an economically strained life, but his children, too, will be deprived of the awesome possibilities of the city their father works to safeguard.

Most jobs aren't in firms like Google and Goldman Sachs. About two-thirds of the jobs in the American economy are in the local service sector, and that number has been steadily growing for fifty years. These are hairstylists and DMV employees and nurses and line cooks and retail workers and real estate agents.[22] They don't see the kinds of wild productivity improvements that tradable goods do because, while one software programmer can write code for a million users, one line cook cannot make food for a million mouths.

But these jobs pay better in dynamic cities. Those Googlers have money to spend. And the consequences here ring out across generations. As the economist Raj Chetty and his team have covered in several papers, upward mobility is in structural decline in the US. In 1940, a child born into an American household had a 92 percent chance of making more money than her parents. But a child born in the 1980s has just a 50 percent chance of surpassing their parents' income.[23] In forty years, the American dream went from being a widespread reality to a coin toss.[24]

Mobility, Chetty found, is a product of place. A child born poor in San Jose has three times the likelihood of ending up wealthy as a child born poor in Charlotte. Among children who moved from a more economically stagnant zip code to a richer neighborhood, Chetty finds that the likelihood of better outcomes improves steadily with every extra year the child spends in their new city, with the kids who moved earliest faring best.[25]

Chetty's team also found that children who moved to a high-innovation area when they were young are much likelier to patent inventions of their own when they matured. The effect was specific to the specialty of the place: "Children who grow up in a neighborhood or family with a high innovation rate in a specific technology class are more likely to patent in exactly the same class," they write.[26]

But that depends on their parents being able to move to high-innovation areas. In the past, higher incomes would attract them.

In the present, sky-high cost of living repels them. A 2017 study by Peter Ganong and Daniel Shoag reveals the scale of what's lost when housing prices gate cities to working-class migrants. From 1880 to 1980, the income gap between residents of different states closed steadily each year. Today, that convergence has dissolved almost entirely.[27] Ganong and Shoag estimate that America's midcentury mobility accounted for more than a third of its midcentury drop in income inequality.[28] Now it is gone. This is the quiet destruction of an ancient path to opportunity.

Consider the fortunes of janitors and lawyers, Ganong and Shoag write. Janitors and lawyers have long made more money working in New York than in the Deep South. As a result, many migrated from the Deep South to New York. But as housing costs in New York rose, the benefits of migration crumbled, at least for the janitors. The lawyers still came out ahead, but the janitors saw housing consume more than 50 percent of their paychecks.[29] It used to be that both high-wage and low-wage workers moved from poorer areas to richer ones. By the 1990s, poorer workers were moving *away* from high-income areas—and from the opportunities they once offered.

It is, then, no surprise that income inequality began rising in the '70s and reached such striking peaks in recent decades. We took a process responsible for much of the march toward income convergence and threw it into reverse. We made mobility into an engine of inequality, and we did it on purpose, using policy levers that made life in dynamic cities too costly for the poor to afford.

But the "we" here is hiding some uncomfortable culprits. It is liberals—and particularly a strain of liberalism that began to develop in the '60s and '70s—that bears much of the blame.

The Problem with
Lawn-Sign Liberalism

There is an old finding in political science that Americans are "symbolically" conservative but "operationally" liberal.[30] Americans talk like conservatives but want to be governed like liberals. The Tea Party–era sign saying "Keep your government hands off my Medicare" is perhaps the most famous example of this divided soul. Americans like both the rhetoric and reality of low taxes, but they also like the programs that taxes fund. They thrill to politicians who talk of personal responsibility but want a safety net tightened if they, or those they know and love, fall.

This dynamic is so well known, so easy to see, that we miss how often it gets reality backward. In many blue states, voters exhibit the same split political personality, but in reverse: they are symbolically liberal but operationally conservative.

In much of San Francisco, you can't walk twenty feet without seeing a multicolored sign declaring that Black Lives Matter, Kindness Is Everything, and No Human Being Is Illegal. Those signs sit in yards zoned for single families, in communities that organize against efforts to add the new homes that would bring those values closer to reality. San Francisco's Black population has fallen in every Census count since 1970. Poorer families—disproportionately nonwhite and immigrant—are pushed into long commutes, overcrowded housing, and street homelessness.

Texas has been the single largest beneficiary of California's housing crisis. And that is, in part, because Texas is California's mirror image on housing. The Austin metro area led the nation in housing permits in 2022, permitting 18 new homes for every 1,000 residents. Los Angeles's and San Francisco's metro areas permitted only 2.5 units per 1,000 residents.[31] In our political typologies, it is liberals who embrace change and conservatives who cling to stasis. But that is not how things work when you compare red-state and blue-state housing policies.

To be fair to California, change is messy and uncomfortable everywhere. Any growing community that likes itself roughly the way it is faces a problem. If more people want to live in that community, then developers will build places for them to live. Worse, they might build dense places for them to live. A plot of land that houses a large single-family house could become a plot of land housing a small building with six units. You can make more money, typically, selling homes to six families than to one family, so it's relatively easy for the developer to offer the family living there now a good price for their home, raze the building, stack six units atop each other, and make a profit. This can be done in many places at once, fairly quickly, and the community will soon wake to find that it is unrecognizable to itself.

But how do you stop people from selling homes they own and developers from building on land they own and people from moving to a city they would like to be part of? Who invented this whole business of cutting cities into "zones" and creating rules about what can and can't be built there? The answer takes us back more than one hundred years.

In the 1800s, no American city had zoning rules, the economist William Fischel writes in his aptly titled book *Zoning Rules!* In the early 1900s, Los Angeles adopted a small package of regulations that divided the city between zones for industrial buildings and residential construction. New York City followed, and soon enough, so did almost everywhere else. "Eight cities had zoning by the end of 1916," Fischel writes. "By 1926, 68 more cities had adopted it, and between 1926 and 1936, zoning was adopted by 1,246 additional municipalities."[32] The concept of zoning, unheard-of in 1900, covered 70 percent of the US population by 1933.

Fischel's explanation begins with trucks and buses, which forever changed the spatial geometry of the city. Before big, gas-powered vehicles took over the streets, it was easy to keep the different functions of the city separate. If you didn't want to live near a manufacturing plant or the masses of workers who worked in it, you could always live (or build) somewhere else. Trucks and buses changed that. "The truck liberated heavy industry from close proximity to downtown railroad stations and docks," Fischel writes.[33] Factories could now be located anywhere. Buses liberated urban workers, too. They didn't have to live within walking distance of their jobs or on a streetcar line. They could reside anywhere, and working-class apartments could be built anywhere. Homeowners could no longer rely on geography to protect them from the people and producers they wanted to avoid. If distance couldn't keep them safe, rules would have to do so instead.

The first zoning rules did little to prevent housing construction at scale. Instead they dictated what kind of buildings could go where. James Metzenbaum, an Ohio litigator, compared these early rules to good housekeeping in the 1930s. "It keeps the kitchen stove out of the parlor, the bookcase out of the pantry," he said.[34] Of course, the rules also often kept non-white Americans out of owning in rich parts of the city.

But the American zoning experiment wasn't finished—not even close. What came next is what really put the clamps on housing supply: zoning as a form of anti-growth regulation. It is this form of zoning that still governs cities and suburbs today.

Two communities in California trace the rise of the anti-growth movement. After World War II, millions of veterans returned from the European and Pacific theaters. They started families in a hurry. Birth rates spiked, and young parents balancing babies in their arms scoured the country for houses. No suburban development epitomized this go-go era more than Lakewood, California, a planned community built on open farmland just north of Long Beach. Between 1950 and 1953, more than 17,000 homes went up.[35] At its most furious pace, the city's builders finished a new home once every seven and a half minutes.[36]

The houses sold almost as fast as they were built. On March 24, 1950, thirty thousand people lined up to check out the inventory at Lakewood's grand opening. In July, the first resident—a Navy veteran named Jim Huffman—moved in with his family.[37] Through the end of the year, twenty more families bought a Lakewood home, on average, every day. By the spring of 1954, a sparse farmland for sugar beets and lima beans had been transformed into one of California's twenty largest cities.

Two decades later, several hundred miles north of Lakewood, another city revealed how rapidly the politics of housing were changing. Petaluma is nestled in the windy hills north of San Francisco, where a gap in the coastal mountain ranges pulls cool, moist marine air into the farmland. Petaluma also saw its population bloom after the war. But unlike Lakewood, the city became famous for stopping growth rather than for welcoming it.

In 1971, city officials introduced the Petaluma Plan. It included a growth rate cap of 500 annual new housing units and an urban growth boundary to prevent sprawl. Despite facing several legal challenges, the law was largely upheld in the courts. In the following decades, the Petaluma Plan offered a useful formula for Californians who wanted to freeze development in their neighborhoods, and other cities quickly adopted its quota system for building permits.

Today, California is more Petaluma than Lakewood. In the 1950s and 1960s, California routinely built more than 200,000 homes each year.[38] Since 2007, California has never once permitted more than 150,000 new homes.[39] "In Los Angeles, fewer homes were built in the seventies than in the sixties, fewer in the eighties than in the seventies, and fewer in the nineties than in the eighties, even as the city's overall population grew," the historian Jacob Anbinder writes in "Cities of Amber," his study of the rise of anti-growth liberalism. In fact, Anbinder points out, much of America has become more Petaluma than Lakewood.

A slew of new zoning laws in Westchester County, New York, reduced the maximum permissible population of the county by 1.4 million people, largely by banning forms of home construction other than large-lot single-family houses. Bergen County, New Jersey, made it illegal by 1970 to build apartments on all but 131 acres of land. A 1973 survey of city and county governments found that one in five had passed laws in the previous two years that limited new residential development by halting expansions of public sewer systems. New York City's first historic district was created in 1965; three decades later, more than fifteen thousand buildings were protected from redevelopment by its landmarks law. By the nineteen nineties, 71 percent of cities and 77 percent of counties in California practiced some form of growth control, with hundreds of such measures enacted in the eighties alone.[40]

In 2020, with home prices at record levels, the Petaluma Plan reached its logical end point. For the first time in the history of the state, California—which, as late as the 1960s, was growing twice as fast as the rest of the country—shrank. The state is dominated by Democrats, but many of the people Democrats claim to care about most can't afford to live there. In the same progressive zip codes where homeowners press signs into the soil of their front lawns bearing the message Kindness Is Everything, affordable housing can't be found—and homelessness is endemic.

This Is Your State on a Housing Shortage

In 2015, when the California Legislative Analyst's Office investigated the cause of the state's housing cost and availability crisis, the authors were unambiguous in their diagnosis. "First and foremost, far less housing has been built in California's coastal areas than people demand," they wrote.[41] Little has changed since the publication of that document. Since 2015, the state has authorized construction on about half as many housing units as Texas, despite it now having 9 million more residents.[42]

California has about 12 percent of the nation's population, 30 percent of the nation's homeless population, and about 50 percent of its unsheltered homeless population.[43] To walk the streets of the Tenderloin in San Francisco or Skid Row in Los Angeles is to tumble into the dystopia tucked amid the plenty of these cities. Tents line the buildings, feces line the sidewalks, needles crunch underfoot. This is not what anyone trying to preserve the idyllic conditions of

California's central coast wanted. But it is what they got. It is what they made.

Homelessness has been particular grist for conservatives who see, in California's homelessness crisis, the roosting of liberal licentiousness. "Failure to enforce basic standards of public behavior has made one of America's great cities increasingly unlivable," wrote Heather Mac Donald, of the Manhattan Institute.[44] Mac Donald is mistaken. San Francisco is eminently livable, which is why the average apartment sells for more than a million dollars. If San Francisco were unlivable, and people ceased to want to live there, the price of homes would plummet, and so too would the ranks of the homeless.

There have been many explanations offered for the severity of California's homelessness crisis. Perhaps it's the nice weather, which makes sleeping on the streets comfortable even in winter. But then why is homelessness so much less prevalent in Houston, where the winters are yet warmer? Perhaps it's the generosity of California's social services. Perhaps it's liberal drug and policing policies. Perhaps it's something to do with mental health. Perhaps California is a magnet of social-service compassion attracting all the rest of the country's homeless.

In their book *Homelessness Is a Housing Problem,* Gregg Colburn and Clayton Page Aldern test these and other explanations and find them worse than lacking. When we tell the stories of the homeless, we focus on the individual events that pockmarked a life path: the loss of the job, the workplace injury, the onset of schizophrenia, the first glow of an opioid high. But what Colburn and Aldern wanted to understand is why homelessness varies so much across cities and regions. If a driver of homelessness doesn't predict these differences, then it is probably not a cause of mass homelessness. It might explain why an individual became home-less in a particular place, but it cannot explain why one place has a homelessness crisis and another does not.

And so they begin ticking through the list and testing them against the data. An obvious place to start is poverty rates. Does more poverty predict more homelessness? No. A number of cit-ies with high rates of poverty—Detroit, Miami, Dallas, Cincinnati, and Philadelphia—have low rates of homelessness.[45] It is richer cities with low overall poverty rates that see more homelessness. A similar story emerges for unemployment: homelessness is low where unemployment is high and high where unemployment is low.[46] Odd.

Then Colburn and Aldern move on to mental illness. It is hard to find reliable data on the rates of mental illness across cities, but the US Department of Health and Human Services does collect data across states. Here, too, the obvious relationship eludes us. Homelessness is slightly less common in the states with the high-est rates of mental illness, and vice versa. Hawaii, which has among the lowest rates of serious mental illness, has among the highest rates of homelessness. There's a slightly positive relationship be-tween measured drug use and homelessness, but not much of one: more drug use explains only about 5 percent of the difference be-tween places.[47]

So what does explain homelessness? The availability and cost of housing. When Colburn and Aldern begin testing these variables, their charts, which had just been masses of disconnected bubbles, coalesce into lockstep lines. As the cost of rent rises, so too does the number of homeless. As the vacancy rate plummets—meaning that the housing market is tight, with too many buyers and too few sellers—homelessness rises.

The way to think about homelessness, they write, is to imagine a game of musical chairs. With ten chairs and ten people, everyone will find a chair when the music stops. That will be true even if one of the players is on crutches. With nine chairs, someone will inevitably be left out. That's when individual life circumstances begin to predict homelessness. If you live in a city with too few homes, poverty and drug abuse and unemployment and mental illness make it likelier that you will be among those who end up without a home. But the cause of homelessness isn't the poverty or the addiction or the unemployment. All those conditions are far more prevalent in, say, West Virginia than in California, and yet California has six times the per capita homelessness of West Virginia.

This leads to a reality many prefer not to acknowledge. If homelessness is a housing problem, it is also a policy choice—or, more accurately, the result of many, many, many small policy choices. The writer Matthew Yglesias, who spent a decade trying to persuade liberals of where they've gone wrong on housing,[48] illustrated this nicely in a 2021 essay.[49]

Yglesias quotes the urban planner Payton Chung's description of the 1951 sci-fi classic *The Day the Earth Stood Still*, which features Klaatu, an alien, escaping captivity at what was then known as Walter Reed General Hospital and moving into a Washington, DC, boardinghouse at Fourteenth and Harvard Streets. Boardinghouses were a common place for adults to live through much of American history. They worked something like today's college dorms: The rooms were small, the bathrooms and kitchenettes shared, and the cost was low. They weren't as nice to live in as a single-family home with a detached garage, but they were far nicer than a tent in the middle of an encampment in the dark of winter. So where did they go?

The answer is that they were made, in most jurisdictions, functionally illegal. By the 1950s, rooming houses were already a target for city planners looking to maintain high home prices and orderly neighborhoods. "If rooming houses are permitted to spread to the city's one- and two-family neighborhoods, there is not much use in talking brave words about fighting blight," wrote the *St. Louis Post-Dispatch* in 1957. "Rooming houses are not compatible with one- and two-family districts. When the rooming houses come in, the families move out—and the whole area starts down hill."[50]

A report from the American Society of Planning Officials that same year offered guidance to planners looking to creatively rid their cities or neighborhoods of such nuisances: "Zoning is not the only tool available to control the blighting effects of rooming houses. Housing codes in an increasing number of cities require that decent—though often minimal—standards be maintained in them. Besides protecting the roomers, enforcement of these codes can do a great deal to assure that rooming houses do not harm districts in which they are properly located."[51]

Over time, planners did exactly that: Zoning and building codes required homes to be built with ever more features and amenities. Minimum parking requirements were added and maximum residency limits appeared. Some of this was done to upgrade housing stock or protect health and safety. Some of it was done to eliminate entire forms of housing that gave the poor or the unlucky a continued toehold in richer neighborhoods. Does it really "protect the roomers" to move them from a boarding home without parking spaces to a tent beneath the overpass?

"It took a while, but over the generations, the planners have been very successful at mostly eliminating the accommodations for down-and-outers with the consequence that if you are down and out in a city where real estate is expensive, you end up on the street," Yglesias writes.[52]

The point is not that cities wanted the homelessness crises they now face. They didn't. Their hope was that people who couldn't afford the kind of housing they allowed would leave. Many did exactly that, of course. But some had nowhere else to go. Others needed to stay near their families or jobs. And these policies did not generate crisis in a single year, or even a single decade. It took time before choices to limit housing led to mass homelessness. But it is not surprising that choices to limit housing led to mass homelessness. And it is not even surprising that cities often choose to limit the forms of housing, or even the amount of housing, that can be built nearby. After all, if you already own a home, scarcity makes the asset you own all the more valuable.

What Happened in the 1970s?

There's an odd website called WTF Happened in 1971? It's a long stack of charts, gathered magpie-like from all manner of books and papers and articles, recording the many ways society began to tilt on its axis as the '70s dawned. The most convincing of them are economic: starting in the '70s, wages began to stagnate, inequality began to soar, inflation began to rise, and housing prices began their inexorable march upward.

Our favorite of these charts shows how many years an average wage earner would presumably need to save to buy a home. In 1950, it's 2.3 years. In 1960, it's 2.6 years. In 1970, it's 2.4 years. But then something happens. By 1980, it's 3.8 years. By 1990, it's 5.4 years. By 2000, it's 7 years.[53] And this forward march is hiding the regional differences: that home you could buy with 2.4 years of labor in 1970 was in a different kind of city than that home you could buy after even 7 years of work at median wages in 2000.

Real wages stagnated over these decades, but they didn't fall. The action was in housing prices, which rose and rose. This was something new. Prior to 1970, housing wasn't a prime asset. You bought a home to live in it. But that changed in the 1970s. Inflation was part of the reason. One of the main aims of federal housing policy has been to make possible the thirty-year fixed-rate mortgage, a peculiar financial device that wouldn't survive a day in the economic wild. What lender in their right mind would hand out thirty-year loans on fixed terms to virtually anybody with a job? But the federal government backed those mortgages and made the interest payments on them into large tax deductions, and so they became the cornerstone of the American housing market. But they became something else, too: a hedge against inflation. A fixed-rate mortgage holds payments flat on an appreciating asset. While inflation eats away at the real value of those payments, the value of the thing the payments are going toward—the house—just goes up and up.

From 1955 to 1970, owner-occupied housing held at about 21 percent of total household net wealth.[54] Between 1970 and 1979, it climbed to 30 percent of net wealth. For those who owned a home, it was much more of their total wealth than that. But a home is a peculiar form of wealth. You typically need to live in it. Selling stocks or bonds liquidates an asset you don't use in your day-to-day life. Selling a home liquidates the place you sleep, the walls within which you may have raised your children or grown to adulthood yourself. Financial interest merges with sentimental attachment and daily need. But it gets worse, as Fischel explains:

It is worth a moment to consider how financially problematic an owner-occupied home was at the beginning of the twentieth century—and remains to the present. An investment advisor whom you have consulted looks at your middle-income portfolio and tells you that you should put almost all of your liquid assets in a single investment. It is not a diversified mutual fund; it is a single firm, and the firm makes only one product in a single location. It has a great upside in that its returns are almost entirely untaxed under federal and state income tax laws, and it insures you against rent increases by the landlord. But its asset value is subject to a multitude of risks. Not least are those from the neighborhood and the single municipality in which the firm is located. Bad events next door, down the street, at the school district, and in city hall can put your life savings in a tailspin.[55]

In the '70s, rising inflation and slowing home building turned the homes people did own into the center of their wealth. But how do you protect the value of that asset? You can insure a home against fire, but you can't insure it against rising crime rates or local schools slipping in quality or a public housing complex being built down the block.

To manage those risks, you need to control what happens around your home. You do that through zoning and organizing. You do it through restricting how many homes and what kinds of homes can be built near you. You do it by making the minimum allowable lot sizes bigger and the parking requirements more expansive because both those rules ensure that only wealthier people will be able to buy into your community. You do it through organizing at planning meetings to defeat proposals for apartment buildings—they'll change the character of the neighborhood, and think of the traffic!—and refusing to expand sewer systems to areas where developers might want to build new homes.

In her essay "The Homeownership Society Was a Mistake," Jerusalem Demsas, who covers housing at the *Atlantic*, traces the politics of treating homes as assets. Housing is often spoken of as a safe investment, but it's not. Homes rise in price when there are too few of them to go around. The greater the gap between supply and demand, the higher the returns for homeowners. "At the core of American housing policy is a secret hiding in plain sight," she writes. "Homeownership works for some because it cannot work for all. If we want to make housing affordable for everyone, then it needs to be cheap and widely available. And if we want that housing to act as a wealth-building vehicle, home values have to increase significantly over time. How do we ensure that housing is both appreciating in value for homeowners but cheap enough for all would-be homeowners to buy in? We can't."

The logic of this is inescapable, and the politics it creates predictable. "[A] home's value is directly tied to the scarcity of housing for other people," Demsas says. "This system by its nature pits incumbents against newcomers."[56]

The '70s were a period of ferment for this form of politics. The run-up in housing prices was part of it. But Fischel emphasizes a few other forces. The Interstate Highway System, coupled with the growth of car use, allowed people to live farther from their workplaces than was possible even a few decades before. Then came civil rights legislation that made it illegal to directly discriminate against homebuyers based on race. Communities that wanted to—in the sanitized language of real estate—"preserve their character" needed to find other means by which to do it. And they did, through rules like setting a large minimum lot size for new construction.

"Lot-size requirements forced developers to build fewer and more expensive homes, in turn guaranteeing that the homes would be sold to wealthier, whiter buyers," writes Anbinder. He quotes a homeowner in Greenwich, Connecticut, giving up the game in 1967. "It's like going into Tiffany and demanding a ring for $12.50," said the homeowner. "Tiffany doesn't have rings for $12.50. Well, Greenwich is like Tiffany."[57] If you zone Greenwich so the only people who can afford homes are multimillionaires, then only multimillionaires will live in Greenwich.

Fischel is an economist, so he takes a materialist view of what was happening here. To him, the core of the story is home prices, and the desire of homeowners to keep those prices rising, and everything else was more or less a rationalization. "Economic advantage is a powerful private motivator, but it plays poorly in public discourse," he writes. "It is considered gauche (I have tried it) to mention in a public meeting that a particular public policy will raise or lower home values, even though what is acceptable to mention—traffic, crime, walkable streets, local pollution—pretty clearly maps onto home values. Something less obviously selfish is required to get other community residents to rally around the cause."[58]

But while there was plenty of selfishness in the housing politics of the '70s, something less obviously selfish was going on, too. Something noble and even necessary. The story of rising housing prices in America isn't a simple morality play of greedy homeowners and feckless city planners. This is a story, at least in part, of how the solutions of one era created the problems of the next.

America the Ugly

In May 1964, Lyndon B. Johnson stepped onto the podium at the University of Michigan to deliver that year's commencement address. The president began with a capsule history of the country he now led. "For a century we labored to settle and to subdue a continent," he said. "For half a century we called upon unbounded invention and untiring industry to create an order of plenty for all of our people." But the age of untrammeled growth—the whirlwind economic expansion that the New Dealers had set into motion—was revealing its limits. What was the cost of all this plenty?

"The catalog of ills is long: there is the decay of the centers and the despoiling of the suburbs," he said. "There is not enough housing for our people or transportation for our traffic. Open land is vanishing and old landmarks are violated."

> Worst of all, expansion is eroding the precious and time-honored values of community with neighbors and communion with nature. . . .
>
> We have always prided ourselves on being not only America the strong and America the free, but America the beautiful. Today that beauty is in danger. The water we drink, the food we eat, the very air that we breathe, are threatened with pollution. Our parks are overcrowded, our seashores overburdened. Green fields and dense forests are disappearing.
>
> A few years ago we were greatly concerned about the "Ugly American." Today we must act to prevent an ugly America.[59]

The problem the New Deal faced was straightforward. People had too little and they needed much more. But by the time Johnson took office, the difficulties of deprivation had been joined by diseases of affluence. In his 1958 bestseller *The Affluent Society*, John Kenneth Galbraith described an America cosseted by new comforts yet unable to shake a sense that something had gone fundamentally awry:

> The family which takes its mauve and cerise, air-conditioned, power-steered and power-braked automobile out for a tour passes through cities that are badly paved, made hideous by litter, blighted buildings, billboards, and posts for wires that should long since have been put underground. . . . They picnic on exquisitely packaged food from a portable icebox by a polluted stream and go on to spend the night at a park which is a menace to public health and morals. Just before dozing off on an air mattress, beneath a nylon tent, amid the stench of decaying refuse, they may reflect vaguely on the curious unevenness of their blessings. Is this, indeed, the American genius?[60]

Modern American liberalism may have been born in the New Deal. But it was reborn in its aftermath. It matured into a political movement with a divided soul. Much of midcentury liberalism evolved in reaction to the excesses and consequences of New Deal liberalism. "One of the most consequential conflicts in postwar America was between two systems of values," writes Jake Anbinder in "Cities of Amber." "An older *growth politics* which extolled the benefits of metropolitan development, and a newer *antigrowth politics* which rejected the idea that such development improved society."[61]

It is hard, now, to imagine how quickly the built environment of America changed in these years. In 1900, there were scarcely 8,000 cars in the entire country.[62] By 1970, 118 million cars sluiced through a nearly completed Interstate Highway System. In 1900, no one had ever flown in an airplane. By 1970, millions of passengers boarded wide-body jetliners like the Boeing 747 to travel across the oceans to thousands of airports around the world. To a previous generation, this technology would have been indistinguishable from sorcery. As every reader of fantasy novels knows, great magic carries a terrible price.

In 1943, Los Angeles residents woke up to air so dark and noxious that they feared the Japanese had launched a gas attack.[63] Five years later, a lethal smog in Donora, Pennsylvania, caused by industrial pollutants from zinc-smelting plants and a temperature inversion that trapped toxins in the air[64] killed twenty people and sickened thousands.[65] In New Hampshire, the Merrimack River, lined with textile mills in Manchester and Nashua, ran in different colors by the day, as dyes and chemicals dumped into the river tinged the water red, then green, then yellow.[66] In Cleveland, Ohio, on June 22, 1969, oily waste and debris were ignited, possibly by a flare thrown onto the Cuyahoga River, sparking a fire as tall as a four-story building.[67] In Pittsburgh, midcentury drivers had to use their windshield wipers to clear away the soot so they could see the road.[68] America in the 1950s and '60s was paradoxically the richest superpower in world history and functioned as a kind of mass-industrial conspiracy to kill its own residents.

The toxicity of growth triggered a reaction among intellectuals and, later, within government. In 1962, Rachel Carson, a marine biologist suffering from breast cancer, published *Silent Spring*, which argued that chemical pesticides were devastating our ecosystems and destabilizing the biosphere. The book is broadly credited with founding the environmental movement, but like any founding document, it hit a nerve because it concretized anxieties that already existed. Environmentalism soon permeated the broader culture. In the late 1960s, Gaylord Nelson, the senator from Wisconsin, who had been closely watching the student-led protests around the Vietnam War, was inspired to channel that energy and enthusiasm to protest on behalf of the environment. He hired a young activist named Denis Hayes, who came up with the idea of a walkout on the first day of spring, which they would call Earth Day. On April 22, 1970, more than 20 million people—roughly 10 percent of the US population—poured into the streets. It was the largest single demonstration in American history.

Between 1966 and 1973, the US passed almost a dozen laws that required the government to be more responsive to local citizens and the environment. They were the National Historic Preservation Act (1966), the Department of Transportation Act, the Federal-Aid Highway Act of 1968, the National Environmental Policy Act, the Clean Air Act of 1970, the Uniform Relocation Assistance and Real Property Acquisition Policies Act, the Noise Control Act of 1972, the Clean Water Act, the Federal-Aid Highway Act of 1973, and the Endangered Species Act. In seven years, America compiled an arsenal of regulation to slow or outright stop the era of big government building.

These were not partisan fights. To read President Richard Nixon's State of the Union address from 1970 is to tumble into a politics very different than our own, where Republicans talked in ways that even few Democrats dare speak today:

The great question of the seventies is, shall we surrender to our surroundings, or shall we make our peace with nature and begin to make reparations for the damage we have done to our air, to our land, and to our water?

Restoring nature to its natural state is a cause beyond party and beyond factions. It has become a common cause of all the people of this country. It is a cause of particular concern to young Americans, because they more than we will reap the grim consequences of our failure to act on programs which are needed now if we are to prevent disaster later.

Clean air, clean water, open spaces—these should once again be the birthright of every American. If we act now, they can be.

We still think of air as free. But clean air is not free, and neither is clean water. The price tag on pollution control is high. Through our years of past carelessness we incurred a debt to nature, and now that debt is being called.

Nixon promised that "the program I shall propose to Congress will be the most comprehensive and costly program in this field in America's history." He was as good as his word. He went on to sign the National Environmental Policy Act, the Clean Air Act, and the Endangered Species Act, and he created the Environmental Protection Agency, making him arguably the most important environmentalist president of the twentieth century.

But Nixon was not aberrant as a Republican taking the environmental worries of the moment seriously. "I might be letting you in on a little secret—as a matter of fact, one of the best-kept secrets in Washington," President Ronald Reagan told the nation in 1984. He went on to describe California's leadership role in passing environmental legislation. He talked about how the nation had followed California's lead. And then he delivered the punch line. "The secret

I mentioned is that I happened to have been Governor of California back when much of this was being done," Reagan said.[69]

In "Cities of Amber," Anbinder tells the story in more detail. Reagan signed the California Environmental Quality Act—CEQA, as it's called—into law in 1970. But he did not know what he was signing, and the legislature did not know what it was passing. The bill was thought to be modest. Despite the environmental consciousness rising in the state and in the media at the moment, the *Los Angeles Times* didn't devote a single full article to the legislation.

Then, in 1972, came a case called *Friends of Mammoth v. Board of Supervisors of Mono County*. A developer had proposed to build six buildings' worth of condominiums and shops and restaurants near Mammoth Lakes, one of California's beloved ski resort areas. Friends of Mammoth, a homeowners' association, sued to stop the build, arguing that it would strain water and sewage resources. The novelty of their argument was that they sued under CEQA. The legislation, as passed, held that government entities in California needed to produce environmental impact reports before embarking on major new projects. But the developer of the proposed Mammoth Lakes condos was not an arm of the California state, and this was not a public project. The argument of the Mammoth homeowners held that yes, actually, it was, because any development that required public permits to be built was inherently a public project.

Friends of Mammoth lost the case in the lower courts but appealed up to the state Supreme Court, which ruled in their favor in a 6-to-1 decision. CEQA, the court held, applies "not only [to] situations in which the government itself engages in construction, acquisition or other development, but also [in] those instances in which the state regulates private activity."[70] That meant it applied to, well, almost anything that anyone might try to build in the state of California. As a lobbyist for the Sierra Club put it, CEQA now covered "anybody engaged commercially in putting two sticks of wood together."[71]

The *Sacramento Bee* called the decision "probably . . . the most important such ruling by any court in the field of environmental concern since the daisy-pickers came out of the woods and plunged into the tangle of government influence."[72] San Francisco froze all new plumbing, building, and electrical permits until it could fully understand the scope of the ruling. As Anbinder dryly notes, "Having been informed of what the law they had passed two years earlier actually said . . . the legislature moved quickly to impose a four-month moratorium on CEQA's implementation so that worksites across the state would not come to a complete standstill."[73]

A couple of years later, government agencies in California were reviewing more than four thousand environmental impact statements annually—four times more than the entire federal government was generating under the facially similar National Environmental Policy Act. CEQA became a potent weapon against the construction of new homes. "Between 1972 and 1975, twenty-nine thousand proposed homes in the Bay Area—roughly a fifth of the region's total housing production at the time—were subject to environmental litigation," Anbinder writes.[74]

The Plague of Growth

We think now of the Interstate Highway System as one of the grand achievements of the postwar era. The reaction at the time, particularly among liberals, was more mixed. "The most charitable thing to assume about [the highway bill] is that they hadn't the faintest notion of what they were doing," the critic and historian Lewis Mumford wrote in 1958. "Within the next fifteen years they will doubtless find out; but by that time it will be too late to correct all the damage to our cities and our countryside."[75]

Robert Caro published *The Power Broker*, his study of how Robert Moses carved up New York, in 1974. Much of what Moses was building was highways. And he was not alone. Moses might have been distinctive in his power, but planners were slicing highways through communities all across the nation. Cities fought back, culminating in the so-called highway revolts, in which residents organized to block the roads being cut into their neighborhoods—and, in doing, built connections and coalitions and tactics for opposing all manner of development.

California was ground zero for both the possibilities and the predations of growth. In the 1950s, the five fastest-growing municipalities were all in California.[76] New suburbs sprung like poppies across the state. Before Californication was a Red Hot Chili Peppers song or a TV series starring David Duchovny, it was shorthand, Anbinder writes, for "the moral bankruptcy that many believed was inextricable from the physical form of sprawl itself."[77] In 1972, *Time* reported on the conversations happening in other western states, where "legislators, scientists and citizens are now openly concerned about the threat of 'Californication.'"[78] This was growth unleavened by concern for beauty or community or conservation. The term "ticky-tacky" comes from a song recorded by Malvina Reynolds and covered by Pete Seeger, describing the soulless, same-same tract housing covering the hills of Daly City, just south of San Francisco.

Anti-growth politics could, and often did, tip into a kind of misanthropy aimed at newcomers. Those who already lived in a place were its stewards, its guardians, its voice. Those who wanted to move to that place were recast as a consumptive horde. Harold Gilliam, who wrote the "This Land" column for the *San Francisco Chronicle*, put it grimly. "Ultimately, every conservation problem is a population problem. Every effort to save some vestige of California's pristine splendor, every campaign to preserve the bay or the hills or a natural coastline or a grove of redwoods, every attempt to curb galloping slurbanism or to save breathing space for the future, would be defeated by the unending advance of new hordes of population like a swarm of locusts devouring everything in sight."[79]

But what could you do about it?

2

Build

NO LESS THAN HOUSING, CLIMATE CHANGE MAKES A HASH OF OUR traditional political categories. Here it is typically the right that is willing to leap into the unknown, confident that humanity can adapt to unimaginable change. Here it is largely the left that wants to conserve the climate that the entirety of human civilization has known.

But to conserve our climate requires more than mere inaction. To do nothing—to let greenhouse gas emissions accelerate as they would if we kept burning coal and oil and gas heedlessly—is to welcome warming of four or five or six degrees Celsius. These are numbers that diverge from the climate of the eighteenth century as sharply as the climate of the eighteenth century diverges from the Ice Age.[1] These are numbers inside which the planetary systems that sustain us break.

To maintain the climate we have had, or anything close to it, requires us to remake the world we have built. One vision that is popular in some corners of the left is called "degrowth." It holds that climate change reflects humanity's thrall to an impossible dream of endless growth. Rich countries must accept stasis, shuttering or scaling down major industries, and poorer countries must grow more gently and prudently.

Degrowth is simultaneously much more and much less than an answer to the climate crisis. It is much more than an answer because it is not really about climate at all. It is an anti-materialist philosophy that holds that humanity made its fundamental errors hundreds of years ago, trading the animism of our ancestors for Christianity's promise of dominion over nature. The problem is not simply greenhouse gas emissions or microplastics. It is Cartesian dualism and American-style capitalism and everything these systems of thought and practice have taught us to value and prize and want.

"Those who sought to pave the way for capitalism in the sixteenth century first had to destroy other, more holistic ways of seeing the world, and either convince or force people to become dualists," writes Jason Hickel in *Less Is More: How Degrowth Will Save the World*. "Dualist philosophy was leveraged to cheapen life for the sake of growth; and it is responsible at a deep level for our ecological crisis."[2]

Hickel compares the scale of the philosophical and economic revolution degrowth imagines to Darwin persuading the world of evolution or Copernicus spreading the knowledge that the earth revolves around the sun.[3] He envisions a wholesale shift in humanity's relationship to other living things—and to itself. But shifts of that size take decades or centuries to play out. In the case of evolution, the victory is yet only partial. We do not have decades or centuries to convince the world to act on climate change.

To the extent that degrowth has a specific climate plan, it is to shut off or scale down areas of production it deems destructive, like military investment, meat and dairy production, advertising, and fast fashion. There is some appeal to this. All of us can identify some aspect of the global production system that seems wasteful, unnecessary, or harmful. The problem is that few of us identify the same aspects of the global production system.

Take meat and dairy production. When we think of humanity's land footprint, we mostly think of buildings and roadways. But only 2 or 3 percent of habitable land is taken up by cities. We do not primarily use land to live on. We primarily use land to feed ourselves. About half of all habitable land is used for agriculture. Of that, three-quarters is given over to raising livestock or growing feed for livestock. It is difficult to find an environmental challenge that is not tied up in raising animals for our consumption. It is a driver of climate change. It is a driver of deforestation. It is a driver of mass extinction, as the land we turn over to cows and sheep and goats is the land that other species need to survive. It is a driver of drought and water scarcity, as it takes about 1,800 gallons of water to produce a single pound of boneless beef.

To the vegetarians and vegans among us, this is an obvious target for elimination. Humans thrive on a vegetarian diet, and the factory farms that produce most of our meat are abattoirs of unimaginable cruelty and suffering. Industrial animal agriculture is more than a climate problem. It is a moral stain upon modernity. There is probably no single change that would do more for our interlinked environmental problems than for the world to cease using cows and goats and sheep for food.

But to suggest such a thing is to court political ruin. People want to eat meat, and they want that meat to be cheap and plentiful. The right accuses the left of scheming to ban hamburgers for a reason. The left denies those accusations and leaves direct confrontation with the meat industry out of its legislation for the same reason. There is no near-term politics that will ban meat consumption or redistribute it from richer countries to poorer countries.

For all the radicalism of his book, even Hickel flinches from the task he sets for himself. He does not suggest anything akin to ridding the world of the factory farms that produce most of our beef. Instead, he proposes "to end the subsidies high-income countries give to beef farmers" and notes that "researchers are also testing proposals for a tax on red meat."[4] Fine proposals. But not the revolutionary upheaval that will cut our emissions rapidly enough to limit global temperature rise to 1.5 degrees Celsius.[5] And that is even assuming you could pass a global or multinational tax on meat. Which you could not.

Degrowth criticizes other approaches as unrealistic, noting the ease with which countries slip from their climate commitments or the ways that clean energy may allow other human cruelties to persist. In a telling passage, Hickel imagines what would happen if we perfected and deployed nuclear fusion tomorrow, bringing to life the clean energy economy of green dreams. "What would we do with it?" he asks.[6] "Exactly what we are doing with fossil fuels: raze more forests, trawl more fish, mine more mountains, build more roads, expand industrial farming, and send more waste to landfill."

In this sense, degrowth recognizes the difficulty that politics poses to climate policy. It knows people want more of what they have, and although it blames capitalism and plutocracy for these wants, it sees the challenges these wants pose to traditional climate politics. But those challenges apply to the degrowth vision with even greater force. If you cannot imagine convincing people to change their desires in the presence of energy abundance, how do you imagine convincing them to accept the rapid, collective scarcity that degrowth demands?

We know what it looks like when governments face the political fury of rising energy prices or fuel rationing. In 2022, ninety countries and territories experienced often violent protests over the rising price of fuel between January and September, according to a BBC analysis.[7] In Sri Lanka—a country that Hickel holds out as a model for degrowth development—those protests led to the collapse of the ruling government.

It is not much easier in rich countries, where degrowthers insist on the most radical restrictions in energy use. In France, the 2018 "yellow vest" protests followed a modest hike in the fuel tax. In America, rising energy costs resulting from sanctions against Russia forced the Biden administration to open up domestic fossil fuel production and beg Saudi Arabia for more oil.[8] Germany's government tried to ban fossil fuel heating systems in favor of greener heat pumps; the outcry nearly split the ruling coalition and the compromised, cut-up bill that ultimately passed was a shadow of the initial proposal. In 2023, a wave of electoral defeats for the UK's Conservative Party were blamed on high energy costs, leading Prime Minister Rishi Sunak to delay a suite of climate policies. In the 2024 election, Vice President Kamala Harris emphasized the record levels of oil and gas production achieved under the Biden administration far more than the historic climate investments she helped pass into law.

When Erik Voeten, a political scientist, picked through the political consequences of recent climate policies, he found that "people who bear the cost of climate policies increasingly flock to the far right."[9] The only policy that seemed to blunt the backlash was directly compensating the people who suffer under green policies.

But you can't both compensate residents of rich countries for lost growth and cut growth in those same countries. Turning global politics into a zero-sum contest for allotted energy rations will not deliver a greener future.

The cost of trying and failing to implement the degrowth vision would not merely be missing our climate targets by a few tenths of a percentage point. It is to deliver a future of populist authoritarians who drill and burn their way back to a false prosperity. It is to discredit parties that care about climate change and empower strongmen who will give people what they have always wanted: the gift of abundant energy.

"We Just Burned It"

"Take any variable of human well-being—longevity, nutrition, income, mortality, overall population—and draw a graph of its value over time," Charles Mann writes in *The Wizard and the Prophet*. "In almost every case it skitters along at a low level for thousands of years, then rises abruptly in the eighteenth and nineteenth centuries, as humans learn to wield the trapped solar power in coal, oil and natural gas."[10]

Without energy, even material splendor has sharp limits. Mann notes that visitors to the Palace of Versailles in February 1695 marveled at the furs worn to dinners with the king and the ice that collected on the glassware. It was frigid in Versailles, and no treasury could warm it. A hundred years later, Thomas Jefferson had a vast wine collection and library in Monticello and the forced labor of more than a hundred slaves,[11] but his ink still froze to the tip of his pen during winter.[12]

Today, heating is a solved problem for many. But not for all. There are few inequalities more fundamental than energy inequality. The late demographer Hans Rosling had a vivid way of framing this. In 2010, he argued that you could group humanity by the energy people had access to. At the time, roughly 2 billion people had little or no access to electricity and still cooked food and heated water by fire. About 3 billion had access to enough electricity to power electric lights. An additional billion or so had the energy and wealth for laborsaving appliances like washing machines. It's only the richest billion people who could afford to fly, and we used around half of global energy.[13] Energy is the nucleus of wealth.

Can we all be energetically wealthy? Not if we're burning coal and oil. The stocks of fossil fuels are finite and their continued combustion is lethal. This would be true even if climate change was a hoax. Air pollution kills between 7 million and 9 million people each year; that is six or seven times the death toll from traffic accidents and hundreds of times the death toll from war or terrorism or all natural disasters combined. It is deadliest where people cook by burning wood or charcoal and farm by burning the end of the last season's crops. That is to say, it is deadliest where people are energy poor, because where people are energy poor, they burn fuel and breathe in the byproducts.

For most of human history there was no other choice. That is why nearly every society that has become rich since the industrial revolution has seen air pollution build to crisis levels. Human beings choked on smog in London in the nineteenth century and in New York and Los Angeles in the twentieth century. A few years ago, Beijing's air quality was an international scandal, and now the same is true for Delhi. But notice: the problem passes. Los Angeles got richer and its residents now breathe clean air. The same is true

63

in London, where air pollution in the eighteenth century was worse than Delhi is today.[14]

"Environmental action is often framed as at odds with the economy," writes Hannah Ritchie in *Not the End of the World*. "It's either climate action or economic growth. Pollution versus the market. This is just wrong."[15] As societies become economically and technologically rich, they clean their air and water. Air pollution is not a problem of using too much energy or pursuing too much growth. It is a problem of using dirty energy because you do not have the money or the technology to grow another way.

The same is true for climate change. We did not always know how to power economies without using fossil fuels. We do now. This is the technological miracle of our age. The cost of solar energy fell by about 90 percent from 2010 to 2020. The cost of wind power fell by nearly 70 percent.[16] Solar power does not choke the lungs. Wind power does not sting the eyes. Neither of them warms the planet. Two decades ago, it was not possible to imagine that modernity was compatible with renewable energy. Now we need not imagine it.

The world installed more solar power in 2023 than it did between 1954 and 2017. We have seen repeated periods in California and Texas of "negative energy prices"—moments where consumers are, mind-bendingly, paid to consume electricity because there is more of it than the system needs. The cost of solar is falling so fast that for much of the day it will be effectively free, in much of the world, by 2030. "I simply cannot believe where we are with solar," Jenny Chase, the BloombergNEF analyst, told the *New York Times*. "And if you'd told me nearly 20 years ago what would be the case now, 20 years later, I would have just said you were crazy. I would have laughed in your face. There is genuinely a revolution happening."[17]

In a thrilling paper with the very un-thrilling title "Empirically Grounded Technology Forecasts and the Energy Transition," a team of researchers found that the price of oil, gas, and coal, after adjusting for inflation, is about what it was 140 years ago.[18] But renewable energy keeps crushing expectations. The authors looked at 2,905 projections for solar costs made by the most popular forecasting models and found that solar costs were expected to fall by 2.6 percent a year and never by more than 6 percent. In reality, they fell by 15 percent per year, year after year. In 2022, the US Energy Information Administration released a report estimating life-cycle costs for new energy installations in the coming decades. Solar was already cheaper than natural gas. Wind was a dollar more. Both were about half the price of coal.[19]

As the climate writer and activist Bill McKibben put it, "In the place of those fires we keep lit day and night, it's possible for us to rely on the fact that there is a fire in the sky—a great ball of burning gas about ninety-three million miles away, whose energy can be collected in photovoltaic panels, and which differentially heats the Earth, driving winds whose energy can now be harnessed with great efficiency by turbines. The electricity they produce can warm and cool our homes, cook our food, and power our cars and bikes and buses. The sun burns, so we don't need to."[20]

To this miracle one might add humanity's harnessing of nuclear power, or our growing ability to tap the geothermal energy pulsing beneath the earth or the hydropower generated by the waves. So much clean energy is possible, and available, if we can muster the ingenuity and the will to harness it.

And so there is nothing inevitable about the pace of greenhouse gas emissions. To see this clearly does not require imagining any new energy technology; it simply requires looking at the way different countries power themselves now. America emits about 15 tons of carbon per person, per year. Canada and Australia belch out nearly the same. In Germany and Japan, it's 8 tons. In France and the United Kingdom, it's less than 5 tons.[21] These are vast differences across similar lifestyles. A wanderer in London or Paris or Tokyo or Berlin would not notice material deprivation compared to Toronto or Sydney or Houston.

What is true across space is also true across time. In 1979, Americans pumped out 22.7 tons of CO_2 per person; Canadians, 18.2; Germans, 14.3; Australians, 13.2; the UK, 11.5, France, 10.[22] All these countries are richer today than they were then, and yet they emit less carbon, per person, than they did then. Nor is it the case that their emissions have simply been offshored to the developing countries that manufacture many of the goods that richer countries buy. Researchers use trading data to track the movement of manufacturing emissions. Adjusting for offshore manufacturing blunts the cuts to emissions somewhat—in the United States, a 21 percent drop becomes a 14 percent drop, while in Germany, there's almost no difference—but it doesn't come close to erasing it.[23]

What is changing, in all these countries, is the source of power. "In 1900, nearly all of the UK's energy came from coal, and by 1950 it was still supplying over 90%," writes Ritchie. "Now coal supplies less than 2% of our electricity, and the government has pledged to phase it out completely by 2025."[24] Indeed, the last coal-fired power station operating in the UK shuttered in September 2024.[25]

It is possible to power a modern economy with clean energy. It is possible to develop an economy with clean energy. And it will be possible to go beyond where any economy is today with clean energy. While we were writing this book, researchers at the Lawrence

Livermore National Laboratory generated more energy than they used in a test of laser-ignited nuclear fusion.[26] We know nuclear fusion can work: it is how stars generate power. We have never known if we can make it work here on earth—at least not affordably and at scale. But we are getting closer.

It is tempting to assume we in the United States sit at the terminus of what energy can achieve and all that is left is for the rest of the world to catch up. We do not. We are early in the story of humanity's relationship with energy. Today's technologies will come to seem comical, even barbaric. "In 100 or 200 years, everything will look radically different," says Melissa Lott, the former director of research at Columbia University's Center on Global Energy Policy. "Folks will look back and be blown away by how we used energy today. They'll say, 'Wait, you just burned it?'"[27]

Too many see clearly the costs that dirty energy can impose on the environment but do not dare imagine the possibilities clean and abundant energy unlocks for it. In a paper imagining "energy superabundance"—which they define modestly, as simply every human being having access to the energy that residents of Iceland enjoy—Austin Vernon and Eli Dourado sketch out some of the near-term possibilities. Vertical greenhouses could feed far more people while using far less land. Desalination is a major contributor to water supplies in Israel now and could supply more than half of the demand in Singapore by the middle of the century. The technology could become affordable for poorer, populous nations that need new water sources most. Directly removing carbon dioxide from the air would become more plausible, giving us a path to reversing climate change over time.

But the first step to building the clean economy of tomorrow is building the clean economy of today. That is a daunting task.

Electrify Everything

Start with the major ways that most US households warm the planet. We drive. We heat homes. We cook food. We dry clothes. These activities require millions and millions of machines, most of which now run on fossil fuels. To decarbonize, they all will need to run on electricity.

The energy analysts Sam Calisch and Saul Griffith estimate that in the next few years consumers will need to replace about *one billion machines* with clean alternatives.[28] That means when old cars give out, they will be replaced by electric vehicles. It means when old furnaces cough their last breath, they are replaced by heat pumps. It means trading gas stoves for induction stoves and clothes dryers that run on natural gas for dryers that work off heat pumps.[29]

Producing all these new machines is itself a steep manufacturing challenge. It is also a persuasion challenge. People need to *want* these alternatives. That means the alternatives need to be excellent, which in many cases they now are. Electric cars accelerate faster and run quieter than cars powered by combustion engines. Induction stoves boil water in a fraction of the time it takes those little licks of fire. Because these advantages are not universally known—and because new technologies are more expensive than mature ones—subsidies need to be generous, and advertising needs to be everywhere. Making these replacement decisions needs to be a no-brainer, every time. But assume that challenge can be met, fully or partially. Now we have a billion more machines using more electricity than ever before. Where is all that electricity coming from?

About 60 percent of the electricity generated in the United

States in 2022 came from fossil fuels.[30] The precise mix varies by state. South Dakota gets 84 percent of its power from renewables, mainly wind,[31] and Washington gets 74 percent from renewables,[32] thanks to hydropower. But Nevada gets 56 percent of its electricity from natural gas.[33] Wyoming gets 71 percent from coal.[34] Florida gets only around 6 percent of its electricity from solar.[35] So much for the Sunshine State.

The first task is to convert that 60 percent of energy coming from fossil fuels to something closer to 0 percent—or at least 0 percent coming from energy that releases carbon emissions into the atmosphere, which could leave a role for natural gas with carbon capture.

That would be task enough. But with one billion new machines plugging into the country's grid, we don't just need the electricity we generate now to be clean. We need much more of it. "One way to put that is for every fifteen years from 2020 to 2050, we need to build the entirety of our electricity grid worth of supply again," says Jesse Jenkins, an energy expert at Princeton University.[36] And we need to build it out of solar panels and wind turbines and storage batteries.

Jenkins's team has modeled that build-out in detail. A plausible path to decarbonization sees wind and solar installations spanning up to 590,000 square kilometers. That is roughly equal to the landmass of Connecticut, Illinois, Indiana, Kentucky, Massachusetts, Ohio, Rhode Island, and Tennessee.[37] And we need to do it fast. In their 2023 paper "The Greens' Dilemma," J. B. Ruhl and James Salzman, professors of environmental law at Vanderbilt and UCLA, respectively, put this vividly. "Consider that the largest solar facility currently online in the United States is capable of generating 580 MW [megawatts]," they write. "To meet even a middle-road renewable energy scenario would require bringing online two new 400 MW solar power facilities—each taking up at least 2,000 acres—*every week for the next 30 years*."[38]

Installing that much wind and solar capacity isn't just a manufacturing challenge; it's a political one. Wind and solar require far more land than coal or natural gas to produce the same amount of energy. Some of the viable land is open and easy to purchase. Much of it isn't. Neighbors have fears about a wind farm rising near their homes, and communities have concerns about becoming the site of a major solar array. If the land is publicly owned, the project has to negotiate with an overlapping set of federal and state authorities. It can take years to merely get the plans and permits approved.

Once we've generated this electricity, we'll have to move it. This will sometimes require sending power across vast distances. The wind blows harder in Oklahoma than in Oregon, and the sun shines brighter in Arizona than in Maine, but a fully electric economy will require these far-flung states to be connected by an integrated energy grid. The name for the infrastructure that moves electricity from one place to another is transmission lines, and we've never completed more than 4,100 miles of transmission lines in one year, ever.[39] We'd have to build more than that, year after year, to hit these goals. Transmission projects often come in late and over budget, and many planned projects stall. A 2016 report by Lawrence Berkeley National Laboratory looked at five major transmission projects with projected completion dates of 2021. Only one of them has been completed. Construction hasn't even begun on the other four.[40]

For decades, American liberalism has measured its successes in how near it could come to the social welfare system of Denmark. Liberals fought for expansions of health insurance and paid vacation leave and paid sick days and a heftier earned-income tax credit and an expanded child tax credit and decent retirement benefits. Worthy causes, all. But those victories could be won, when they were won, largely inside the tax code and the regulatory state. Building a social insurance program does occasionally require new buildings. But it rarely requires that many of them. This was, and is, a liberalism that changed the world through the writing of new rules and the moving about of money.

The climate crisis demands something different. It demands a liberalism that builds. The Infrastructure and Investment Jobs Act, the Inflation Reduction Act, and the CHIPS and Science Act add up to about $450 billion in clean energy investments, subsidies, and loan guarantees. This is how the scale of such bills is normally described in Washington: by a price tag. The more money, the bigger the bill. That is an incomplete measure, at best.

If we could build faster, the numbers could rise. If we could build cheaper, the money would go further. That $450 billion is only an estimate. Many of the subsidies in these bills are open-ended. They will go to as many projects as can use them. These bills could spend trillions of dollars if we can build that infrastructure fast enough. They could spend far less than $450 billion if projects become too hard to permit. They could waste tens or hundreds of billions on projects that are never completed. What matters is not what gets spent. What matters is what gets built.

California's No-Speed Rail

In 1982, Governor Jerry Brown signed a bill to study what it would take to build a high-speed rail system across California. Californians liked what they saw. In 1996, California formed a high-speed rail authority to plan for the construction of what would be America's fastest rail system. Planners imagined a silver shell whistling along beams of steel, carrying millions of parents, children, Silicon Valley entrepreneurs, Hollywood actors, and solo travelers through America's largest state at speeds reaching 220 miles per hour. Goodbye, traffic and pollution-choked freeways. Hello, classy dining cars and reclinable seats.

High-speed rail is not some futuristic technology like cold fusion or flying cars. France and Japan broke ground on these projects back in the 1960s. Both of us have boarded bullet trains in foreign countries, taking the TGV from Paris to Bordeaux and the Shinkansen from Tokyo to Kyoto.

Ah, but California. The years ticked by. The governors came and went. In 2008, voters approved a plan to build the first segments by 2020 for $33 billion. Then, in 2011, high-speed rail's foremost champion returned when Brown improbably won back the governor's mansion, almost thirty years after last leaving it. In his 2012 State of the State address, he marked high-speed rail as his signature project. "If you believe that California will continue to grow, as I do, and that millions more people will be living in our state, this is a wise investment," he said. And California was ready to make it. "We are within weeks of a revised business plan that will enable us to begin initial construction before the year is out," he promised.

This time, Brown had allies. In 2009, President Barack Obama signed the American Recovery and Reinvestment Act into law. The "Recovery" bit was obvious: A housing bubble had caused a financial crisis. A financial crisis had caused mass joblessness. The economy needed help, and it needed it now. But the administration wanted to do more than mere stimulus. They wanted a legacy. They wanted the kinds of ambitious projects upon which another century of American might and prosperity could be built. "You never want a serious crisis to go to waste," Rahm Emanuel, Obama's chief of staff, said. "And what I mean by that is an opportunity to do things that you think you could not do before."[41]

This was the "Reinvestment" side of the bill: hundreds of billions of dollars to build the infrastructure of the future. And high-speed rail was the glitzy, headline project at the center of it. "Imagine boarding a train in the center of a city," Obama said in April 2009. "No racing to an airport and across a terminal, no delays, no sitting on the tarmac, no lost luggage, no taking off your shoes. Imagine whisking through towns at speeds over one hundred miles an hour, walking only a few steps to public transportation, and ending up just blocks from your destination. Imagine what a great project that would be to rebuild America. Now, all of you know this is not some fanciful, pie-in-the-sky vision of the future. It is now. It is happening right now. It's been happening for decades. The problem is it's been happening elsewhere, not here."[42] Obama wanted it to happen here.

The most obvious place was California, where, Obama continued, "voters have already chosen to move forward with their own high-speed rail system, a system of new stations and 220-mile-per-hour trains that links big cities to inland towns; that alleviates crippling congestion on highways and at airports; and that makes travel from San Francisco to Los Angeles possible in two and a half hours."

In 2009, then, this was the status of high-speed rail in California: It was a signature project of the president of the United States. A signature project of the most powerful governor California had in decades. Voters in California had set aside billions to make it real. And the federal government was adding billions more. It is hard to imagine a more favorable climate for the project. A spokesman for the California High-Speed Rail Authority joined a call-in radio show and told listeners that they'd be "able to ride that train from San Francisco to LA in the year 2020."

But progress crawled and costs ballooned. In his final State of the State address, in 2018, Brown tried to rally Californians to the task. "Difficulties challenge us but they can't discourage or stop us," he said.[43] The next year, Gavin Newsom, who had served as lieutenant governor, succeeded Brown. "Let's be real," Newsom said in his first State of the State. "The project, as currently planned, would cost too much and take too long. There's been too little oversight and not enough transparency. Right now, there simply isn't a path to get from Sacramento to San Diego, let alone from San Francisco to LA. I wish there were."[44]

Ambitions were cut. No longer was California trying to build high-speed rail to connect the megacities of San Francisco and Los Angeles. Now it was trying to salvage something, anything: A line between the agricultural centers of Merced and Bakersfield. A line no one would have authorized if it had been the plan presented in the first place. The scaled-down plan was estimated at $22 billion.[45] But even the price tag on that line has ballooned. The latest estimate is it will cost $35 billion to complete, and it won't begin carrying passengers until sometime between 2030 and 2033.[46] If all goes well.

The US has contributed as much to rail technology as any other country in the world—or more than any other country. Americans invented the air brake[47] and led the world in rail construction at the end of the 1800s. California businessmen helming the Central Pacific Railroad Company built all but a few hundred miles of the western portion of the Transcontinental Railroad in the 1860s. The project spanned nearly 1,800 miles. It took just six years to finish.

These days, six years is roughly the amount of time it takes California to realize that its bullet train needs to be pushed back by another decade. In the time California has spent failing to complete its 500-mile high-speed rail system, China has built more than 23,000 miles of high-speed rail.[48]

In October 2023, one of us—okay, it was Ezra—went to Fresno, California, and toured the miles of rail infrastructure that the California High-Speed Rail Authority has built.[49] The project is caught in a strange limbo between political fantasy and physical fact. The agency doesn't have anywhere near the money or political capital it would need to complete the Los Angeles–to–San Francisco system Californians actually want. It doesn't even have the money to complete the Bakersfield-to-Merced system that Newsom proposed. It has no line of sight on how it will get that money or that political capital. But since it has some money and some political capital, it is building anyway, in the hopes that Californians will want to finish what they started.

As Ezra walked the path of the track with the engineers who built it, he heard less about engineering problems than political problems. He stood on a patch of the 99 freeway that had been moved in order to clear the hoped-for train's path. Not far from there had been a Derrel's Mini Storage. In folk imagination, eminent domain is a simple process by which the state simply tells you it wants your land and then gives you some money and takes it from you. In reality, it took the High-Speed Rail Authority four separate requests for possession, and two and a half years of legal wrangling, to get the land.

That story repeated and repeated again and again. There are parts of the build that intersect with the freight rail lines. But the freight rail lines are so busy in the holiday season that some impose a construction moratorium from October to December. So in those areas no construction can happen for a large chunk of the year. Trains are cleaner than cars, but high-speed rail has had to clear every inch of its route through environmental reviews, with lawsuits lurking around every corner. The environmental review process began in 2012, and by 2024 it still wasn't finished. "I'm always amazed the staff has been working on these segments for a decade or longer to get through the environmental process," Brian Kelly, who served as CEO of the High-Speed Rail Authority from 2018 to 2024, says.[50]

What has taken so long on high-speed rail is not hammering nails or pouring concrete. It's negotiating. Negotiating with courts, with funders, with business owners, with homeowners, with farm owners. Those negotiations cost time, which costs money. Those negotiations lead to changes in the route or the build or the design, which costs money. Those negotiations lead to public disappointment and frustration, which leads to loss of money that might otherwise have been approved if the project were speeding toward completion.

There is one school of thought that says it is worth taking the time to do these projects right. If the reviews and the negotiations and the consultations take a few more years, those are years well spent. But they carry a price tag. "Time is a killer on the estimate of a project's cost," Kelly said. "When you don't have funding and can't make decisions and can't drive to get operational and you can't move the ball—the cost is huge. Two to three percent a year, and in higher inflation periods, like we just had, five percent." As delays mount, costs keep rising. The project becomes more expensive to finish. The public loses faith. The politicians begin second-guessing.

Governor Newsom knows how bad this looks. He knows how

bad this is. "I watched as a mayor and then a lieutenant governor and now governor as years became decades on high-speed rail," he says. "People are losing trust and confidence in our ability to build big things. People look at me all the time and ask, 'What the hell happened to the California of the '50s and '60s?'"[51]

But it's not just California. Democrats today are as searing in their criticisms of public sclerosis as any Republican. John Podesta, the graybeard who oversaw the rollout of the Inflation Reduction Act for Joe Biden, bemoaned that "delays are pervasive at every level of government—federal, state, and local. We got so good at stopping projects that we forgot how to build things in America."[52] Brian Deese, then the director of Biden's National Economic Council, noted in April 2022 that the Empire State Building was completed in a little over a year and said that government needs to "demonstrate that America can build—fast, as we've done before, and fairly, as we've sometimes failed to do."[53]

One response—the typical Republican response—is that government is intrinsically inefficient. But the data doesn't bear that out. The Transit Costs Project tracks the price tags on rail projects in different countries. It's hard to get an apples-to-apples comparison here, because different projects are, well, different, and it matters whether they include, say, a tunnel, which is expensive for all the obvious reasons.

Even so, the United States is notable for how much we spend and how little we get. It costs about $609 million to build a kilometer (about 0.6 miles) of rail here. Germany builds a kilometer of rail for $384 million. Canada gets it done for $295 million. Japan clocks in at $267 million. Portugal is the cheapest country in the database, at $96 million. All those countries build more tunnels than we do,[54] perhaps because they retain the confidence to regularly try. The better you are at building infrastructure, the more ambitious you can be when imagining infrastructure to build.

We looked into it, and it turns out that all those countries also have governments. So the problem cannot simply be government. Nor is the problem unions—another favored bugaboo of the right. Union density is higher in all those countries than it is in the United States.

The Construction Puzzle

Think of the technology we have today that we didn't have in the 1970s. The new generations of power tools and computer modeling and teleconferencing and advanced machinery and prefab materials and global shipping. You'd think we could build so much more, so much faster, for so much less money, than in the past. But we can't. Or, at least, we don't.

Throughout the 1950s and 1960s, productivity in the construction sector—how much more could be done given the same number of workers and machines and the same amount of land—grew faster than productivity in the rest of the economy. Then, around 1970, it began to fall, even as economy-wide productivity kept rising. Today, a chasm yawns. A construction worker in 2020 produced less than a construction worker in 1970, at least according to the official statistics. Contrast that with the economy overall, where labor productivity rose by 290 percent between 1950 and 2020, or to the manufacturing sector, which saw a stunning ninefold increase in productivity.

In the piquantly titled "The Strange and Awful Path of Productivity in the U.S. Construction Sector," Austan Goolsbee, the president of the Chicago Federal Reserve and a former chairman of the Council of Economic Advisers under President Barack Obama, and Chad Syverson, an economist at the University of Chicago's Booth School of Business, set out to uncover whether this is all just a trick of statistics, and if not, what has gone wrong.

Their paper works by process of elimination. First, they look at whether there has been less capital investment in construction than elsewhere in the economy. Nope. Then they examine whether we're mismeasuring construction—which would mean that sometime starting in the 1970s we began overestimating the labor or materials the construction industry used or underestimating how much it built with them, or both. They test this a few different ways, but the most interesting is to look at how many houses were built per worker, adjusted for square footage. There, the trend looks more flat than negative, and maybe slightly positive for single-family homes, but it's far from bringing construction productivity anywhere near level with the rest of the economy.[55]

This isn't a quirk of American recordkeeping. The slowdown is international. The Organisation for Economic Co-operation and Development tracked construction productivity in twenty-nine countries between 1996 and 2019. In 55 percent of them, productivity fell during that time. The only countries in which productivity rose at more than 2 percentage points per year were the Slovak Republic, Latvia, Estonia, and Lithuania—poorer countries rebuilding after the crackup of the Soviet Union and the Soviet bloc.[56]

So if it's not underinvestment and it's not a statistical illusion, what is it? Here, Goolsbee and Syverson seem stumped. The Wharton School, for example, tracks building regulations across cities, and Goolsbee and Syverson tested regulatory burden against construction productivity. There was a slight relationship, but nothing impressive. They looked at which states saw the highest and lowest rates of productivity increases. The worst performers, Syverson said, were Alaska, Idaho, Wyoming, Delaware, and Michigan. The relative stars were Georgia, North Carolina, South Carolina, Virginia, and Colorado. That doesn't lend itself to a clean story of red states and blue states or urban states and rural states.

Syverson, for one, is skeptical that there's any single answer. "I don't know how you get 50 years of decline without having multiple problems," he said. "Everyone has their pet theory. But everyone has a different pet."[57]

But Goolsbee and Syverson are economists. Maybe the cause is obvious to industry insiders. Ed Zarenski worked in construction, largely as an estimator, for more than forty years and now runs the market analysis firm Construction Analytics. Zarenski, who tracks construction costs and business volume closely, agrees that there has been a slowdown. And he agrees that there is no single cause for it. But when he thinks back on what the construction industry looked like when he began his career, and what it looks like now, the anecdotes tumble out.

"When I first started back in the '70s, you did one estimate on a project," he said. "You put it in, you got your bid, and if you won, you began construction. By the time I left in 2014, you did three estimates for every job before you even put the bid in. That becomes part of the cost of the job."

Or take the job site, he said. "The safety features on jobs when I started in the industry were not even noticeable. Safety on a job today is incredibly different. You don't walk across a beam; you walk around on a pathway marked for you to stay safe so you don't fall off the side of the building. By the time I retired, one thing that took place every day, on every job site, was a mandatory 15 minutes of calisthenics before you start your workday. That's totally non-productive, but it led to fewer work site injuries during the day."

And behind all that is paperwork, and paperwork, and more paperwork. "The work we do today takes hundreds more people in the office to track and bring to completion," he said. "The level of reporting that you have to send to the government, to the insurance companies, to the owner, to show you're meeting all the requirements on the job site, all of that has increased. And so the number of people you need to produce that has increased."[58]

The Organizations of Affluence

The economist Mancur Olson's famous 1982 book *The Rise and Decline of Nations* begins with its own productivity mystery: After World War II, Germany's and Japan's cities were bombed out, their people dispirited, their economies wrecked. The question of the age, Olson writes, was "whether these abjectly defeated societies would be able to provide themselves with even the rudiments of survival."[59] Instead, West Germany and Japan thrived, growing far faster in that era than Britain, which had emerged victorious from the war.

Olson was known for seminal work on how groups cooperate—and why, so often, they don't. In *The Rise and Decline of Nations*, he developed a deeper theory of why nations often stagnate amid affluence yet thrive in the aftermath of chaos. His key insight is that groups capable of collective action—imagine the Sierra Club or the Chamber of Commerce—are slow to build but powerful and persistent when they coalesce. America has long had seniors, but the emergence of the AARP gave them a new level of political power. Workers become far stronger once they organize into unions. Forming these groups is difficult, but power creates persistence: once a group is successfully organized, it can fight for its own survival and invest in its future strength. And so, Olson suggests, "if organizations and collusions for collective action usually emerge only in favorable circumstances and develop strength over time, a stable society will see more organization for collective action as time passes."[60]

The more organized groups you have, Olson says, the more fights over distribution you'll have, the more lobbying you'll have, the more complex regulations you'll have, the more bargaining you'll get between groups, and the harder it will be to get complex projects done. Affluent, stable societies have more negotiations. And that means they have more negotiators. There's great good in that. It means people's concerns can be voiced, their needs can be met, their ideas can be integrated, their insights can be shared. It also means that it becomes difficult to get much of anything done. This is why China can build tens of thousands of miles of high-speed rail in the time it takes California to fail to build hundreds of miles of high-speed rail. China does not spend years debating with judges over whether it needs to move a storage facility. That power leads to abuse and imperiousness. It also leads to high-speed rail.

The Rise and Decline of Nations is a classic economics text. But time has exposed gaps in the theory. Japan has gone from economic poster child to growth laggard. Olson's argument would seem to imply that the United States, with its geographic protection against invasion and its long history of continuity, would be far more sclerotic than Germany, but it isn't. And Olson has no real answer for why so few countries that fall into crisis subsequently grow into affluence.

Olson's biggest error is his assumption that groups organize around redistribution. Olson almost completely missed the post-materialist turn in the politics of affluent countries. Some groups seek to fill their coffers, but others organize to protect the environment, to increase safety standards, to preserve the feel of their communities, or to express their values. These kinds of groups have been engines of social progress. Their existence is a gift of affluence, not a disease of affluence.

But Olson, who died in 1998, was right when he said that affluence is a gift that comes with costs. And those costs concentrate in the areas of the economy in which the number of groups that have to be consulted mounts. From this perspective, the productivity woes in the construction industry don't seem so puzzling. It's relatively easy to build inside the confines of computer code. It's harder, but manageable, to manipulate matter within the four walls of a factory. When you construct a new building or subway tunnel or highway, you have to navigate neighbors and communities and existing roads and emergency access vehicles and politicians and beloved views of the park and the possibility of earthquakes and on and on. Construction may well be the industry with the most exposure to Olson's thesis. And construction of public projects, like high-speed rail, is almost uniquely vulnerable. It is the government's job, after all, to balance society's many competing perspectives. They need to do more than turn a profit or satisfy shareholders.

Zarenski's experience often felt like a narrativization of Olson's thesis. "There are so many people who want to have some say over a project," he said. "You have to meet so many parking spaces, per unit. It needs to be this far back from the sight lines. You have to use this much reclaimed water. You didn't have 30 people sitting in a hearing room for the approval of a permit 40 years ago."[61]

Syverson told a similar story. "There are a million veto points," he said. "There are a lot of mouths at the trough that need to be fed to get anything started or done. So many people can gum up the works."[62] That's particularly true in richer areas. There's a reason so much of the housing construction in Washington, DC, since 2000 has happened in the city's Southwest, rather than in Georgetown. When richer residents want something stopped, they know how to organize—and they often already have the organizations, to say nothing of the lobbyists and access, needed to stop it.

These dynamics help explain the curious finding that ends Syverson and Goolsbee's paper. After looking at the states with the highest construction productivity, they note that the more productive states don't seem to gain market share in the construction industry. That doesn't make much sense if you assume that the difficulties of construction are primarily the organization of manpower and materials. It makes more sense if you assume that the frictions are in navigating local regulations, community considerations, neighbors' qualms, and politicians' interests. Developers are often fixtures in the local political scene. They have to be.

"My feeling is the guys that know the system have a much easier time getting through the system," Zarenski said. "They know ahead of time what they have to come into the party with and how to speak to those people and how to satisfy them, and so it goes a lot smoother for them."[63] But a thorough knowledge of one city or state, and establishing relationships with its decision-makers, won't necessarily translate to success in another.

In a separate paper, Ed Glaeser and four coauthors add to this story.[64] They begin with an astonishing fact: from 1935 to 1970, the number of homes produced per construction worker increased at the same pace as, and sometimes even faster than, the number of cars produced per automobile industry worker or the total manufactured output per industrial worker.[65] The world we live in—where manufacturing productivity rises and rises even as construction productivity falls—is a new phenomenon, not a historical inevitability.

Glaeser and his colleagues go on to look at the size of the firms involved. It turns out that big home construction companies are much more efficient than small home construction companies. No surprise there. But the market in home construction is dominated by small firms: more than 60 percent of employment in single-family home construction is in firms with fewer than 10 employees; in manufacturing, most employees work in firms of more than 500 people.[66]

Why is home construction in America dominated by such small firms? The researchers pick through the data and find that firms are allowed to build on less and less land, and are subject to more and more land use regulations, in ways that choke off their ability to grow and scale their work across cities and states. A manufacturing plant can locate in one place and sell everywhere. Builders have to negotiate through the regulations and interest groups and political relationships of each parcel of land they work on individually.

One of Olson's insights is that a complex society begins to reward those who can best navigate complexity. That creates an incentive for its best and brightest to become navigators of complexity and perhaps creators of further complexity. "Every society, whatever its institutions and governing ideology, gives greater rewards to the fittest—the fittest for *that* society," Olson writes.[67] A young country that is still in its building phase creates opportunities for engineers and architects. A mature country that has entered its negotiations phase creates opportunities for lawyers and management consultants.

Then there's the incentive to avoid bureaucracy and its attendant frustrations. Patrick Collison, the CEO of the online payments behemoth Stripe, was once asked whether too much talent was flowing into Silicon Valley. "I don't think that the ambitious upstarts who go into high-speed rail (in America, anyway) are going to have a great time or have much success in convincing their friends to follow them. And I suspect that, for various reasons, too many domains look somewhat like high-speed rail. . . . There's a view that the internet is a frontier-of-last-resort and I don't think it's totally wrong."[68]

Nader's Raiders

America's postwar politics are often shorthanded as the rise of New Deal liberalism and then the backlash of small-government conservatism. But it wasn't just conservatives who came to think the government reckless and dangerous and in need of new rules and strictures. Liberals did, too.

After World War II, as highway construction grew, vehicle sales soared. So did road deaths. Motor vehicle fatalities rose from about 30,000 in 1946 to more than 50,000 in the late 1960s. In 1965, a lawyer named Ralph Nader published the book *Unsafe at Any Speed*, a blistering exposé of car manufacturers resisting safety improvements while blaming individual drivers for rising fatalities. The book was a sensation. In 1966, Lyndon Johnson signed the National Traffic and Motor Vehicle Safety Act and the Highway Safety Act, which mandated a new set of auto safety standards.[69] Nader soon became one of the most famous lawyers in America.

To replicate his success, he recruited teams of young activists to join the cause of bird-dogging government and big business on behalf of consumers. His disciples, known as Nader's Raiders, transformed politics, with their blend of expertise and advocacy.[70] "So far as anyone can remember, nothing quite like this has happened in Washington before," a *Christian Science Monitor* reporter wrote in 1969. "A group of unofficial but informed outsiders . . . as a sort of civilian posse, has descended on a rather stuffy government commission, poked under sofas, and asked some rough questions."[71]

As the historian Paul Sabin writes in his book *Public Citizens*, reformers like Ralph Nader were right to concentrate their fury on government and its safety record in the 1960s. "The government *was* allowing strip mines to ravage the Appalachian Mountains and leaving coal miners to suffer from black lung disease with little compensation," he writes. "Government policies *were* permitting oil refineries to freely dump toxic emissions into low-income communities of color, and letting oil spills pollute the nation's waterways and coasts."[72]

Nader didn't just criticize the government. He launched a movement to tame it. His Raiders contributed to some of the most important environmental laws in history, including the Clean Water Act. With each win, they made it easier for more citizens and groups to sue the government for wrongdoing. But what they were building was an arm of liberalism—with associated institutions, laws, and leaders—designed to relentlessly sue the government itself, and that would go on to fight for more bills and rules that would widen the opportunities to sue the government. Sabin writes:

Litigation by leading public interest environmental law firms in the early 1970s almost exclusively targeted the government for legal action. The Sierra Club Legal Defense Fund boasted of seventy-seven legal accomplishments between 1971 and 1973. Approximately seventy sought to block government actions, or to intervene in public proceedings to influence government regulatory and permitting practices. The Environmental Defense Fund similarly began its 1972 case summary with a list of acronyms for the ten federal agencies named in its legal interventions. In more than sixty of its sixty-five listed legal actions, the Environmental Defense Fund either intervened in public proceedings, such as government permitting processes for private projects, or directly assailed a government-led initiative. Fewer than five of EDF's legal actions directly targeted companies or private parties. Similarly, only three out of twenty-nine of NRDC [Natural Resources Defense Council]'s legal action initiatives from its first seven months directly named a corporate defendant.[73]

The environmentalist movement succeeded brilliantly. Between 1970 and 2020, the combined emissions of the six most common pollutants—which include lead, carbon monoxide, and sulfur dioxide—dropped by roughly 80 percent. New cars, SUVs, and trucks that run on gas today are more than 99 percent cleaner than in 1970.[74] The benefits of the Clean Air Act, which was amended in 1977 and 1990, have prevented between 400,000 and several million premature deaths in the last fifty years.[75] The reduction in lead furthermore saved tens of thousands from senseless poisoning and saved millions of IQ points. The number of "very unhealthy or hazardous air days" in Los Angeles fell from 160 in 1981 to an average of 2 in the 2010s.[76]

But behind these victories, Nader's revolution created a new layer of government: democracy by lawsuit. The number of lawyers and cases soared in the 1970s and 1980s. The result, Sabin argues, was a new kind of liberalism, which regarded government not as a partner in the solution of societal problems but rather as the source of those very problems.[77]

When the PBS news anchor Jim Lehrer asked Nader why he was qualified to be president in 2000, Nader told him, "I don't know anybody who has sued more [agencies and departments]."[78] Nader and his Raiders believed in government. They defended it from conservative assault. When they criticized it—when they fought it, sued it, restrained it—they did so to try to make it better. But those same laws and processes were available for anyone else to use, too. You can bog clean energy projects down in environmental reviews. You can use a process meant to stop the government from building a highway through your town to keep a nonprofit developer from building affordable housing down the block. "It was as if liberals took a bicycle apart to fix it but never quite figured out how to get it running properly again," Sabin writes.[79]

Liberalism's Lawyers Problem

Nicholas Bagley, a law professor at the University of Michigan, has seen the broken bicycle up close. When he served as Governor Gretchen Whitmer's chief legal counsel, he noticed that Republicans were consistent in the way they tried to weaken the government. They would bury it in paperwork and procedure and hearings and disclosure demands and lawsuits. It was as if the right had studied the tactics of Nader's Raiders and adopted them for their own purposes.

The 2017 Regulatory Accountability Act, which Republicans proposed but couldn't pass,[80] was a good example. For every major regulation, it would have forced the government to open a period of comment and solicit alternative approaches from the public, given those affected the opportunity to cross-examine the agency proposing the rule at an oral hearing, forced the publication of on-going frameworks for evaluation, and much more. Some of these ideas sound fine in theory but multiplied across the entire swath of major regulations the government proposes or carries out, the burden of compliance would become overwhelming.

Democrats would defend the government against these salvos, but they didn't seem to notice what the defenses implied. If Republicans were proposing more paperwork and process to make the government less effective, wasn't it likely that less paperwork and process would make government more effective? Or as Bagley asked, "If new administrative procedures can be used to advance a libertarian agenda, might not relaxing existing administrative constraints advance progressive ones?"[81]

In 2019, Bagley published an incendiary article in the *Michigan Law Review*, which he later turned into a policy paper for the Niskanen Center. "The Procedure Fetish" argued that something had gone wrong inside government, inside liberalism, inside Bagley's own profession. Liberal legalism—and through it, liberal government—had become process-obsessed rather than outcomes-oriented. It had convinced itself that the state's legitimacy would be earned through compliance with an endless catalog of rules and restraints rather than through getting things done for the people it claimed to serve.

"Inflexible procedural rules are a hallmark of the American state," Bagley wrote. "The ubiquity of court challenges, the artificial rigors of notice-and-comment rulemaking, zealous environmental review, pre-enforcement review of agency rules, picayune legal rules governing hiring and procurement, nationwide court injunctions—the list goes on and on. Collectively, these procedures frustrate the very government action that progressives demand to address the urgent problems that now confront us."[82]

Behind these procedures, Bagley suggested, were two very real concerns: legitimacy and accountability. How can a government as powerful and vast as that of the United States maintain legitimacy? How could it maintain accountability to citizens?

These fears reflect, in part, the age in which the rules were written. The 1946 Administrative Procedure Act, which governs much of the federal government's bureaucratic workings, was adopted "to soothe the jangled nerves of legal and business communities alarmed by the New Deal and the muscular wartime exercise of state power."[83] Then came the buildup of procedural architecture in the '70s, when liberal lawyers, inspired by the courtroom heroics of the civil rights movement, turned to the legal system to make sure that the government actually worked on behalf of the people.

The system we developed is unique. Decisions that are often made by bureaucracies in other countries are made by judges in our country. Robert Kagan, a law professor at the University of California, Berkeley, calls it adversarial legalism. "It is only a slight oversimplification to say that in the United States, lawyers, legal rights, judges, and lawsuits become functional equivalents for the large central bureaucracies that dominate governance in the activist states of Western Europe," he writes.[84]

There's a reason, Kagan thinks, that America has ended up with the system we have. Americans have always mistrusted the government. They've particularly mistrusted centralized power. But they also need a government able to wield power. They want the good a government can do. The tension became unbearable after the New Deal and the Great Society. "Between 1965 and 1977, responding to the new political movements, Congress passed 25 major environmental and civil rights acts, plus far-reaching statutes regulating workplace safety, consumer lending, product safety, private pension funds, and local public education," Kagan writes. "It created federal regulatory agencies or bureaus to issue implementing regulations, binding on millions of business firms. But to enforce those laws and regulations, Congress was compelled to bow to the inherited demands for decentralization of government."[85]

Americans were asking the government to do more than it ever had but they were not willing to give the government the trust and authority it needed to do it. But reformers could not simply devolve power to state and local governments. Liberals had just seen, in the fight against Jim Crow, that you could not trust the states, much less the localities, to do what the federal government asked. And so they turned to the courts, which had, under Chief Justice Earl Warren, become newly beloved by liberals. Adversarial legalism was a way of reconciling the government we wanted with the suspicions we harbored.

America is unusually legalistic. It always has been. In 1835, Alexis de Tocqueville wrote, "Scarcely any political question arises in the United States that is not resolved, sooner or later, into a judicial question."[86] What was true then is truer now. America has twice as many lawyers per capita as Germany and four times as many as France. Much of this energy is now devoted to suing the government. In 1967, there were 3 cases per 100,000 Americans directed at enforcing federal laws. By 1976, there were 13. By 2014, there were 40.[87]

The prevalence of lawyers in American life is unusual. But their dominance at the top of American politics is startling. "Though they make up less than 1 percent of the population, lawyers currently constitute more than one-third of the House of Representatives and more than half the Senate. Fully half of the last ten presidents were lawyers, as are more than a third of the officials now serving in the states as governor, lieutenant governor, and secretary of state," Bagley writes.[88] In the Democratic Party, every presidential and vice presidential nominee from Walter Mondale to Kamala Harris attended law school (Tim Walz, in this respect, was an almost radical break with tradition). When you make legal training the default training for a political career, you make legal thinking the default thinking in politics. And legal thinking centers around statutory language and commitment to process, not results and outcomes.

Olson predicted that a thriving, successful society would become more complex to navigate over time. There would be more groups and voices and laws and processes. Those who succeeded would be those best suited to operating at the nexus of that complexity. In the economy, that might be management consultants and financiers. In politics, it will be lawyers. There is nothing wrong with lawyers. There might be something wrong with a country or a political system that needs so many of them and that makes them so central to its operations. That might be a system so consumed trying to balance its manifold interests that it can no longer perceive what is in the public's interest.

"Legitimacy is not solely—not even primarily—a product of the procedures that agencies follow," Bagley writes. "Legitimacy arises more generally from the perception that government is capable, informed, prompt, responsive, and fair."[89] And that is where government is failing. California's High-Speed Rail Authority has been scrupulous in following the law but has been unable to deliver a train. The result is less, not more, faith in government.

The Pew Research Center has aggregated decades of polls tracking the public's trust in government. The high mark on the chart is in 1964, when 77 percent of the public believed that the government would do the right thing all or most of the time. Confidence plummets from there. In the '70s, after Watergate, it sits in the 30s. It rebounds into the 40s in the '80s and briefly brushes the 60s after 9/11, but the downward trend is undeniable. By 2023 it sat at 16 percent.[90] This is not, in our view, attributable solely or even mainly to cumbersome government processes. But the collapse in trust across the same decades that so many processes were being built to affirm that government could be trusted should make us question whether we have yoked the state to a failed theory of legitimacy.

Now the government has taken on the task of decarbonization and the responsibility of coordinating a once-in-a-century transformation of America's built landscape. But it is doing so with laws and agencies and habits that are better designed to block green construction than to allow it.[91]

The Green Dilemma

In 2020, J. B. Ruhl and James Salzman published a paper titled "What Happens When the New Green Deal Meets the Old Green

Laws?" They began by imagining a presidential debate in which two opposing candidates describe their vision for remaking America's energy infrastructure. One candidate proposes doubling down on oil and gas production, building more freeways, and crisscrossing the country in natural gas pipelines. The other candidate imagines an all-out race to an economy built atop renewables, with electric vehicle chargers everywhere and a national high-speed rail system anchoring American transit. "These two infrastructure agendas could not be more different in vision, but they are very much alike in one key respect," Ruhl and Salzman noted. "Each is an environmental impact assessment and project permitting nightmare."[92]

The problem, Ruhl and Salzman argued, is that "the Green New Deal must undertake multiple national-scale infrastructure initiatives of magnitudes never before processed through existing siting and environmental law standards and procedures." There was little reason to believe that was possible. Examples were piling up of renewable projects being stalled or killed by coalitions akin to those that formed against dirty energy projects, and deploying the same environmental laws and rules. "Most people do not like the idea of an oil pipeline or electric transmission line running through their backyard," write Ruhl and Salzman. "Guess what—they do not like the idea of wind turbines or solar panels in their backyard, either."[93]

In their follow-up, "The Greens' Dilemma," Ruhl and Salzman tried to diagnose the problem more precisely. The raft of environmental laws in the 1970s, they said, represented a "Grand Bargain" of sorts.[94] "The quid pro quo for a cleaner environment was that development would become slower and more expensive due both to permitting and to the litigation that often ensued. In many respects, this has turned out to be a good deal. Apart from greenhouse gases, which effectively have been unregulated, every major air pollutant has decreased significantly over the past five decades, from carbon monoxide and sulfur dioxide to airborne lead and others. Surface water quality has similarly improved substantially since the 1970s."[95]

But that bargain has broken down. The problem we faced in the 1970s was that we were building too much and too heedlessly. The problem we face in the 2020s is that we are building too little and we are too often paralyzed by process. And this is not just the view of a few law professors.

"The environmentalist movement evolved to stop bad people from destroying the world, and so we have perfected the art of saying no," says Larry Selzer, the president and CEO of the Conservation Fund. "But we can't 'no' our way to the kind of growth we need. The Interstate Highway System is forty-nine thousand miles of road. The interstate clean-energy system—the solar farms, the wind turbines, the geothermal land, the transmission lines, the pipes—will touch more than five hundred thousand miles of land. This will be an enormous project. We have to build, and build, and build."[96]

Ruhl and Salzman, for their part, believe we need new laws. The problem with the laws we have is that they are indiscriminate. It is as easy to obstruct an oil refinery as a wind farm. The National Environmental Policy Act (NEPA) gets much of the attention here, but the problem is really the profusion of different, overlapping policies and authorities. Beyond NEPA, Ruhl and Salman note the Endangered Species Act, the Migratory Bird Treaty Act, the Marine Mammal Protection Act, the Coastal Zone Management Act, the Clean Water Act, the Federal Land Policy and Management Act, and the National Forest Management Act. "All told," they write, "over sixty federal permitting programs operate in the infrastructure approval regime. And that is just the federal system—state and local approvals and impact assessments could also apply to any project."[97]

The Chokecherry and Sierra Madre Wind Energy Project, which is intended for federal land in Wyoming, would be the largest wind farm in US history. Building it has meant navigating a morass of federal, state, and local permitting and siting authorities, as well as environmental challenges. If all goes well from here, it will be completed in 2026—eighteen years after it was proposed, Ruhl and Salzman note. Timetables like that will not meet the climate emergency we now face. Either we build faster or we accept catastrophe. There is no third option.

In his paper "Getting Infrastructure Built: The Law and Economics of Permitting," Zachary Liscow notes that the United States performs below the average of OECD states in environmental quality but also performs below average in confidence in government. "So, despite its participatory ethos, the United States does not succeed in producing more trust."[98]

What we are leaders in is the cost of public construction. In separate work with Leah Brooks, Liscow has found the cost of building a mile of interstate highway tripled in the back half of the twentieth century. "Though the data are fairly sparse, available data show that the U.S. Interstates built in the 1980s and 1990s were more expensive (in real terms) than any projects built elsewhere at any time—and that the highways built since 2010 are far more expensive than highway projects elsewhere in the world," he writes.[99]

To many environmentalists, that's a victory. It should be harder to build highways. But that same architecture of law affects the infrastructure they care about, too. "It is important to keep in mind what is actually expected to be permitted in the coming decades," Liscow continues. "Among projects seeking to connect to the grid (which is one indicator—though an imperfect one—of what will ultimately be built), 95% of the capacity is solar, battery storage, or wind." That's a dramatic change from 1969, "when 81% of the electricity supply was petrochemical and only 19% was zero-emission."[100]

New problems and new solutions require new laws. Ruhl and Salzman favor past models by which certain kinds of projects have been fast-tracked past environmental and legal challenges. A 1996 law offered this favoritism to border security, and the Trump administration used it to great effect in constructing parts of their border wall. In another example, Congress recognized that we had too many military bases after the Cold War and that closing them through the normal congressional process would be politically impossible. So they created an independent base-closing commission that received recommendations from the Department of Defense, proposed plans for closure based on those recommendations, and ensured those plans got simple and fast up-and-down votes. In October 2024, President Biden signed legislation exempting semiconductor-manufacturing facilities receiving subsidies under the CHIPS and Science Act from environmental review.[101]

Something similar could be created for green infrastructure, Ruhl and Salzman suggest, with projects deemed important to our climate goals fast-tracked past a slew of normal hurdles. Something akin to this system would, in their thinking, update our environmental laws for a new age, tuning them to meet the challenge of today rather than the challenge of yesteryear.

But no individual law will address this many different blockages at this many points in the system. What is needed here is a change in political culture, not just a change in legislation. Liberalism acted across many different levels and branches of government in the 1970s to slow the system down so the instances of abuse could be seen and stopped. Now it will need to act across many different levels and branches of government to speed up the system. It needs to see the problem in what it has been taught to see as the solution. Nothing about this is easy, and it is not always clear how to strike the right balance. But a balance that does not allow us to meet our climate goals has to be the wrong one.

3

Govern

TAHANAN, AT 833 BRYANT STREET IN THE SOMA NEIGHBORHOOD OF San Francisco, is 145 studio units of permanent supportive housing for the chronically homeless. Completed in 2021, it's a cheerful, efficient building that bears the hopes and scars of the population it serves. The curated murals and architectural flourishes are pockmarked by extensive water damage inflicted when a resident on an upper floor reportedly slept with the faucets running. Social workers stride purposefully through the halls, and well-loved dogs are being walked everywhere you turn.

But what makes Tahanan notable isn't its aesthetic. It's the way it was built. Tahanan went up in three years, for less than $400,000 per unit.[1] Affordable housing projects in the Bay Area routinely take twice as long and can cost almost twice as much. "Development timelines for affordable projects in San Francisco have typically stretched to 6 years or longer and development costs have reached $600,000 to $700,000 per unit," reported the Terner Center for

Housing Innovation at the University of California, Berkeley.[2] San Francisco cannot dent its housing crisis at the speed and cost at which it is building affordable units now. But if the pace and price of Tahanan were the norm, the outlook would brighten.

So how did Tahanan do it? The answer, for liberals, is depressing: It used private money to avoid the pile of rules and regulations that taking government money triggers. But it could only do that because it had the support of city and state officials who streamlined zoning and cut deals to make it possible. Tahanan reveals a confusion in the way we talk of the government. The government is a plural posing as a singular. Different factions and officials and regulations and processes push in different directions. It is often the case that no one is more frustrated by how the government works than the people who work in it or who are charged with running it.

Tahanan was built on the former site of a parking lot and temporary bail bond office. Sounds easy enough to build on. But it wasn't zoned for affordable housing. The project could get off the ground only because of legislation passed by State Senator Scott Wiener in 2017 that fast-tracked certain kinds of affordable housing projects in California past the local approval process.[3] "This project didn't have to go before the planning department for discretionary review or the Board of Supervisors," Rebecca Foster, the chief executive of the Housing Accelerator Fund, which led the development of Tahanan, said. "We got our entitlements in four months, which is unheard-of."

But that merely means you can begin the process of building. When you're building affordable housing, you're typically using public money. When you're using public money, you have to abide by public requirements. Take the Local Business Enterprise and Non-Discrimination in Contracting Ordinance, also known as 14B.[4]

These requirements began in 1984 as a preference for minority- and female-owned contractors. But in 1996, California passed Proposition 209, which held that "the state shall not discriminate against, or grant preferential treatment to, any individual or group on the basis of race, sex, color, ethnicity, or national origin in the operation of public employment, public education, or public contracting."[5]

Instead of scrapping the contracting requirements, San Francisco rewrote them to favor small businesses. "The public has an interest in fostering a strong and vibrant network of small and very small micro businesses in San Francisco," the ordinance says. To qualify as one of the favored "Micro-Local Business Enterprises" under 14B, a contractor must have less than $12 million in average annual gross revenue.[6] This cap creates a few problems. One is that it means public housing efforts in San Francisco are, by definition, discouraged from working with large contractors that have grown in size and revenue precisely because they are good at delivering projects on time and under budget. Another is that San Francisco has a tight labor market and an even tighter construction market. There aren't a lot of capable small contractors sitting around with nothing to do.

In practice, Foster said, a few small contractors end up attached to a large number of affordable housing jobs, causing delays and cost overruns. Then, of course, there's the cost of compliance—of proving to the city you're following the 14B rules. Foster's team estimates that requirements like 14B could add six to nine months and millions of dollars to building an affordable housing project the size of Tahanan.

It's not just 14B. There are local hiring requirements. The Arts Commission does a separate review of your design. You need an additional review from the Mayor's Office on Disability. Who could oppose that? But these projects already have to comply with the Americans with Disabilities Act, and the additional review takes time and comes at a cost. "They come in when you're done," Foster said. "And they'll say, 'That threshold is two centimeters off, and it is in all of your doors.' And so that delays people moving in for another couple of months. And it might mean that you miss a financing deadline and have an adjuster on your tax credit fees that are another $2 million. So it just has a big ripple impact."[7]

Tahanan is the first affordable housing project in San Francisco built using modular housing. All the units above the ground floor were fabricated at a factory in Vallejo, California. "That definitely helped with meeting the time- and cost-saving goals," Foster said. But some local unions were furious, even though the factory in Vallejo is unionized. Here, then, is another place where progressive goals conflict. Local union jobs are a good thing. Modular housing can make construction cheaper and faster in a state facing a severe housing shortage. Which do you choose?

What made Tahanan possible was a $65 million grant from Charles and Helen Schwab.[8] The grant's conditions were that the housing had to be built in under three years and for under $400,000 a unit. By using private financing, the project avoided the standards and rules that public money carries. That isn't to say the political system in San Francisco was against the project. The Board of Supervisors approved a crucial lease to keep the development operating into the future. But private money was the secret sauce.

It is damning that you can build affordable housing so much more cheaply and swiftly by forgoing public funds. Shouldn't things happen faster when they are backed by the might and money of the government?

A False Divide

We are used to understanding the battle lines of American politics as cleaving liberals who believe in a strong, active government from conservatives who doubt it. The truth is far more complicated. Liberals speak as if they believe in government and then pass policy after policy hamstringing what it can actually do. Conservatives talk as if they want a small state but support a national security and surveillance apparatus of terrifying scope and power. Both sides are attached to a rhetoric of government that is routinely betrayed by their actions. The big government–small government divide is often more a matter of sentiment than substance.

Neither side focuses on what scholars call "state capacity": the ability of the state to achieve its goals. Sometimes that requires more government. Sometimes it requires less government. But it always requires a focus on what the state is trying to achieve and what is in its way. In the absence of that focus, absurdity reigns.

Across Europe, government-administered health-care systems negotiate down the prices of drugs and treatments. In America, our fear of socialized medicine has led to a hodgepodge of private and public insurers who do not coordinate and do not effectively negotiate. The weight-loss drug Ozempic, for instance, costs about ten times as much in America as it does in Britain or France.[9] Those countries have national health-care systems that restrict what pharmaceutical companies can charge, and we do not. As a result, taxpayers in Europe spend less on health care, as a percentage of GDP, than taxpayers in America. And then Americans have enormous private bills atop our public spending. Keeping the American health-care state weak has made the American government larger and left Americans poorer.

But liberals lose sight of their goals, too. In response to the Tahanan story, Bob Kuttner, the cofounder of the stalwart liberal publication *The American Prospect*, tried to jam the problem into a container that the left is more comfortable with. "We have a very modest social-housing sector in the US and limited funds for housing subsidies. We are largely at the mercy of developers. We could eliminate zoning restrictions and make it easier to build multifamily housing, and that would solve only a small portion of the affordable-housing shortage." There is a comfort here with solutions that put more faith in government (public, or social, housing) and a discomfort with solutions that seem to align with markets (being at the "mercy" of developers, eliminating zoning restrictions).

The reality of housing development doesn't track along such neat ideological lines. Kuttner says that eliminating zoning restrictions and making it easier to build multifamily housing would make only a modest difference in our problems. He does not provide any evidence for this claim, but there is evidence against it. Houston has no zoning rules at all, though it does have some land use regulations.[10] As a result, it is dramatically easier to build in Houston than to build in Los Angeles or San Francisco or Seattle or Boston.

In 2023, the San Francisco metro area issued about 7,500 new housing permits. The Boston metro area issued 10,500. New York City, Newark, and Jersey City—together—issued slightly fewer than 40,000. The Houston metro area issued almost 70,000.[11] This divergence is decades old, and its consequences are clear. Houston has the lowest homelessness rate of any major US city. Officials estimate that it costs $17,000 to $19,000 to house a homeless resident of Houston, with about $12,000 of that going to housing and the rest to wraparound services.[12] In San Francisco, the cost is between $40,000 and $47,000 annually, with about $35,000 going to housing costs alone. This tracks the broader difference between the two cities: in Houston, the median home costs a bit over $300,000 rather than a bit over $1.7 million in San Francisco.[13] Houston is not free of affordability problems. But it is not facing the crises of homelessness and housing affordability seen in the superstar cities of many blue states.

Liberals lament that private developers want to build profitable developments when what is needed most is affordable housing. But even aside from how much housing is built, one way to make housing more affordable is to make it cheaper to build. The problem is many liberal jurisdictions have layered on rules and regulations that make housing pricier even when it is constructed—and that, of course, makes it less affordable. In San Francisco, a 2023 state report found that it took 523 days, on average, to get clearance to construct new housing, and another 605 days to get building permits—and that's for the projects that aren't killed by community opposition during the planning process.[14] A project needs to be quite profitable to make it through that gauntlet—and it needs to be acceptable to its wealthy neighbors—and that pushes developers toward luxury condos.

But the grim absurdity of liberal housing policy comes clearest when you focus on the kind of housing liberals claim to support: affordable housing built by nonprofit developers with the backing of both voters and local government. In 2016, the people of Los Angeles overwhelmingly passed Proposition HHH, a ballot measure that raised $1.2 billion through a higher property tax to create

10,000 new apartments for the homeless. "The voters of Los Angeles have radically reshaped our future," Mayor Eric Garcetti said, "giving us a mandate to end street homelessness over the next decade."[15]

By March 2024, the city had built 4,344 units under HHH.[16] A 2022 audit found the units cost, on average, around $600,000[17]— almost twice the cost of the median sale price for a home in Houston. There have been many problems with Prop HHH, but the real problem predates it: the way that taking advantage of public money layers on requirements, delays, and additional goals, slowing down construction and raising costs.

HHH is designed to provide some, but not all, of the money for developments. Defenders of HHH are quick to point out that the average cost per unit includes around only $134,000 of HHH funds.[18] The program is designed to seed projects that can find other financing, too. That sounds good: by leveraging outside money, the taxpayer's dollar can go further. In reality, it means affordable housing projects need to line up four or five or six different funders, cobbling together tax credits and philanthropic donations and state and local incentives.

"Everyone wants to be able to say we spent only $50,000 on this apartment—that means I have to go through the process four or five times," Yasmin Tong, the founder of CTY Housing, a consultancy on affordable housing projects, says. "I've seen projects with as many as ten funding sources. It takes time to do that."[19]

The different financing sources come with different demands, all of which make the project more complex. "The developer has to hopscotch from one funding source to another to another," Tong said. "So you start by saying we'll serve low-income families at this development. But the funding falls through. So you put in veterans' units. Or try to house domestic violence survivors in here. There's this constant restructuring of the project as the funding sources come and go."

Ron Galperin was the Los Angeles city controller from 2013 to 2022. His office was responsible for auditing HHH. His office tracked how much each unit cost and where the money came from and whether the program was achieving its aims. You might expect him to praise HHH's effort to match each dollar with five dollars from other funders. In fact, he's furious at the way the money was structured.

"If you look at the inflated cost that comes along with all of the regulations and rules and restrictions and limitations," Galperin said, "then basically all of this money is going to feed the beast of covering the cost of the regulations. Yes, they get $134,000 on average from the city, but the hoops that have to be jumped through to get it very well may exceed the $134,000. We've created an absolutely insane system."[20]

Then there are the higher standards that public money requires developers to meet. "We're required to pay prevailing wage, so there's at least a 20 or 30 percent premium on the labor costs," Tong says. "We have sustainability requirements we need to maintain. I've had projects where the planning department required a higher-quality air ventilation system because we were a certain distance from the freeway. All the affordable housing development is subject to green building requirements. The standards in California are higher than anywhere else in the country. And you're not just required to build to the standard, you also need to hire a consultant to confirm you've built to the standard. That adds costs."[21]

Every one of these is a worthy goal. But so too is building a lot of affordable housing quickly and cheaply. Los Angeles is failing, and failing badly, at doing that. Given that failure, does it make sense to be asking for special air filtration systems for developments near freeways when the alternative, for many of the would-be residents, is a tent beneath the freeway? To pose the question sounds callous. But to refuse to pose the question, given the need for more housing, is cruel.

These additions do not come only from planning boards trying to upgrade the quality of the housing. They also come from neighbors who would prefer it never got built at all. In Venice, home of the legendary boardwalk, the Venice Dell Community project is trying to turn a parking lot owned by the city into a 140-unit building for homeless residents, low-income artists, and families, all of it designed by a star architect.[22] The development is being fought and even sued by a collection of local homeowners who complain that "Venice desperately needs this parcel to address our chronic parking shortage," that the new housing would be "an eyesore completely divorced from sound architectural principles," and that it is being developed "with no environmental review in a designated tsunami zone and FEMA Special Flood Hazard Zone."[23] (When do Angelenos want affordable housing? Now! Where do they want it? Not here!)

Surviving local opposition often means agreeing to a range of demands that send costs ballooning. To try to neutralize local attacks, developers hire pricey architects, redo plans repeatedly, make all kinds of aesthetic and architectural concessions or additions, hire extra lawyers and auditors, and on and on. Even if a project does survive all this, it does so at a higher per-unit cost, which then, of course, becomes one more data point that gets wielded in opposition to the next project.

Perhaps, as Kuttner suggests, the problem is simply that we don't have enough public (or, as it's been rebranded, "social") housing. In Singapore, almost 80 percent of the population lives in public housing. These projects have a bad reputation in the United States, but beautiful developments have opened in places like Montgomery County, Maryland, and larger cities like Atlanta are experimenting with using public projects to expand their housing stock. But social housing will rise or fail for the same reasons that all building projects rise or fail. It doesn't matter whether the worker hammering in nails is a public employee or a private contractor. The government still needs to build those homes affordably and quickly. And that's not possible under the rules and strictures that liberals have designed within the governments they run.

Heidi Marston led the Los Angeles Homeless Services Authority from late 2019 until April 2022, when she resigned in frustration. "We had thirty-eight unique funding sources coming in when I was there," Marston says, "and each of those had annual or biannual audits of not just us, but the nonprofits we were funding." Those audits were meant to show that the money was being spent exactly as intended. But that was part of the problem.

"Federal funding is probably more restrictive than any other," Marston continued. "Every year we get money from the Department of Housing and Urban Development. The city often gives their share to us, but on top of the auditing and tracking that the federal money comes with, they add on their own conditions, like we can't use it for staffing. Just all this stuff that gets added on in the process."[24]

It is easy enough to imagine how these conditions emerge. The city wants to show that it is using its money to build houses rather than expand its head count. HUD has no end of priorities and is trying to satisfy the desires and demands of the members of Congress who control its funding. Tax credits are added to the code to address real and wrenching problems, like the rise in homelessness among veterans. Grant makers want to show donors that their money is being used well, and the only way to prove that is through audits. Everyone, everywhere, is afraid of being implicated in fraud or waste or having their funding cut or seeing the public turn on them.

Each individual decision is rational. The collective consequences are maddening. We hire skilled, dedicated people to do the public's work and then make it impossible for them to do that work well. We ask people to work on society's hardest problems—often making much less than they could make in the private sector—and then rob them of the discretion and agility they need to solve them. And then we wonder why so many of them leave.

"There's tons of money that goes into homelessness, particularly in Los Angeles," Marston says. "My budget was almost a billion dollars. But the money comes with such confined requirements that it's almost impossible to spend. If you give me a billion dollars and the ability to spend it, it would be a different story."[25]

It is hard to hear Marston's story without being reminded of Nicholas Bagley's argument that liberalism has become obsessed with procedure rather than with outcomes, that it seeks legitimacy through rule following rather than through the enactment of the public's will. Homelessness in Los Angeles is a catastrophe. The public is furious at the sluggish, ineffective response. And the lead agency on homelessness is spending its time filling out audit forms and making sure each dollar is spent in strict accordance with the specific demands of funders.

The Problem with
Everything-Bagel Liberalism

In his 2022 article "A Time for Triage," Michael Gerrard, the founder of Columbia Law School's Sabin Center for Climate Change Law, considered why it has proven so hard for liberals to build the kind of climate infrastructure they believe is needed. "Rather than climate denial, the environmental community has tradeoff denial. We don't recognize that it's too late to preserve everything we consider precious, and to linger in making decisions. Society has run out of time to save everything we want to save, and to mull things over for years."[26]

One problem liberals are facing at every level where they govern is that they often add too many goals to a single project. A government that tries to accomplish too much all at once often ends up accomplishing nothing at all. (Conservatives are not immune from piling on procedure and stricture, but they often do so in a purposeful attempt to make government work poorly, and so failure and inefficiency become a perverse form of success.)

Call this "everything-bagel liberalism." The everything bagel is, of course, the best bagel. But that is because it adds just enough to the bagel and no more. It does not, actually, pile everything atop the bagel. In the Oscar-winning movie *Everything Everywhere All at Once*, there is an attempt to create a true everything bagel, and it becomes a black hole from which nothing can escape. The same is true for public projects. When the government adds the right number of goals, standards, and rules, much can be accomplished. When it adds too many, the project can collapse under its own weight, as has happened to high-speed rail in California.

In 2022, President Biden signed the CHIPS and Science Act into law. The Biden administration believed semiconductors would be to the twenty-first century what oil was to the twentieth century and that America must be a leader again in manufacturing them. "This is first and foremost and primarily a national security initiative," Gina Raimondo, the secretary of commerce, said. "We have national security goals we must achieve. Period. Full stop. No compromise."[27]

The semiconductor industry was invented in America—the "silicon" in Silicon Valley refers to the material that semiconductors are made from—but we long ago lost our dominant position in making what we invented. A report by the Semiconductor Industry Association says that the US share of global semiconductor-manufacturing capacity dropped from 37 percent in 1990 to 12 percent in 2020.[28] Part of the reason is cost. The association estimates that building and operating a semiconductor-manufacturing facility in the United States costs about 30 percent more over ten years than it does in Taiwan, South Korea, or Singapore.[29]

In 2023, the Biden administration released its Notice of Funding Opportunity for the $39 billion it intended to hand out to semiconductor manufacturers to locate new fabs in the United States. Reading the NOFO was a strange experience. Here was the US government trying to recapture an industry it had lost in part because it had become cost-prohibitive to manufacture semiconductors domestically. But the NOFO did not seem laser-focused on the cost problem. To be honest, it did not seem laser-focused on any problem.

Page 12 encouraged a pre-application that includes an environmental questionnaire "to assess the likely level of review under the National Environmental Policy Act." Page 20 mandated that applicants prepare "an equity strategy, in concert with their partners, to create equitable work force pathways for economically disadvantaged individuals in their region," which should include "building new pipelines for workers, including specific efforts to attract economically disadvantaged individuals and promote diversity, equity, inclusion, and accessibility." Pages 21 and 22 asked for a plan "to include women and other economically disadvantaged individuals in the construction industry" and encouraged the use of project labor agreements and sets out requirements for "access to child care for facility and construction workers."

Pages 24, 25, and 26 asked applicants to detail how they would include minority-, veteran- and female-owned businesses, as well as small businesses, in their supply chain, and offered seven bullet points detailing how this might be done, including dividing supply chain requirements "into smaller tasks or quantities to expand access" and "establishing delivery schedules for subcontractors that encourage participation by small, minority-owned, veteran-owned, and women-owned businesses." Then there are requirements for "a climate and environmental responsibility plan," as well as community investments in areas like transit, affordable housing, and schools.[30]

Many of these are good goals. But are they good goals to include in this project? There is no discussion in the NOFO of trade-offs. Nor was there any admission by the administration that anything they were asking for even represented a trade-off.

"Every one of the requirements—or they're not really requirements—nudges—are for criteria or factors we think relate directly to the effectiveness of the project," Raimondo said. "You want to build a new fab that will require between 7,000 and 9,000 workers. The unemployment rate in the building trades is basically zero. If you don't find a way to attract women to become builders and pipe fitters and welders, you will not be successful. So you have to be thinking about child care."[31]

But do Taiwanese semiconductor firms really know how to expand the role of women in the construction industry? How good will they be, really, at diversifying supply chains? These are all worthwhile goals. But there is some margin at which trying to do more means ultimately achieving less.

It is impossible to read these bills and guidelines and not notice that the additions are rarely matched by deletions. Process is enthusiastically added but seldom lifted. You can imagine a version of the CHIPS bill that lifted immigration rules to make it easier for skilled semiconductor workers to come to the United States. That would have been the most direct way to address the shortage of skilled workers hindering the construction and operation of the fabs. You could have imagined rules exempting the semiconductor fabs from NEPA or giving them some kind of fast-track process. (In late 2024, the Biden administration signed a bill from Senators Mark Kelly and Ted Cruz to do exactly that, after warning that environmental review could add "years" to the construction timeline.)

To be clear, there is nothing unusual in the way the Biden administration approached the CHIPS and Science Act. The federal government often tries to make the subsidies it offers serve an array of goals and constituencies. California's high-speed rail was shaped by this dynamic, too. Many Californians were confused that construction had begun in the Central Valley, which was far less populated than the corridors near Los Angeles or San Francisco.[32] Why start there?

When California applied for federal money under the terms of the American Recovery and Reinvestment Act, the Obama administration gave preference to bids that would improve air quality in poor communities. And so the $3 billion the federal government offered was not really to build high-speed rail. It was to begin building high-speed rail in ways that addressed air pollution in specific places. The Central Valley is poorer and more polluted than coastal California, so federal funding went there, and so did the initial construction. California is building high-speed rail in a place that makes it less likely that it will generate the ridership, political support, and financial backing to ever finish. The irony is that it's not just bad for the high-speed rail project. It's also bad for air pollution across the state.

It Should Not Be This Hard to Serve the Public

Since 1960, federal government spending has risen more than five-fold—and yes, that's accounting for inflation.[33] But the size of the federal civilian workforce has barely budged. It was slightly fewer than 2 million people in 1960 and it's slightly over 2 million people today. In countries like China and Singapore, civil service is held in high esteem, and the brightest graduates compete in nationwide tests to win government jobs. In the United States, the word "bureaucrat" is tossed around as an epithet. Republicans have spent decades demonizing government, and they have largely won the argument. The dominant belief is that anything that can be outsourced or privatized should be. Government is bloated. The private sector is efficient.

Democrats may not believe what Republicans believe about government, but they often act as if they do. In 2008, when

California began building its high-speed rail system in earnest, the state's High-Speed Rail Authority had just ten workers. One of them was responsible for designing graphics for social media. The job was turned over to a vast assemblage of consultancies. It was one of these consultants—WSP—that estimated the system would cost only $33 billion and take only twelve years to build. But WSP was joined by Project Finance Advisory, Cambridge Systematics, Arup, TYLin, HNTB, PGH Wong Engineering, Harris & Associates, Arcadis, STV, Sener, and Parsons Corporation. The outsourcing "proved to be a foundational error in the project's execution— a miscalculation that has resulted in the California High-Speed Rail Authority being overly reliant on a network of high-cost consultants who have consistently underestimated the difficulty of the task," reported Ralph Vartabedian in the *Los Angeles Times*.[34]

California is one of the richest polities in the world. It was building one of the most ambitious rail projects in the world. But it did not hire the best rail designers and engineers to provide in-house expertise and manage the project. California was financing and overseeing a program it did not have the capacity to plan, manage, or even truly understand. "There was an ideology at the Authority some time ago that was like, 'Let's keep this small and in-house and we'll rely on consultants to build this,'" Brian Kelly, the High-Speed Rail Authority's CEO, said. "My philosophy when I got here was the state is the owner of this project and so we need to build state capacity. When I started, the authority was seventy percent consultants, thirty percent state. Now it's fifty-five percent state and forty-five percent consultant."[35]

In the Bay Area, a different story played out. In 2012, Bay Area Rapid Transit (BART) signed a contract with Alstom, a French rail car manufacturer, to deliver 775 cars for $2.58 billion.[36] By 2023, though, something unusual had happened: the cars were coming in faster, and cheaper, than expected. The cost estimate was slashed by almost $400 million.[37] One major source of savings, reported trains.com, was "BART's decision to have its own staff do more of the engineering work in house. The project team has included engineers who have successfully completed new rail car projects at other agencies."[38] Nor is this an isolated anecdote. Zachary Liscow's research found that increasing employment in state departments of transportation by 1 employee per 1,000 residents reduced the cost-per-mile of highway construction by 26 percent.[39] Government cannot do everything itself. But it needs enough know-how to oversee the projects it is doing.

Jen Pahlka is the founder of Code for America, a civic tech group that tried to build a bridge between the technology industry and the government in a bid to upgrade government services. The work was hard, fruitful, important, frustrating. She went on to advise on digitizing government in the Obama White House. She is something of a godmother to a generation of idealistic technologists who tried, or are trying, to make government work the way it should work. Her memoir of this work, *Recoding America*, is a compendium of their stories. It is painful to read.

In January 2020, Pahlka had stepped away from her role at Code for America. She needed some time away from the problems of digitizing government. But then came the pandemic, and the lockdowns, and the millions of people suddenly out of work. Those people were all, unexpectedly, now reliant on unemployment insurance, which is managed by the states. And those systems were not prepared for anything like this level of demand. California's system, administered by the state's Employment Development Department, fell into particular chaos, with millions of people seeing their benefits wrongly delayed or denied.[40] Pahlka was asked to co-lead a task force that would rescue it.

Technologically, there was nothing particularly novel in the challenge. Unemployment insurance is fairly simple. People apply. They are accepted or rejected. Then checks are sent out. By the standards of the technology sector, this is a solved problem. "Privately, some California officials told me they thought the EDD staff was just incompetent at technology and our team would find the problems easy to fix," Pahlka writes. But that wasn't how the task force saw it. "Privately, we wondered if we could help at all."[41]

Pahlka has come to think of government technology—and the regulations that control it—as layers of sediment. As new problems emerge, new layers are added. But the older ones are rarely removed. "Each successive layer is constrained by the limitations of the earlier technologies," she writes. "The system is not so much updated as it is tacked on to."[42] The challenge of updating government technology is the challenge of updating, harmonizing, or terminating the functions of these old systems. And all of it must be done while following procurement and contracting rules that no private technology company would ever impose on itself.

At the EDD, the core technological layer was called the single client database, which runs on an IBM mainframe from the '80s.[43] Parts of it are written in a programming language called COBOL, which dates back to 1959. COBOL is almost never used today, and it is hard to find engineers who know how to program in it. Making matters worse, parts of the single client database were designed to run on those old monochrome displays that showed green text on a black background. Because nobody makes those displays any longer, the staff used virtual emulators to access the system—they would run software on new computers that could mimic the constraints of old computers.

Then came more layers. In 2002, the EDD contracted with Deloitte to bring their work online. Deloitte built one system to access the IBM mainframe through a web browser. It built another system to corral and manage applications flagged for manual identity verification. It built a third system that acts as the public-facing website for people to apply for benefits. All these systems had their own subsystems. And within those subsystems, applications could pool and get trapped in places no one was really looking. Pahlka and her team were told the number of backlogged applications was around 230,000. It took them seven weeks to organize the databases such that they could be precisely counted. The true number was 1.2 million.

The EDD doesn't build or manage its own technology. Nor is that technology built or managed by a centralized team of software engineers in the state government. It is done by external firms chosen and managed through a labyrinthine procurement process. At the time of the meltdown, the EDD had been working on a modernization contract for ten years that it was theoretically just weeks away from awarding. Read that again: They had not been working on modernizing their technology stack for ten years. They had been working for ten years on the massive contract they would award to outside firms to modernize and manage their technology stack. That contract was expected to take eleven years to execute.

The sedimentary chaos at the EDD was not at all unusual. California spent ten years and $500 million trying to bring its courts onto a common document management system before abandoning the effort.[44] The State Department's Bureau of Consular Affairs has been trying to modernize and consolidate its visa and passport systems since 2009.[45] The IRS began trying to replace one of its core systems—the Individual Master File—in 2000. The work is now projected to be completed in 2030.[46]

"The public servants responsible for the interminably drawn-out modernization efforts are neither lazy, stupid, nor malicious," Pahlka writes. "I've met hundreds of them, and they are overwhelmingly dedicated, conscientious, and often quite creative. IRS employees managed to send monthly child tax-credit payments to nearly forty million families and to mail out over $800 billion in stimulus checks during the pandemic, all while relying on systems that were never designed to change so quickly or handle such enormous volume." The problem is that the systems they are updating have become "complex beyond our ability to imagine," as has "the complexity of all the rules these public servants need to follow to do that updating."[47]

The worst of the EDD backlog was in the system that managed manual identity verification. But working in that system required years of experience, accreditation, and testing. When the EDD crisis had begun, elected officials demanded the EDD hire more people. So the EDD signed another contract with Deloitte to bring on another five thousand workers. The governor touted the new hires. But it would have taken years to train those workers to face down the backlog the EDD was facing. And their questions and confusion were taking up the time of the workers who could work on the backlog. Pahlka's team calculated that it was now taking two to five times as long to clear those files as it had before the pandemic.

Letting go of thousands of new hires is cheaper and easier than training them. But that wasn't how the agency's leadership saw it. "Hiring as fast as they possibly could had been the one consistent directive coming from everyone above them: the governor's office, the legislature, the federal Department of Labor, and every oversight body with jurisdiction over the EDD's operations," Pahlka was told.[48] Telling all those overseers they were wrong was not in anyone's interest. And no one believed they would listen anyway. Firing workers during a crisis of EDD performance would look terrible.

There was another option. The system was choking over manual verification. Manual verification was typically triggered when the information an applicant filled out on their form didn't precisely match some other piece of information the EDD had about them. Perhaps you write "Jonathan" on legal forms but your employer pays you under "John." Perhaps you mistyped a digit in your Social Security number. It makes sense why this would lead to a manual check. But there was no real relationship between these tiny errors and fraud. Out of the 183,167 claims flagged in the previous quarter, only 804 were ultimately judged invalid.[49]

If anything, there was more fraud in the perfect applications. "Our world is awash in databases of stolen identities from breaches at credit monitoring services, retailers, and employers, and these stolen identities are freely traded on the dark web. Fraudulent applications using these sources will not get flagged: the data entered on the application will exactly match the sources the EDD checks against, because it is usually a copy of precisely that data," Pahlka writes.[50]

The EDD was implementing a new system of identity verification that would be quicker and more effective, but it needed to do something about the backlog that was building daily. The obvious answer was to loosen the rules that would lead to manual verification. But even though the process wasn't working, it was still the process. To follow it was safe. To evade it was risky. Fraud was really happening, and when its full extent was known, there was going to be a furor, and it would fall particularly heavily on anyone who loosened the anti-fraud rules, even if the rules they loosened were failing to catch fraud and causing the huge backlogs that were crashing the system.

What the EDD eventually did was simply stop taking applications altogether. For weeks, they shut down the portal for new applications. The EDD reassigned the bulk of its staff to clearing the backlog and setting up the new identity verification program.

Amid all this, Pahlka recalls, a member of the California Assembly introduced legislation requiring the EDD to make its applications and communications available in over a dozen languages. Most of those languages were already required by a 1973 state law. They were also required by multiple federal laws and rules. The EDD wasn't in compliance with all these older rules. It wasn't even serving English speakers effectively. It was not able to do what it was already required to do. Now it was being instructed to do more.

What was needed was subtraction. What Pahlka and her team found, again and again, was that the rules and regulations that governed California's unemployment insurance system and that had been written into its code had just kept growing. That made the code more complex and harder to update. It made new hires harder to find and harder to train. It made backlogs harder to clear. "Lawmakers often have good intentions, but they continually add policy layers with too little understanding of (and, sometimes, regard for) how what they add will interact with the layers that are already cluttering the delivery environment," she concluded.[51] For government to do more—or even for it to just do what it is already doing—sometimes it first needs permission to do much less.

A Government That Chooses Is a Government That Works

On June 11, 2023, a tanker truck carrying 8,500 gallons of gasoline flipped over. The truck ignited underneath the I-95 bridge in Philadelphia, killing the driver and melting the steel beams undergirding it. The I-95 bridge, which carries 160,000 cars daily, collapsed. This wasn't just a crisis for a roadway. It was a crisis for a region. I-95 is one of the main transportation arteries on the East Coast. It's a crucial connector between New York and Washington. Officials, including Pennsylvania governor Josh Shapiro, warned that rebuilding it would take months.

And it would have taken months, or longer, under Pennsylvania's normal rules. "We would hire a consultant to design it," Mike Carroll, the Pennsylvania secretary of transportation, says. "We'd need final design approved by the Federal Highway Administration. Then there'd be bidding from interested contractors. Then we'd process the bids. Then we'd issue a contract. That'd take about twelve to twenty-four months."[52]

But Shapiro signed a declaration of emergency that exempted the rebuilding process from the rules and requirements that slow so many public projects down.[53] Speed was the priority here. There would be no environmental impact statement. There would be no lengthy bidding process. The procurement rules were shunted aside. When Carroll arrived at the disaster, C. Abbonizio Contractors, a firm the state had worked with before, was already at the bridge on another job. They were chosen to oversee the demolition. Rob Buckley, of the highway contractor Buckley & Company, was also nearby, working on another project. His firm was pulled in, too. "The emergency declaration gave us the ability to engage contractors without bidding," Carroll said. "Work commenced the moment the fire department released the scene—that same day."

All the labor Pennsylvania used was union labor. And they pushed hard: work went on twenty-four hours a day, seven days a week.[54] A twenty-four-hour live cam trained on the site allowed the public to follow along. Shapiro took to giving updates on Twitter and TikTok. He turned the I-95 rebuild into a crucible for his governorship and an object lesson in something few still believed: That government could build big things fast. That it could do so using union labor. That it could move at the speed of an emergency rather than according to its own rules.

"The common denominator with all these decisions was let's get this thing done as fast as possible," Carroll said. He recalled a moment he came across a bunch of Abbonizio workers using a screwdriver to disassemble a highway sign. He asked what they were doing, and they told him they were saving the sign for the Department of Transportation in case they wanted to reuse it. "I said turn the machine on and knock the goddam thing over," he said with a chuckle. On another night Carroll saw rain forecast over the next few days. He told the team to pave anyway, in contravention of the Department of Transportation's rules, because the rain was light that night and could grow heavier soon.[55] If they waited, they might be waiting for days. "The emergency declaration was a game changer," Carroll says. "I took calculated risks that I'd have not taken in a normal project. It could've gone badly, but it didn't."

It's worth taking seriously what Carroll says there. These were risks. There are reasons these rules are in place. No-bid contracts can enable corruption as well as speed. There are reasons not to put down asphalt when it's raining. But in turning these questions from choices into rules, we have taken discretion and judgment away from people like Carroll. We prefer that projects go badly by the book. We minimize some risks but make delay and high costs routine.

The emergency declaration allowed Shapiro to make choices. He chose to use union labor but to gore a lot of other interests and processes. I-95 reopened in just twelve days—not the "months" initially forecasted. Shapiro did "one heck of a job," President Biden said.[56] His popularity swelled, and he began to be mentioned as a possible future presidential candidate. Turns out people like it when their government gets things done.

The *Washington Post* asked Shapiro to write an op-ed reflecting on lessons he'd learned. The first lesson, he said, was "empower strong leadership." The key to the rebuild was that the people in charge of the rebuild could act. "Managers of every component of the project were empowered to be decisive, take ownership and make a call when necessary—not defer and delay to the often-circular bureaucracy," Shapiro wrote.[57] The process Shapiro used would typically be illegal. Yet national Democrats and Pennsylvania voters alike loved it. What does that say about the typical process?

In his paper "State Capacity: What Is It, How We Lost It, and How to Get It Back," Brink Lindsey puts it well:

What is needed most is a change in ideas: namely, a reversal of those intellectual trends of the past 50 years or so that have brought us to the current pass. On the right, this means abandoning the knee-jerk anti-statism of recent decades, embracing the legitimacy of a large, complex welfare and regulatory state, and recognizing the vital role played by the nation's public servants (not just the police and military). On the left, it means reconsidering the decentralized, legalistic model of governance that has guided progressive-led state expansion since the 1960s, reducing the veto power that activist groups exercise in the courts, and shifting the focus of policy design from ensuring that power is subject to progressive checks to ensuring that power can actually be exercised effectively.[58]

Liberals have chosen to trust elected politicians and government workers less and trust regulatory and judicial processes more to ensure that government delivers. That may have made sense in a past era, but given the problems we face now, it is a mistake. Whether government is bigger or smaller is the wrong question. What it needs to be is better. It needs to justify itself not through the rules it follows but through the outcomes it delivers.

4

Invent

KATALIN KARIKÓ WAS BORN IN A SMALL VILLAGE IN THE NORTHERN Great Plain of Hungary. Her home, built of clay and straw, had no running water. It drew heat from a sheet metal stove that burned leftover sawdust from a local toy store.[1] Her first science lesson as a child did not come from a classroom but rather from the small garden next to the house. One year, an infestation of *Leptinotarsa decemlineata*, or what Americans call Colorado potato beetle, blighted her family's crop of potatoes. On her hands and knees, she plucked the black-and-white bugs, one by one, from the tubers and scraped off the smear of their pink eggs to preserve the crop. The work was "tedious and sometimes gross," she wrote years later;[2] no fun for a kid, perhaps, but fitting practice for a career in medicine.

As a young woman, Karikó became a scientist at the Biological Research Centre in Szeged, near Hungary's southern border.[3] When the center lost its state funding, she sold her car for nine hundred British pounds and sewed the cash into her daughter's teddy bear to elude Hungarian currency-control laws. She moved to Pennsylvania with her family. For the first few years in America, Karikó was an academic tumbleweed. She bounced around several university labs before she was hired by the University of Pennsylvania.

When Karikó arrived at Penn, a great gusher of money was flowing to DNA, as scientists hoped to directly edit the instruction manual of the human body.[4] Karikó developed a different interest: messenger ribonucleic acid, or mRNA. If DNA was the king of the biotech landscape, mRNA was a frail courier: a single-stranded molecule that ferried information from the nucleus to the part of the cell that made new proteins. Upon accomplishing this, mRNA disintegrated.

DNA had many technical advantages over mRNA, including its centrality to the genome. But in Karikó's mind, mRNA's apparent weakness, its structural frailty, was a strength. With human-edited mRNA, she thought, scientists could theoretically turn human cells into factories for producing any protein under the sun—to repair organs, or to fight disease—and then, *poof*, the therapy would disappear from the body without a trace. "People didn't understand why I was so interested in RNA," Karikó said. "They didn't see any potential. Nobody saw it as suitable for making medicine."[5]

At the University of Pennsylvania, Karikó submitted dozens of grants, including to the National Institutes of Health, the largest and most important scientific body in the US—and, by extension, in the world. For two years, she submitted a new grant application almost every month. The rejections were relentless. "Every night I was working: grant, grant, grant," she said. "And it came back always no, no, no."[6] Sometimes the NIH told her that her work was too risky. Sometimes they said she didn't have enough data to prove that her experiments would work. Other times, her grants scored so poorly that she received no feedback at all.

Throughout these years of failure and disappointment, Karikó stayed motivated. She loved science: the painstaking discovery of the new, the long and winding road out of ignorance. On her wall hung a Leonardo da Vinci quote that offered inspiration during the dark years when the rejections piled one on top of another: *Experiments never err, only your expectations do.*[7] "I was a scientist through and through," she writes in her memoir. "I wanted more than anything else to understand how the world works."[8]

But after five years of relentless rejection, Karikó hadn't brought in any federal grants, which are the lifeblood of American science. The NIH and other funding agencies rejected her work so many times she lost count. Penn demoted her to "senior research investigator." The position was so powerless that it seemed practically made-up, as she didn't know anybody at the university with the same title. By the mid-1990s, Katalin Karikó's future as a scientist—and the future of mRNA science itself—had hit a dead end. Rejected, ignored, and unfunded, her work seemed destined to wither away in that great invisible graveyard of ideas that die a silent death, thrilling their creator and then petering out into oblivion.

In 2020, decades after Karikó's demotion, a novel coronavirus pandemic was rampaging around the world. With frantic desperation, countries experimented with a variety of policies to contain it. Some ideas worked in some places. Few ideas worked everywhere. Italy implemented a strict national lockdown, while Sweden allowed many businesses to stay open. In the US, the response was scattershot. Pennsylvania's state rules permitted indoor dining in the summer, while in Philadelphia, a November city ordinance made it illegal for neighbors to sip beer on a porch.[9]

A year into the pandemic, researchers were still debating the most elemental questions, such as: Do masking rules even work? In 2021, a group of scientists from Yale, Stanford, and other august institutions published the final results of a randomized study of masking, which included data from roughly 350,000 people in 600 villages in Bangladesh.[10] The researchers concluded that villages randomized to receive surgical masks saw less symptomatic infection. But two years later, the coauthor of a large analysis of global masking research concluded that "there is just no evidence that [masks] make any difference, full stop."[11] To bring the pandemic to heel, the world needed something more universally applicable than a rule, or a law, or a border control policy. We needed a global fix: a medicine that would achieve immunity protection at scale.

What happened next is a kind of miracle. Before 2020, no vaccine in American history had ever gone from the lab to the public in less than three years.[12] The COVID vaccines achieved this feat in about ten months. In December, the US Food and Drug Administration issued an emergency authorization for two COVID therapies based on mRNA technology—the very same idea that the science establishment rejected when Katalin Karikó had suggested it, decades earlier.[13] The first vaccine came from Pfizer, working with the German firm BioNTech. The second came from Moderna, a biotech start-up based in the US. Unlike most behavioral interventions, the vaccines were immediately and obviously effective at reducing mortality for adults in every age cohort and in every country. Every study testified to their effectiveness at reducing severe illness, especially for the elderly. In the US, one year after the vaccines were first granted authorization, unvaccinated seniors were dying at more than ten times the rate of vaccinated seniors.[14] In Britain, an analysis by Imperial College London estimated that between 10 million and 20 million lives were saved worldwide by the shots in the first year of the vaccination program.[15]

In our first chapters, we recounted the many ways that America has gotten in the way of building what we need to flourish in the twenty-first century, from homes to clean energy. But the pandemic was a different kind of challenge. Here was a problem we couldn't regulate, or subsidize, or merely build our way out of. No number of masks for shoppers or plastic dividers in restaurants could do what the vaccines did. The end of the health emergency required the summoning into existence of something fully new. To defeat COVID, it wasn't possible to build our way out of the problem.

We had to invent our way out.

The Politics of Invention

Invention—the act of solving problems by bringing new products, systems, and ideas into existence—is the basis of human progress. Consider a thought experiment. The average lifespan of an American today is about eighty years. The world of 2025 is therefore just three modern lifetimes away from the world of 1785—three eighty-year-olds holding hands across time. To travel back three lifetimes to the 1780s is to enter a world without a car, toilet paper, or large-scale production of soap. In the realm of food, it is a world before can openers, pasteurization, or modern refrigeration. In medicine, it is a world without antibiotics, anesthesia, or a single vaccine. What principally distinguishes the past from the present is not biology, nor psychology, but rather technology. If the world has changed, it's because we have changed the world.

Modern liberal politics is made possible by invention. Almost every product or service that liberals seek to make universal today depends on technology that did not exist three lifetimes ago—or, in some cases, half a lifetime ago. Medicare and Medicaid guarantee the elderly and poor access to modern hospitals, where many essential technologies—such as plastic IV bags, MRI and CT scan machines, and pulse oximeters—are inventions of the last sixty years. It is tempting to say that, with these essentials already in existence, it is time for society to focus at last only on the fair distribution of existing resources rather than the creation of new ideas. But this would be worse than a failure of imagination; it would be a kind of generational theft. When we claim the world cannot improve, we are stealing from the future something invaluable, which is the possibility of progress. Without that possibility, progressive politics is dead. Politics itself becomes a mere smash-and-grab war over scarce goods, where one man's win implies another man's loss.

The world is filled with problems we cannot solve without more invention. In the fight against climate change, the clean energy revolution will require building out the renewable energy that we have already developed. But decarbonization will also require technology that doesn't exist yet at scale: clean jet fuel, less carbon-intensive ways to manufacture cement, and machines to remove millions of tons of carbon from the atmosphere.

In health care, the last few centuries of invention have turned a death planet—where disease ran rampant and, before 1850, one in two babies perished before their sixteenth birthday—into a world where people can look forward to generation-over-generation increases in life expectancy. But there are still so many mysteries that require fresh breakthroughs. We've made disappointingly little progress with many cancers. Complex diseases like Alzheimer's and schizophrenia elude treatment or even basic comprehension. The cellular process of aging is a deep mystery. We still don't have effective vaccines for adult tuberculosis or hepatitis C, or vaccine platforms that we can immediately scale up in the event of a new pandemic. Decades from now, our children may gawk in horror that people with chronic pain or lingering illness in the early twenty-first century couldn't take a simple all-purpose saliva or blood test to answer the basic question *Why do I feel sick?* If disease is a universe of mysteries, we have scarcely explored one minor solar system of its cosmos.

Inventions that may seem outlandish today may soon feel essential to our lives. Streets filled with electric self-driving cars that give us mobility without emissions and free us from the vast number of deaths caused by faulty human reflexes or judgment. Gigantic desalination facilities that transform our oceans into drinkable tap water. An economy with robots that build our houses and machines that take on our most dangerous and soul-draining work. Wearable devices to scan our bodies for diseases. Vaccines that we can rub on our skin rather than inject at the end of a needle. As unrealistic, or even ludicrous, as some of these ideas might seem, they are not much more ludicrous than a rejected, ignored, and unfunded mRNA theory that came out of nowhere to save millions of lives in a pandemic. To make these things possible and useful in our lifetime requires a political movement that takes invention more seriously.[16]

So, where is that movement? Invention rarely plays a central role in American politics. In health care, for example, Democrats have spent decades fighting for universal insurance, while Republicans have consistently fought its expansion. But while the dominant fight in Washington is typically about how we *buy* health care, we rarely talk about the health care that *exists to be bought*. After all, in the future, progressives don't just want everyone to have an insurance card; they want that card to provide access to a world of treatments that liberates patients from unnecessary disease and debilitating pain. Technology expands the value of universalist policies.

If progressives underrate the centrality of invention in their politics, conservatives often underrate the necessity of government policy in invention. "The government has outlawed technology," the investor and entrepreneur Peter Thiel said in a debate with Google CEO Eric Schmidt in 2014, echoing a popular view among techno-optimists and libertarians that government laws mostly block innovation. But many of Silicon Valley's most important achievements have relied on government largesse. Elon Musk is now a vociferous critic of progressive policy. But he has also been a beneficiary of it. In 2010, when Tesla needed cash to launch its first family-friendly sedan, the Model S, the company received a $465 million loan from the Obama administration Department of Energy.[17] His rocket-launching company, SpaceX, has received billions of dollars from NASA under Democratic and Republican administrations. Musk has become a lightning rod in debates over whether technological progress comes from public policy or private ingenuity. But he is a walking advertisement for what public will and private genius can unlock when they work together.

Beyond merely regulating technology, the state is often a key actor in its creation. An American who microwaves food for breakfast before using a smartphone to order a car to take them to the airport is engaging with a sequence of technologies and systems—the microwave, the smartphone, the highway, the modern jetliner—in which government policies played a starring role in their invention or development. Federal science spending is so fundamental to the overall economy that a 2023 study found that government-funded research and development have been responsible for 25 percent of productivity growth in the US since the end of World War II.[18] "There is widespread agreement that scientific research and invention are the key driver of economic growth and improvements in human well-being," the Dartmouth economist Heidi Williams said. "But I think researchers do a poor job of communicating its importance to lawmakers, and lawmakers do a poor job of making science policy a major focus."[19]

The pandemic proved the necessity of invention yet again. The mRNA COVID vaccines saved millions of lives and spared the US more than $1 trillion in medical costs.[20] But they might have never existed if it weren't for Karikó's force of will—and the cosmic luck of an extremely well-placed Xerox machine.

A Shot to Save the World

One day in the fall of 1997, after her demotion at the University of Pennsylvania, Katalin Karikó left her small office in the building for neurosurgery to make photocopies of several articles from science journals. The nearest large Xerox machine was in a different hall, inside Robert Wood Johnson Pavilion, which housed the biomedical library.[21] Waiting to use the photocopier, she struck up a conversation with an immunologist named Drew Weissman.[22] Karikó told him about her interest in mRNA as a therapy. Weissman told her he was working on an elusive HIV vaccine. Their brief interaction sparked an idea. What if synthetic mRNA, with its power to teach the body to make specific proteins, could trigger an immune response that fought off a virus like HIV?

When they teamed up, their partnership felt like kismet. "Each of us had exactly the knowledge and skills that the other needed," Karikó wrote.[23] "I was an RNA scientist who didn't know much about immunology. He was an immunologist without RNA experience."

But progress was painfully slow, and the NIH rejected practically all of their grant applications. "People were not interested in mRNA," Weissman said. "The people who reviewed the grants said, 'mRNA will not be a good therapeutic, so don't bother.'"[24] They cobbled together funds from other projects. Weissman had federal grant money coming in for his research on HIV, which he pulled over into the mRNA project. Meanwhile, Karikó made do with bits of funding that had been awarded to her Penn colleagues. For years, the science wasn't going much better than the fundraising. In their first experiments, mRNA injections in mice caused terrible inflammation.

After several years of trial and error, they finally broke through in the early 2000s, by creating an mRNA therapy that could enter the cell without sending the immune system into a frenzy. "I was absolutely elated," Karikó wrote.[25] But the scientific community largely ignored their discovery. When they submitted their findings to the leading science journal *Nature*, the editors rejected the paper entirely. The specialty journal *Immunity* agreed to publish it in 2005 only after extensive edits. The night before the paper came out, Weissman told Karikó that "starting tomorrow, your phone is going to ring off the hook."[26] He was wrong. In the years following publication, Karikó received only two speaking invitations. "Our breakthrough had apparently failed to break through," she wrote. Rather than make Karikó a science rock star, the tepid response to her mRNA discovery made her a target for firing. In 2013, when it was clear that she wasn't bringing in enough outside funds to justify a tenured faculty position, she left academia for good. "I was kicked out, forced to retire," she said.[27]

If mRNA was failing to impress the scientific establishment, its reception in the private sector was a different story. In the US, Karikó and Weissman's work caught the attention of a brash group of postdoctoral researchers, professors, and venture capitalists. They had started a company whose name smushed the words *modified* and *RNA*: Moderna. In Germany, Ugur Sahin and Özlem Türeci, a married couple with backgrounds in immunotherapy research, also saw huge potential in Karikó and Weissman's work. They founded several companies, including one to research mRNA-based treatments for cancer: BioNTech. In 2013, they made Karikó a vice president. "There was a lot of skepticism in the industry when we started, because this was a new technology with no approved products," Türeci said. "Drug development is highly regulated, so people don't like to deviate from paths with which they have experience." BioNTech and Moderna pressed on for years without approved products, thanks to the support of investors and philanthropy groups, such as the Bill & Melinda Gates Foundation.

By the time the coronavirus outbreak shut down the city of Wuhan in China, Moderna and BioNTech had spent years finetuning their technology, which explains how they solved the mystery of SARS-CoV-2 with such speed. It turned out that mRNA offered the perfect key to pick the lock of the virus that caused COVID. Coronaviruses are named after a crown, or "corona," of proteins that surrounds the virus particle, like spikes around a ball. Synthetic mRNA therapies send detailed instructions to a person's cells to make duplicates of the distinctive "spike protein," which the immune system trains itself to attack. Later, if the same person confronts the full-blown virus, the body recognizes the spike protein again and blitzes it with the precision of a well-trained military, reducing the risk of severe illness.[28]

With COVID, the science of mRNA proved its value almost immediately. On January 11, 2020, Chinese researchers published the genetic sequence of the virus. Within forty-eight hours, Moderna's mRNA vaccine recipe was finalized. By late February, batches of the vaccine had been shipped to Bethesda, Maryland, for clinical trials. By December, it was approved—the fastest vaccine development in history. Today, several billion mRNA vaccines have been shipped.[29] In 2023, Katalin Karikó and Drew Weissman, who struggled for years to get a dollar of funding from the NIH, won the Nobel Prize in Physiology or Medicine for a technology that saved millions of lives.

The mRNA vaccines were a triumph—for Karikó and Weissman, for Pfizer and Moderna, for all of us. But they are also clearly a cautionary tale for American science. Karikó said she "never got a dime" from the US government to directly support her mRNA projects in her years at Penn.[30] "Even now, I am working on therapies that were part of grant applications that were rejected twenty years ago," she said.[31]

Karikó is not the only scientist to hear "no, no, no" from funding institutions like the NIH on her path to international renown. When he won the Nobel Prize in Physiology or Medicine in 2013, James Rothman told an interviewer that he was grateful to have started work in the 1970s, back when the federal government "was willing to take much bigger risks" on young scientists. "I had five years of failure, really, before I had the first initial sign of success," Rothman said. "I'd like to think that that kind of support existed today, but I think there's less of it."[32]

At the highest levels, American science has become biased against the very thing that drives its progress: the art of taking bold risks. "We have a problem of creaky institutions getting in the way of inventing," the MIT economist Pierre Azoulay said. "It's not so different from housing or clean energy. American science has accumulated a set of processes and norms that favor those who know how to play the system, rather than those who have the most interesting ideas."[33] In short, America—and American science—has a Karikó Problem.

The Karikó Problem and the Great Science Slowdown

By some measures, the business of academia in America has never been bigger. In the 1930s, there were just 80,000 professors across all US universities;[34] today there are more than 1.5 million.[35] The search for knowledge has never been easier. We have more information about our genes, our proteins, and our cells, along with tools to make it easier to search, copy, paste, and organize the data and to run statistical analyses. It is easier than ever to collaborate across large distances on the internet. Surely it seems like, if we value science, our society has done everything right.

And to be sure, the landscape of inventions sparkles with bright spots. The last few years have witnessed the remarkable emergence of new gene therapies, drugs to thwart diabetes and obesity, and a suite of artificial intelligence tools—such as ChatGPT from OpenAI and DeepMind from Alphabet, the parent company of Google— that can perform a wide range of complex tasks, from writing essays and code to predicting the shape of proteins.

But, mysteriously, progress in many fields seems to be slowing down. In April 2020, just as the world was convulsing from the pandemic, a group of economists from Stanford and MIT published a study with the irresistible title "Are Ideas Getting Harder to Find?"[36] Their answer was an unambiguous yes. From medicine to agriculture, basic science is becoming less productive. "Consider what's happened in medicine in the twenty-first century," said Nicholas Bloom, a Stanford economist and coauthor of the paper. "In heart-disease research, the number of journal publications has increased, and the number of clinical trials has soared, but the quantity of lives saved or extended has slowed significantly. As a result, it's taking more and more research to eke out the same extra year of life."[37]

One area where we should expect much more from scientific progress is in the field of cancer research. In 1971, President Richard Nixon signed the National Cancer Act, kicking off what became known as the "War on Cancer." Three decades later, Andrew von Eschenbach, the director of the National Cancer Institute, pledged in 2003 to "eliminate suffering and death due to cancer by 2015."[38] Six years later, President Obama pledged to find "a cure for cancer in our time."[39] Two presidents later, President Biden reinitiated a "Cancer Moonshot" to "end cancer as we know it."[40] But our progress on cancer research has been uneven. While some cancers, such as childhood leukemia, have become much less fatal, the prognoses for others have proven stubbornly resistant to improvement. The death rates of some cancers, such as uterine and pancreatic, are still rising, despite significant investment. Although there are many drugs approved to treat very sick cancer patients, there are shockingly few drugs approved to prevent cancer in the first place.[41] "Especially when you consider the scale of spending, cancer research has been a huge disappointment overall," said Eric Topol, director of the Scripps Research Translational Institute. "There are all these drugs for treatment that mostly just extend people's lives a few months."[42]

How can we possibly account for this puzzle: more scientists, more money, more years of education, more knowledge, more technology, and more papers—but, in many fields, slower progress? In 2008, the Northwestern economist Benjamin Jones proposed an elegant theory to explain the slowdown across science. It starts with two simple observations. First, nobody is born an expert. Second, total expertise in any given domain of knowledge—say, physics or chemistry—grows over time, as we unravel the mysteries of the natural world.[43] As we build expertise in a field like medicine, it's a bit like plucking the lowest-hanging fruit from a tree. The more low-hanging fruit we pick, the higher in the tree we have to climb to pick fruit, and the more resources we need to do it. Jones called this escalating challenge "the burden of knowledge."

The burden of knowledge isn't just plausible. It's practically obvious. To take one simple example: The first element discovered and recorded by a European scientist was phosphorus. The story goes that in the mid-1600s, a German alchemist did a little home experiment, the crux of which involved boiling piss, evaporating the urine, and heating the remains.[44] Out came phosphorus. Almost any high school chemistry student could replicate this experiment today (please don't), but they shouldn't expect it to break open any new scientific frontier. The latest elemental discoveries have been a bit more complicated. Element 117, tennessine, was discovered only when a Tennessee laboratory created an isotope of the rare metal berkelium and sent twenty-two milligrams of the radioactive material to Russia, where a separate group of scientists at a nuclear research facility hit it with a beam of 6 trillion calcium ions per second for 150 days and used specialized equipment to detect the faintest whispers of tennessine flickering into existence for less than a second.[45] While it's hard to say how the next synthetic element will be detected, it is safe to assume that it will not be discovered in a pot of hot urine.

If that example seems a little goofy, try this one. The godfather of genetics was Gregor Mendel. A Czech friar in the mid-1800s, Mendel grew peas of varying shape, color, and flower position in his monastery's garden. He bred the pea plants by cross-pollination over generations and noticed that peas seemed to pass down their traits, producing predictable crossbreeds. Although his 1866 analysis[46] was published to little fanfare, a group of botanists later rediscovered Mendel's work, independently confirmed the principles of inheritance, and cracked open the field of genetics.

One hundred and sixty years later, genetics is a mature scientific domain whose breakthroughs are a bit more complicated than careful gardening. For example, we haven't yet figured out how a complex disease like schizophrenia arises from the interplay between multiple genes and the environment. When an organization like the Broad Institute in Cambridge, Massachusetts, wanted to investigate the genetic building blocks of schizophrenia, scientists sequenced the genomes of thousands of people around the world, looking for commonalities among those who share the disease. Such research—called genome-wide association studies—takes hundreds of geneticists, neuroscientists, computer programmers, assistants, and more working together in organized teams over many years to get us one small step closer to solving the riddle of schizophrenia. It is absurd to imagine that one person, even as brilliant as Gregor Mendel, could do all this alone in his backyard.

That is Jones's point in a nutshell. Scientific progress is a blessing that comes with a curse. The unsolved problems are typically harder than the solved ones.

If keeping up the pace of scientific progress demands more resources, it points to a clear solution: recruit more scientists and spend more money. These aren't bad ideas; they might be great ones. "As a share of the economy, government-funded R&D has declined in the last sixty years," the economist Heidi Williams said.[47] If scientific spending is fundamental to economic growth, this suggests that the US has hugely underinvested in basic research.

Meanwhile, recruiting brilliant immigrants to the US has for decades been the "secret ingredient" to America's success in science and technology, according to Jeremy Neufeld, a fellow at the Institute for Progress. "Some of the greatest achievements in US history, including the Manhattan Project and the Apollo program, are impossible to imagine without the contribution of people who were born abroad," he said.[48] Despite making up only about 14 percent of the US population, immigrants accounted for 23 percent of US patents from 1990 to 2016, 38 percent of US Nobel Prizes in chemistry, medicine, and physics from 2000 to 2023, and more than half of the billion-dollar US start-ups in the last twenty years.[49]

Today, however, this talent pipeline is at risk. As immigration politics has been subsumed by debates about border control policies, the US has quietly made it harder for the typical foreign-born student to stay. America has allowed wait times for green cards to lengthen, while the number of applicants stuck in immigration backlogs has gotten so large that some talented immigrants have stopped waiting and moved away. Since 2007, the share of international students on academic visas applying to stay and work in the US has declined by more than a third.[50]

Neufeld singled out one policy for criticism: the H-1B visa, which is America's primary visa for high-skilled foreign workers. In 1990, the US capped the number of annual H-1B visas at 65,000.[51] The figure was eventually raised to 85,000 in the early 2000s. But in twenty years of immigration fights, it still hasn't increased to match the growth of the population or the urgent need for scientists, engineers, and researchers. This artificial scarcity means many promising foreign students and researchers are forced to leave the US after completing their studies, taking their skills and innovative potential elsewhere. If Katalin Karikó, who moved to the US in 1985, had tried to immigrate just a few years later, the creation of the H-1B visa cap might have prevented her move—and, perhaps, catastrophically delayed the emergence of mRNA research. Strengthening and expanding America's high-skilled immigration program would be a good way to pull the Karikós of the future into the U.S., where they could cook up the next life-saving breakthrough. Doubling the H-1B visa cap, especially while raising the average wage for visa holders, could be transformative for American science and technology,[52] Neufeld said. "We'd have more, and more meaningful, inventions, which would increase productivity, and make the US as a whole richer."[53]

More money and more scientists might help the US fight the knowledge burden. But it doesn't solve what we've called the Karikó Problem. In fact, in the same way that throwing housing vouchers into a market with insufficient supply raises home prices, throwing more money into a flawed science system might exacerbate its problems.

Let's define the Karikó Problem like this: American science funding has become biased against young scientists and risky ideas. What is most obvious is that American science is getting older. In the early 1900s, some of the most famous scientists—Einstein, Heisenberg, Schrödinger—did their breakthrough work in their twenties and thirties. Indeed, their youth may have been critical to their paradigm-busting genius. But these days the twentysomething scientist is an endangered species. The share of NIH-funded scientists who are thirty-five years old or younger declined from 22 percent in 1980 to less than 2 percent by the 2010s.[54]

American science also seems to produce far too many papers that don't create new knowledge while overlooking researchers with promising new ideas. A 2023 study titled "Papers and Patents Are Becoming Less Disruptive Over Time" found that any given paper today is much less likely to become influential than a paper from the same field decades ago.[55] This could be because too many papers are essentially worthless. Or it could mean that scientists feel pressured to herd around the same few safe ideas that will keep them in good standing with their peers.

"When you look at the diminishing returns in medicine, you can say, well, maybe all the easy drugs have been discovered," said James Evans, a sociologist at the University of Chicago. But the more compelling possibility, he said, is that "the very organization of modern science is leading us astray." In Evans's interpretation, the low-hanging fruit hasn't been plucked. The problem is that too many scientists are all looking at the same few trees. "I think there are all kinds of weird trees in the forest that we haven't found, because everybody's looking in the same place, and we're not making enough high-risk, high-reward bets," Evans said. "That has nothing to do with the knowledge burden. That's all about the organization of American science. It's about our policies, our laws, and our rules."[56]

The idea that the NIH has become deeply biased against risky and novel research—and too fixated on funding only those projects that are practically guaranteed to succeed—is so widespread that it has become "the biggest cliché in science," said Azoulay, the MIT economist.[57] In 2012, Gregory Petsko, a biochemist and member of the National Academy of Sciences, published a satirical essay in which King Ferdinand and Queen Isabella of Spain mock Christopher Columbus for not collecting preliminary data about the voyage across the Atlantic. When King Ferdinand suggests that the explorer try a shorter trip—say, to Portugal—Columbus exclaims, "Everybody knows that Portugal is immediately west of Spain. . . . What will you learn from that?" "Not much, if anything," Queen Isabella responds. "But it can't fail, now, can it? Besides, you've sailed to Portugal before, so the Study Section would know you can do it."[58] This satire didn't appear in a personal blog. It ran in *Genome Biology*, one of the most prestigious journals in the field of genetics.

For all its flaws, the NIH has been central to some of the most important scientific discoveries in history. In the 1960s, when scientists developed the first effective treatment of childhood leukemia, they used NIH funding. In the 1980s, when researchers identified the first cancer-causing gene and developed the first HIV blood test, they did it with NIH funding. In the 2000s, when the Human Genome Project cracked open a new frontier in genetic research, the NIH was its leading bankroller. From the human brain to the immune system to the genetic basis of disease, almost every bountiful field of bioscience has been irrigated by the National Institutes of Health.

To understand how a system designed to encourage risk-taking in science ironically became captured by risk aversion, we have to tell the story of the birth of the American innovation system and the creation of the modern NIH itself.

The Growth of the American Innovation System

Before the twentieth century, science and invention had largely been a job for solo entrepreneurs. The cotton gin and the telegraph, icons of eighteenth- and nineteenth-century ingenuity, were made by individual tinkerers who, through trial and error, cobbled their way toward a product that—initially, barely—worked.

In the late 1800s and early 1900s, Thomas Edison proved a new model: the corporate research lab. Inside the two-story shed he built in Menlo Park, New Jersey, Edison oversaw a team of "muckers"—his term for professional experimenters—who fleshed out his sketches and helped him invent, among other things, the incandescent lightbulb and the first instruments for recording sound and video. Edison's team-based success became too obvious to ignore, and other companies copied him, with magical results. In the 1930s, DuPont's Experimental Station developed synthetic rubber, nylon, and Kevlar. Meanwhile, the university scientists who worked outside these labs mostly relied on funding from private philanthropies, such as the Rockefeller Foundation.

In all these triumphs, one actor was notably absent: the federal government. Washington played almost no role in supporting innovation before the 1900s, outside of a few programs that subsidized research in farming, agriculture, and defense. But just as World War II reshaped borders and rules around the world, so too did it reshape the US innovation system.

In June 1940, as the German army invaded and occupied Paris, the eminent engineer Vannevar Bush delivered grave news to President Franklin D. Roosevelt in an urgent White House meeting: America was technologically unprepared to take on the Axis powers.[59] Wiry thin with a narrow face and glasses, Bush dominated several disciplines. A pioneer in early computer research, he published some of the first predictions of the internet, was the dean of the MIT School of Engineering, and was the chairman of the National Advisory Committee for Aeronautics, which was eventually folded into NASA.

He urged Roosevelt to create a new agency to direct American ingenuity toward the war effort, presenting the president with a brief, one-page proposal for a new organization, the likes of which had never existed in US history: a committee to coordinate all the science and technological work that might help defeat the Nazis, which would be funded by the White House. The memo was persuasive. Roosevelt approved the creation of an agency that grew to become the Office of Scientific Research and Development (OSRD)—a multibillion-dollar hydra of wartime science and technology operations that supported the work of thousands of scientists and engineers. OSRD's early work developing an atomic weapon eventually became the Manhattan Project, overseen by J. Robert Oppenheimer. With OSRD funding and guidance, American scientists invented radar, invested in malaria treatments, developed an early influenza vaccine, and built the foundations for early computing.

The country emerged from World War II with a new way of

thinking about science and innovation: *this is a job for the government*. In 1945, Bush drew on the lessons of the war to draft a block-buster report on the future of American innovation titled "Science, the Endless Frontier." The most important idea that emerged from the Bush report was the primacy of "basic research"—a term Bush meant to refer to science at universities and research centers that seeks to understand the world "without thought of practical ends." Bush wrote:

> Basic research leads to new knowledge. It provides scientific capital. It creates the fund from which the practical applications of knowledge must be drawn. New products and new processes do not appear full-grown. They are founded on new principles and new conceptions, which in turn are painstakingly developed by research in the purest realms of science.[60]

It was a dreamy—even radical—depiction of American science. Rather than rely on private philanthropy, or the closed-door laboratories of corporate behemoths, Bush saw the future of science as a kind of hub-and-spoke system, with the federal government directing funds to the most deserving university researchers.

Bush's vision of a government organization for science funding led to the creation of the National Science Foundation (NSF) in 1950. As OSRD wound down—its charter depended on a wartime designation—contracts for medical research were transferred to the National Institutes of Health (NIH).

At the time, the NIH was a fairly insignificant agency. It had evolved out of the Hygienic Laboratory, a meagerly funded facility with no experience coordinating a national research agenda.[61] But this quickly changed. Medical schools, eager to capitalize on a new source of funding, overwhelmed the NIH with new proposals. Between 1945 and 1960, the NIH budget grew rapidly, as it added several specialized institutes, such as the National Heart Institute in 1948 and the National Institute of Mental Health in 1949. By the mid-1950s, the NIH was the world's largest biomedical research organization. In the last seventy years, its budget has increased 1,000-fold.[62]

Today NIH, along with the NSF, are irreplaceable. If these institutions had never been created or expanded, the lives of millions, even billions of people around the world would be shorter than they are today, and people would be sicker. If they disappeared tomorrow, the world would instantly be worse.[63]

But it is precisely because the NIH stands above every bioscience institution in significance that we should scrutinize the way it shapes the practice of science in America and around the world.

There are several popular complaints about the way the NIH has developed over the last few decades. The first problem that emerged with the rise of the NIH echoes the criticism from our chapters on housing, energy, and the difficulty of building things in America: rules have increased, while efficiency has decreased. Immediately after World War II, NIH leaders foresaw that the rising tide of bureaucracy could drown the work of science. In 1946, Cassius Van Slyke, who would soon become deputy director of the NIH,[64] warned in the journal *Science* that he did not want the work of writing research grants to eclipse the work of actually doing science. "It is not desired that the preparation of these reports present any long, tedious burden,"[65] he wrote. Ten years later, James Shannon,[66] himself then one year into the job of NIH director, coauthored an article in *Science* with another ominous warning for his field:

The research-project approach can be pernicious if it is administered so that it produces certain specific end products, or if it provides short periods of support without assuring continuity, or if it applies overt or indirect pressure on the investigator to shift his interests to narrowly defined work set by the source of money, or if it imposes financial and scientific accounting in unreasonable detail.[67]

If we are living in the world that Bush built, we are also living in the world that Shannon feared. As science funding became more entrenched inside the federal government, politicians did what they do best. They created paperwork. In the early 1960s, Congressman Lawrence Fountain, a Democrat from North Carolina, published two reports complaining that the NIH did a lousy job accounting for the money it sent to scientists. He convinced Congress to take the unusual step of cutting the agency's funding.[68] A decade later, Senator William Proxmire, a Wisconsin Democrat, created the Golden Fleece Award to draw negative attention to the worst use of government money in science. The first two Golden Fleece Awards went to studies about human attraction and why mammals clench their jaws when stressed. Proxmire called on government science funding to "get out of the love racket" and declared that these projects "made a monkey out of the American taxpayer."[69]

The NIH got the message. Requirements for paperwork surged. "All of a sudden," one NIH administrator wrote at the time, "a whole series of 'thou shalts' and 'thou shalt nots' were written down."[70] One 1960s *Science* editorial—the headline: "More Paper Work, Less Research"—complained that turning scientists into clerks would "cost the nation millions of dollars in lost time from research."[71] It was a move reminiscent of blue states creating so many rules around permitting and environmental regulations that it became impossible to build necessary housing and energy. The instinct to make science democratically responsible has gunked up the scientific process.

To appreciate the explosion of scientific paperwork requirements, imagine if every scientist working in America contracted a chronic fatigue disorder that made it impossible for them to work for half of the year. We would consider this to be a national tragedy and an emergency. But this make-believe disorder is not so dissimilar to the burden we place on scientists today when it comes to paperwork. Today's scientists spend up to 40 percent of their time working on filling out research grants and follow-up administrative documents, rather than on direct research.[72] Funding agencies sometimes take seven months or longer to review an application or request a resubmission.[73]

"Folks need to understand how broken the system is," said John Doench, the director of research and development in functional genomics at the Broad Institute.[74] "So many really, *really* intelligent people are wasting their time doing really, *really* uninteresting things: writing progress reports, or coming up with modular budgets five years in advance of the science, as if those numbers have any meaning. Universities have whole floors whose main job is to administer these NIH grants. Why are we doing this? Because they're afraid that I'm going to buy a Corvette with the grant money?"[75] The rules exist for a reason, Doench acknowledged. Some scientists in the past probably abused their funding. But just as environmental laws passed in response to twentieth-century problems created a crisis of building in the twenty-first century, the paperwork cure in science is sometimes worse than the disease. "We are very much in danger of falling behind because we are so bloatedly inefficient,"

Doench said. "It's the same truth about how it takes forever to build a mile of subway in New York City. The cracks are emerging, and we are going to lose our edge if our best and brightest people are spending their lives filling out forms rather than focusing on the next great thing."

The second problem coming out of the growth of the NIH is that the onerous process of applying for grants has put a premium on status-seeking rather than pure science. This was a theme of Katalin Karikó's years in the wilderness. "I wasn't very good at kissing butts," Karikó said bluntly. In *Breaking Through*, she wrote that she felt success in academia was more about marketing and status than it was about hard science:

> You needed the ability to sell yourself and your work. You needed to attract funding. You needed the kind of interpersonal savvy that got you invited to speak at conferences or made people eager to mentor and support you. You needed to know how to do things in which I have never had any interest (flattering people, schmoozing, being agreeable when you disagree, even when you are 100 percent certain that you are correct). You needed to know how to climb a political ladder, to value a hierarchy that had always seemed, at best, wholly uninteresting (and, at worst, antithetical to good science). I wasn't interested in those skills.[76]

While Karikó flashed the intelligence of a future Nobel-winning scientist, she wasn't world-class at a skill that Azoulay calls "grantsmanship"—the ability to write winning project proposals.[77] "There is a hidden curriculum for navigating grants, and it is critical for success as a scientist today," Azoulay said. "But those skills are weakly correlated with scientific potential, and they might be negatively correlated."[78] We have—even if by accident—designed a system that often privileges the game of performing the act of science over the actual practice of science.

The final common criticism of the NIH might be the most important piece of the Karikó Problem. While many discoveries depend on high-risk research that departs from the herd—like embracing the potential of mRNA while others rush toward DNA—modern science too often plays it safe.

"I have little doubt that the NIH is biased against high-risk science," said Azoulay. When I asked him how we know for sure that the current system isn't doing a perfect job balancing high-risk bets with important incremental projects, he offered a charmingly humble answer: we *don't* know. Not for sure, at least. "This is one of the most important things that I'm working on, and it's hard to make progress, because the data is crap."[79] He said it's hard to know for sure if there are a few Katalin Karikós in the world or thousands, because the NIH makes it hard for outside researchers to compare the proposals that it funds against the ones it rejects.

The NIH still largely relies on its decades-old peer review system. A small team of independent scientists rates a project's merit, methodology, and significance before offering funding. Without full access to NIH decision-making, a scientist who wanted to study the agency's peer review system might have to do something a bit strange, like build a dummy peer review system in a lab setting. In 2014, a team of researchers from Harvard University did just this. They recruited 142 star medical researchers to act as evaluators in a makeshift grant-review process. They took 150 proposals and gave each one a "novelty score" and randomly assigned multiple proposals to each reviewer. In the final analysis of 2,130 evaluations, highly familiar proposals did all right, and slightly novel proposals did the best. But highly novel ideas received the worst scores by far. "We find that evaluators uniformly and systematically give lower scores to proposals with increasing novelty," the team concluded.[80]

"New ideas no longer fuel American science the way they once did," the economists Mikko Packalen and Jay Bhattacharya write.[81] In a 2020 paper, they showed that NIH funding used to support fresh questions. In the 1990s, for example, the NIH consistently funded medical papers whose key words first appeared in the literature in the previous seven years. But since the 2000s, NIH funding for the youngest vintage of science has declined by more than 25 percent.[82] Once again, either the new ideas in science are getting worse, or we're getting worse at looking for them and funding them.

Bias against novelty, risk, and edgy thinking is a tragedy, because the most important breakthroughs in scientific history are often wild surprises that emerge from bizarre obsessions. "Too many projects get funding because they are probable," said Evans, the University of Chicago sociologist. "But science moves forward one *improbability* at a time."[83] In the 1990s scientists studying the Gila monster, a stocky lizard, discovered a hormone in its venom that allowed the reptile to go months between meals. When they synthesized the hormone in a lab, they produced a medicine called a GLP-1 agonist, which was shown to reduce blood sugar levels in some people with diabetes.[84] Today GLP-1 drugs, like Ozempic, seem to treat not only diabetes but also obesity and a dizzying range of maladies, including heart disease, alcoholism, and drug addiction. The most famous pharmaceutical breakthrough of the last decade is thus built on the foundation of a most delightfully peculiar obsession: lizard spit.

Science is often nonlinear in this way. The most popular COVID tests relied on a technology called polymerase chain reaction. Developed in the 1980s, PCR is a method for amplifying small DNA sequences, which can be used for paternity tests and disease diagnoses. When scientists were initially trying to figure out how to scale PCR, they needed bacterial enzymes that didn't fail at high temperatures. Fortunately, two decades earlier, in the 1960s, biologists in Yellowstone National Park had isolated a hot-springs bacteria that thrived in boiling conditions.[85] The bacteria they isolated was incorporated into PCR research and helped launch a revolution in diagnostics and genetics. Without the bacteria, significant achievements such as the Human Genome Project might have been impossible. (Not to mention other great moments in scientific history, such as "You are not the father!" outbursts on *The Maury Show*.) Nobody building an effective medical test during a pandemic would ever stop to think, *Well, first thing, let's book a flight to Wyoming and take samples from geysers*. But this is how science often works; a broad base of knowledge is built, upon which we piece together disparate fragments of a puzzle to create new breakthroughs.

Another example: CRISPR is a gene-editing function that some scientists believe could one day unlock the cure for any number of genetic diseases. But it was not discovered by a group of geneticists. The first mention of CRISPR in the scientific literature comes from Japanese and Spanish researchers working with bacteria that displayed a peculiar immune reaction when attacked by viruses.[86] This early work did not initially receive many citations. But after twenty years of development, CRISPR now looks like one of the most powerful medical technologies in history. Isaac Newton famously said he saw further by standing "on the shoulders of giants." But clearly, some brilliant ideas are not born giants. They are born as all children are born—small and helpless, requiring care and protection to grow.

"We want the most life-saving, life-enhancing, productivity-expanding inventions and innovations possible," Evans said. "That means we need a system that is designed to take more risks, and accept more failures, as a part of the scientific process."[87] In a strange way, the problem isn't that too much science is "doomed to fail," he said. It's the opposite. Too much science is, in his words, "doomed to succeed"—fated to duplicate what we know rather than risk failure by reaching into the unknown.

Rather than see the NIH as an enemy of risky science, it makes more sense to think of it as a typical bureaucracy whose leaders are doing their best to solve typically bureaucratic problems. In 2017, longtime NIH director Francis Collins acknowledged, in an email to the libertarian venture capitalist Peter Thiel, that NIH needed "to liberate young scientists from training periods that are much too long" and that "some of the ways in which we support" biomedical research are "outdated."[88]

In the last twenty years, NIH has created several grant programs that are earmarked for riskier research and younger scientists. Their High-Risk, High-Reward Research program now includes a Pioneer Award for scientists "pursuing new research directions" and a New Innovator Award for younger academics.[89] "It's so important to be able to fund the people and ideas that might be a little bit out there," said Patricia Labosky, a program leader in

NIH's High-Risk, High-Reward initiative. "You want some science in low- or medium-risk areas where you're confident that you're going to learn something, but you also need this high-risk aspect, where you can learn something different and you can push the envelope." The New Innovator Award initiative, which Labosky oversees, is structured very differently than typical NIH grants, known as R01s. "With a standard grant, you often have to show that you can accomplish everything you're proposing, and you're graded on a very high feasibility level," she said. "For a New Innovator Award, we like to see a little plausibility, sure, but mostly they just need a cool idea and the equipment to plausibly get it done."[90]

The NIH's own research indicates that Pioneer Award recipients seem to produce influential, highly cited research.[91] But despite efforts to help younger scientists, the share of basic NIH funding going to scientists under thirty-five continues to decline. In the 2024 fiscal year, the High-Risk, High-Reward Research program allocated about $200 million to scientists, a moderate decline since 2019. The amount was an almost negligible fraction—less than half of 1 percent—of the NIH's annual budget for that year.

If we want a fully new approach to funding breakthrough science and invention, maybe we should look outside the NIH for the best ideas about how the government can accelerate invention.

The Idea Factories

In October 1957, a strange-looking device breached our planet's atmosphere and entered space. It resembled a kind of robotic daddy longlegs, with four spindly antennas connected to a spherical head made of polished metal. This space-age insectoid robot didn't live a long life. By January, it had fallen back to earth and incinerated. But in its three-month lifespan, the little machine changed the world. Sputnik, as it was called, was the first man-made object to orbit the earth. And to the great astonishment of many Americans, it was not launched by the United States but rather by its chief rival, the Soviet Union.

Sputnik ignited the space race, pushing the US to invest in propulsion and rocket technology that would eventually put an American flag on the moon and leave boot prints in the moondust. It also sparked an innovation race for terrestrial inventions. In 1958, vowing that the US should never again be on the other side of a technological surprise, the Department of Defense established the Advanced Research Projects Agency. Later renamed the Defense Advanced Research Projects Agency, or DARPA, it produced a gaudy résumé of ingenuity. The internet, GPS, personal computers, and self-driving vehicles all trace their roots back to DARPA-funded research. What started as a bureaucratic reaction to a Soviet satellite became the seeds of the communications revolution that would shape the next sixty-five years of American innovation. Years before most people had heard of mRNA vaccines, DARPA invested $25 million in Moderna in 2013.[92]

The science and tech community has fervently debated what makes DARPA so special.[93] With an annual budget of $4 billion[94]—about one-tenth of the NIH—DARPA punches well above its weight. One answer is that DARPA empowers domain experts called program managers to pay scientists and technologists to work together on projects of their own design, "There's no question to me that program managers—especially program managers with vision, creativity, and independence—are the most important part of DARPA," said Erica R. H. Fuchs, a professor of engineering and public policy at Carnegie Mellon.[95] Unlike traditional scientists, these program managers do not face peer review. They can make big counterintuitive bets, are not punished for failure, and are not hauled before congressional committees for supporting weird-sounding projects.

To explain how a successful program manager works, Fuchs pointed to the invention of ARPANET, the world's first internet. In 1962, J. C. R. Licklider, a psychologist and computer scientist from MIT, joined ARPA to lead its information-processing division. Licklider, who had previously sketched out the concept for a global computer network, set out to assemble a dream team of researchers to bring his idea to life. Like a Hollywood producer handpicking his favorite director, designers, and actors to make a new film, Licklider paid far-flung geniuses across the country to work together. Computer scientists at the Carnegie Institute of Technology (now Carnegie Mellon) and engineers at Stanford University collaborated to link computing systems to send coast-to-coast messages. In 1966, Bob Taylor, a psychologist who had worked at NASA, took over Licklider's program. He vastly expanded the network of collaborators, pulling in pioneers of science and engineering from several more universities, engineering firms, and government labs, including MIT, the RAND Corporation, and UCLA. When ARPANET went online in 1969, the world's original—and very basic—internet required the collaboration of individuals and firms who would never have otherwise come together. To invent an online network of information, Licklider and Taylor built an offline network of minds.

Every worthwhile DARPA project is a bit like this, Fuchs said. The agency's most successful people are talent scouts with a vision. "They say, 'If we get this person over here, working with this person over here, and then we bring in this third person, we could solve this unsolvable problem.'" In the early 2000s, the Department of

Defense was worried that Moore's law—the frequent doubling of the density of transistors on a computer chip—was slowing down and threatening the cost and quality of our military software. DARPA was asked to come up with a solution. One program manager Fuchs interviewed at length convened an unlikely alliance of industry giants and academic luminaries.[96] He brought together computer scientists and engineers from Hewlett-Packard and MIT, along with promising California start-ups collaborating with the software firm Sun Microsystems, who collaborated with nanotube experts at Harvard and UCLA; all of them received millions in DARPA funds. This group contributed to a breakthrough in silicon germanium technology, which was ultimately commercialized by IBM. In 2015, IBM told the *Wall Street Journal* that they'd "broken through major bottlenecks" in advancing Moore's law.[97] The announcement was IBM's. But the breakthrough itself began with DARPA.

If the DARPA model holds a lesson, it is that the agency works because it empowers program managers to pursue their most radical ideas with an open-ended budget and vast connections throughout science and industry. By contrast, as John Doench of the Broad Institute said, many scientists seeking funding today are disempowered to the point of infantilization. Their time is colonized by paperwork, and their ambition is pinched by grantsmanship. The American innovation system would benefit from trusting individuals more and bureaucracies less.

DARPA isn't the only midcentury factory of innovation that we can turn to for inspiration. Bell Labs, officially known as Bell Telephone Laboratories, was established in 1925 as the research and development arm of AT&T and Western Electric. Between the 1930s and 1950s, it became one of the most prolific research institutions in the world, responsible for a staggering list of accomplishments.

In 1947, its engineers built the first transistor, which enabled the development of smaller and more efficient electronic devices. In 1954, Bell Labs demonstrated the first practical silicon solar cell, opening the door to solar energy as a viable power source. In 1958, the lab published a paper outlining the principles of the laser.

While DARPA and Bell Labs are both considered icons of innovation, their success took place in very different contexts. DARPA emerged in a period of geopolitical insecurity. Bell Labs thrived in an environment of extraordinary security. As a state-sanctioned monopoly, AT&T could invest in every facet of telecommunications science without concern for short-term profits, which gave its scientists and engineers the freedom to pursue ambitious projects over decades. This long-term security was essential for many of Bell Labs's most important technological advances, such as fiber optics and electronic switching, which took decades to develop.

Bell Labs benefited from a unique moment in history. "After spending six years writing a book about Bell Labs, I've often wondered whether it would be possible to recreate it today," said Jon Gertner, the author of *The Idea Factory*. "My answer is no."[98] After World War II, AT&T was a goliath within a goliath—a huge government-sanctioned monopoly inside a country that dominated fields like chemistry and quantum mechanics when Nazi Germany's assault on Europe forced many of the continent's best minds to flee to America.

But its success still holds lessons for us, as we think about a national invention agenda. "If Bell Labs had a formula, it was to hire the smartest people, give them space and time to work, and make sure that they talk to each other," Gertner said.[99] Like DARPA, the program thrived by identifying brilliant people who wouldn't normally work together and by giving them freedom to pursue their most ambitious ideas together. This blending of minds got scientists to think about their work in new ways. Gertner visited the home of Morris Tanenbaum, who invented the silicon transistor at Bell Labs in the 1950s before he became the first chief executive officer of the AT&T Corporation in the 1980s. "When I was at his house, Tanenbaum brought me upstairs and showed me an entry in his notebook, from the day he had invented the transistor made from silicon. He had written, 'This is the transistor we've been looking for! It should be very manufacturable!'"[100] The journal entry struck Gertner as a microcosm of Bell Labs's unusual approach to science. Here was a chemist, tinkering with the fundamental principles of electrons, thinking about how his invention would become a product that went through factory assembly and ended up in people's houses.

Our institutions shape the way we think, and new institutions can make new kinds of thinking possible. For decades, too many university researchers applying for NIH funding have constrained their own curiosity. The perceived biases of the NIH became their own biases. By contrast, the best DARPA program managers see the world as a set of puzzle pieces to snap together in the creation of a new initiative. The Bell Labs scientists worked in an offshoot of AT&T, which made it natural for them to consider the commercial potential of their work, which might explain how they created so many useful products.

America's innovation system still relies on agencies and habits that were developed in the middle of the twentieth century. Decades have now passed. The world has changed, and today's scientific challenges are getting harder. So, how do we build new centers that are as transformative in our time as DARPA was in its own? Where are the brand-new government research labs for the 2020s?

Such institutions are not guaranteed to succeed, but they represent the sort of risk-taking that American science needs more of.

Experimenting with Experiments

"Scientific research and invention are the key drivers of economic growth and improvements in human well-being," Dartmouth's Heidi Williams said. "This is a fact, and it naturally raises a question: How could we get more of that?"[101] Today's politics is alarmingly vacant when it comes to answering this question. Neither liberals nor conservatives have articulated a clear politics of invention. Neither have prioritized the rigorous analysis of public policy in sciences.

We could do so much better. We could fix the manufactured scarcities of our immigration system and make it easier for the world's most brilliant people—who often graduate from American schools—to stay and work in the US. We could increase federal research and development spending rather than allow it to decline as a share of the economy, as we did for much of the second half of the twentieth century. But perhaps most important, we could fix the incentives of the American innovation system to help each dollar of funding find the right scientist taking the right risk at the right time.

In the last few years, a small group of researchers have advanced a theory of change in American politics that they call "metascience." Their thesis is straightforward. The US government is the single largest source of science funding in the world, and yet we know shockingly little about how science actually works.[102] Our laws, rules, and habits have accreted over decades without much of a grand strategy. A national invention agenda ought to operate from the first principle that *if we don't understand the science of invention at all*, we should do what scientists do. We should run experiments. Lots of experiments.

We could start with the NIH. To reduce the paperwork burden, we could run pilots that eliminate major parts of the application process. Or we could expand programs that prioritize the funding of younger scientists. To mimic the program director's power at DARPA, we could give some NIH panel members a "golden ticket," such that they would have the power to independently approve one proposal each year, regardless of how crazy the idea sounds to their peers. Or, for some applications, we could replace the existing selection process with a random lottery. Or we could announce that, for a lucky group of grantees, no scientists would have to fill out yearly progress reports.

And then, after we run all these experiments, we should have independent scientists study the results. In 2009, several researchers compared a group of typical NIH grant recipients to scientists funded by the Howard Hughes Medical Institute. Whereas the NIH pays scientists for specific projects, HHMI funds scientists without attaching strings to their research. They found that HHMI funding led to more "flops" but also more "hits"—more original discoveries and more high-impact articles.[103] Is it better to fund individual projects, or to give open-ended grants to scientists and hope for the best? As Pierre Azoulay says: We don't know for sure. But we should run the experiment.[104] As we tinker with the basic funding models of science, we could also pay for the creation of new federal research organizations, where full-time scientists pursue ambitious projects over many years without having to stress over quarterly paperwork. The ambition would be to rebottle the magic of midcentury DARPA and Bell Labs. It might not work. But that's what high-risk science does: it takes on projects with a keen possibility of failure.

"You don't want the entire innovation system made up of DARPA, and you don't want the entire innovation system made up of NIH grants, and you don't want it made up of any one thing," Azoulay said. "We want a well-tempered balance of experiments: let a thousand initiatives bloom, track their long-term success, and determine whether there are better ways to finance the sort of scientific breakthroughs that can save or improve millions of lives."[105] This approach to science and invention would be genuinely novel. It would mean creating a layer of the American science system that specializes in self-experimentation. It would mean turning the federal government into a kind of meta-laboratory for the study of science itself.

Generations from now, inventions that we can scarcely imagine will feel core to modern life: all-disease saliva and blood tests, vaccines that wipe out whole classes of virus and disease, materials stronger than steel and lighter than air, infinite clean energy from fusion reactors. If these things are possible in the realm of physical reality, then they are possible to discover; and if they can be discovered in a century, they can be discovered in a decade, or in a year. These achievements will require a level of risk-taking and ambition that we are too effective at snuffing out. For all the wonders of American invention, it is astonishing to realize that we don't know for sure how the process of discovery actually works. We still don't know how to identify and nurture the Katalin Karikós of the world. To find them, we need a better science of science.

5

Deploy

IN THE FALL OF 1928, THE SCOTTISH SCIENTIST ALEXANDER FLEMING returned from a long holiday to his lab in London. He had been working with *staphylococcus*, a bacterium that caused common infections. Deriving its name from the Greek *staphyle*, meaning "a bunch of grapes," and *kokkos*, meaning "berry," its colonies resemble a cluster of white grapes under a microscope. But when Fleming looked closely at his samples, he saw something unexpected in a dish he'd left open to the air. While he was away, a substance of unknown origin had contaminated the sample and killed much of the bacteria.[1] Fleming later identified the mysterious material as a mold belonging to the genus *Penicillium*.[2] As for the bacteria-killing substance it produced, he called it penicillin.

Fleming later claimed that the spore of mold blew into his lab through an unlocked window. If so, it was carried by a heavenly breeze. For millennia, humankind fought bacteria in war after war within our bodies and died by the millions at the hands of the unseen enemy. As late as 1900, bacterial infections were the most common cause of death in the US; more people died of bacterial pneumonia during the 1918 influenza pandemic than from the virus itself. When Fleming tested the mold against other bacteria, he saw it was even more powerful at neutralizing the nemeses of diphtheria and meningococcus. He suspected that he might have something miraculous on his hands. But after several more experiments, his work hit a wall.

In 1939, an Australian-born professor at Oxford University named Howard Florey and a German-born biochemist named Ernst Chain picked up where Fleming left off. Whereas the Scottish scientist had shown that penicillin could zap microbes on glass, Florey and Chain wanted to know if it might do the same inside animals. Their lab divided 150 mice into three groups and injected each with, respectively, *staphylococci*, *streptococci*, and a bacterium that causes gangrene. Half of the mice were left untreated to serve as the control group, and the other half were given penicillin. In the control group, all 75 untreated mice died. In the intervention group, 70 survived.[3] Penicillin seemed quite special indeed.

But people are not mice, and Florey, Chain, and their group had more trouble testing the effect of penicillin in humans. After nearly two years of work, they, too, were stuck. By the spring of 1941, with Europe submerged in war, five human patients in their experiments had been treated with penicillin. Two of them had died.[4]

Let's pause the narrative here, as strange as this interruption might seem. Fleming's discovery of penicillin is world-famous: cherished by scientists and hailed as one of the most significant breakthroughs in the history of health, or any other field. Florey's portrait adorned the Australian $50 note for decades. Chain, along with Fleming and Florey, won the 1945 Nobel Prize in Physiology or Medicine.

For many, progress appears to be a mere timeline of such eureka moments. Our mythology of invention treats the moment of discovery as a sacred scene. In school, students memorize the dates of major inventions, along with the names of the people who made them—Edison, lightbulb, 1879;[5] Wright brothers, airplane, 1903. The great discoverers—Franklin, Bell, Curie, Tesla—get bestselling biographies, and millions of people know their names. You can think of this as the "eureka theory of history." It's the story of progress you might expect to see in Hollywood or to read in nonfiction books that hail the lonely hero whose flash of insight changes the world.

But this approach to history is worse than incomplete; it's downright wrong. Inventions do matter greatly to progress. But too often, when we isolate these famous scenes, we leave out the most important chapters of the story—the ones that follow the initial lightning bolt of discovery. Consider the actual scale of penicillin's achievement in 1941: five human subjects and two deaths. Thirteen years after one of the most famous discoveries in science history, penicillin had accomplished practically nothing.

The Eureka Myth

When a good idea is born, or when the first prototype of an invention is created, we should celebrate its potential to change the world. But progress is more about implementation than it is about invention. An idea going from nonexistence to existence—from zero to one—introduces the possibility of change. But the way individuals, companies, and governments take an idea from one to one billion is the story of how the world actually changes.

And it doesn't always change, even after a truly brilliant discovery. The ten-thousand-year story of human civilization is mostly the story of things not getting better: diseases not being cured, freedoms not being extended, truths not being transmitted, technology not delivering on its promises. Progress is our escape from the status quo of suffering, our ejection seat from history—it is the less common story of how our inventions and institutions reduce disease, poverty, pain, and violence while expanding freedom, happiness, and empowerment. It's a story that has been at risk of grinding to a halt in the United States.[6]

The US has thrown tens of billions of dollars annually into scientific discovery. But it hasn't brought as much progress as we'd expect. As we explained in the previous chapter, we have haphazardly burdened the scientific process with the same flavor of procedural kludge that has slowed down other critical parts of the economy. What's more, as we'll explain in this chapter, we have gotten worse at translating our inventions into domestic industries. To borrow some familiar language, it's not just that ideas are getting harder to find. The problem is also that new ideas are getting harder to use.[7]

What went wrong? There are many answers, but one is that we have become too enthralled by the eureka myth and, more to the point, too inattentive to all the things that must follow a eureka moment. The US has more Nobel Prizes for science than the UK, Germany, France, Japan, Canada, and Austria combined. But if there were a Nobel Prize for the domestic deployment of technology—even technology that we invented—our legacy wouldn't be so sterling.[8]

An American craftsman, Elisha Otis, invented the first safe passenger elevator in 1853.[9] This only deepens the irony that, 170 years later, the US struggles to build tall apartments efficiently, in part because American elevators have become "over-engineered, bespoke, handcrafted and expensive pieces of equipment that are unaffordable in all the places where they are most needed," according to Stephen Jacob Smith, executive director of the Center for Building in North America.[10] Burned by regulations and inattention to cost-effective production, basic elevators cost four times more in New York City than in Switzerland.

Americans invented the world's first nuclear reactor and solar cell. But today, we're well behind various European and Asian countries in deploying and developing these technologies.[11] Thirty years ago, a group at the University of Texas developed next-generation technology to create lithium iron phosphate (LFP) batteries—which car companies need for the top-performing electric vehicles. But in the early 2020s, no American company knew how to manufacture these batteries at scale, and China held a monopoly on the market.[12]

Politics should take technology more seriously. Innovation can make impossible problems possible to solve, and policy can make impossible technologies possible to create. The fundamental link between the two is not at the core of the Democratic or the Republican agenda. Instead, we are stuck between a progressive movement that is too afraid of growth and a conservative movement that is allergic to government intervention.

In the last seventy years, we have too often followed the same playbook—invent, but don't implement. We cannot afford to follow this playbook for the next seventy years. To appreciate the deeper story of progress—and to see how it illuminates America's own problems in the twenty-first century—let's return to the 1940s to watch how penicillin went from a scientific discovery in a lab to a medicine that saved millions of lives.

In 1941, Howard Florey and Ernst Chain were stumped. The British research teams that were investigating the potential for antimicrobial medicine had hit a dead end. Deep in war, England didn't have resources to scale the technology. Florey and Chain needed help from overseas.

By some providence, America had everything the scientists wanted. President Roosevelt had just approved Vannevar Bush's vision of a centralized agency to coordinate wartime innovation. Bush's Office of Scientific Research and Development included a division focused on new treatments that could be useful for soldiers and other military personnel. This agency, called the Committee on Medical Research (CMR), had already invested in malaria medicine and new research on novel influenza vaccines.[13]

CMR took Florey and Chain's science project and turned it into a medical product. First, the US solved penicillin's chemistry problem. It was one thing to make a small batch of penicillin in a little flask. But if you used the same ingredients to make larger amounts, microorganisms would mess up the mixture, producing a worthless sludge. (The historian James Phinney Baxter III elegantly described the irony: "The same accident of contamination which led to the discovery of penicillin very nearly prevented its use.") With OSRD's encouragement, scientists in Peoria, Illinois, discovered that adding "corn steep"—water soaked with corn—could increase penicillin production tenfold.[14] The military collected and tested new strains of mold, which, mixed in the larger vats and with further modifications to the process, made mass production possible.

With the help of the War Production Board, OSRD spent millions of dollars paying firms to set up penicillin plants. Penicillin production went exponential, rising from an average of 10 million units per plant per month in 1942 to 646 million units by June 1945.[15] As production scaled, the cost of making the antibiotic plummeted by more than 95 percent. Meanwhile, CMR conducted clinical trials on penicillin to ensure its effectiveness. In the spring of 1943, with the chemical procedures standardized, the US government turned to distribution. An advisory board and the American Medical Association chose one thousand hospitals across the country to store and distribute the drug, which was also made available to local communities. In December, a report on 209 soldiers and civilians across the country with severe wound and bloodstream infections found that those treated with penicillin experienced both lower mortality rates and shorter hospitalizations. Just as important, the medication obliterated bacteria without any toxic effects.

By March 1945, there was enough penicillin for just about everyone in America. In short order, the little mold that blew in through the window revolutionized modern medicine and life. Bacterial infections become manageable health problems. Surgeries became safer, childbirth less deadly, and war wounds less lethal. Penicillin saved the equivalent of full battalions by reducing the mortality rate of bacterial pneumonia in soldiers from 18 percent to 1 percent. One source estimated that 1 in 7 wounded British soldiers lived thanks to the drug.[16] From 1945 to 2023, considering global disease burden data, and accounting for antibiotic effectiveness against bacterial diseases, it's reasonable to assert that penicillin and its progeny have saved hundreds of millions, if not billions, of lives around the world.

Building What We Invent

The development of penicillin offers a usefully complete story, where humanity triumphed over a natural adversary. The lesson, which the US seems to have forgotten in the last few decades, is that implementation, not mere invention, determines the pace of progress.

In 1941, penicillin was a stalled science project, languishing in the resource-starved labs of warring Europe. It became a lifesaving product only thanks to hundreds of American scientists and engineers. Almost every technology is like this. "Most major inventions initially don't work very well," the economic historian Joel Mokyr said. "They have to be tweaked, the way the steam engine was tinkered with by many engineers over decades. They have to be embodied by infrastructure, the way nuclear fission can't produce useful electricity until it's contained inside a working reactor. And they have to be built at scale, the way Ford's Model T came down in price before it made a big difference to the country."[17]

Tinkering, embodiment, scaling: these are examples of what Mokyr calls *microinventions*, or the incremental improvements needed to turn a new idea into a significant product. These microinventions are often more important than the original breakthrough. For example, it's broadly understood that Thomas Edison "invented" the incandescent lightbulb in his Menlo Park, New Jersey, lab in 1879. But what exactly did he invent? Certainly not electric power. In 1800, the Italian physicist Alessandro Volta reportedly built the first battery with an electric current.[18] Not electric light, either. In 1809, Humphry Davy built the first practical "arc lamp" that sent a span of sparks across two rods.[19] Edison didn't even invent lightbulbs. In 1841, the English inventor Frederick de Moleyns was granted the first patent for a charcoal-powered incandescent lamp.[20]

So, what did Edison actually do? In his chambers, he painstakingly burned hundreds of materials inside a glass vacuum until he settled on a carbonized bamboo to serve as an efficient lightbulb filament. Understanding that electric light required the steady delivery of electricity, Edison also built a system of generators to make power, wires to carry it, sockets and switches to turn it on and off, and meters to measure usage and allow for the billing of customers. Edison did not make electric light possible. But his microinventions did something even more important. Through exhaustive tinkering, embodying, and scaling, he made electric light *useful*.

Making technology useful often means building it at scale. For many decades, however, US policy hasn't taken this lesson as seriously as it should. After World War II, the American approach to innovation has been to throw money at the initial eureka moment, sporadically support its development, and then watch idly as the technological frontier moves to other countries.

In 1954, three American researchers at Bell Labs built the first device for turning sunlight into energy: a silicon-based solar cell. When light struck the silicon chip, electrons in the metal splashed around, as if cannonballed into activity. Lab engineers found a way to convert the electrons into a current: electricity. At last, sunlight from our nearest star could be technologically photosynthesized into energy for human use. On April 25, the laboratory's managers gathered for a press conference to unveil the world's first solar-powered machine, a miniature Ferris wheel. The *New York Times* heralded the demonstration as "the beginning of a new era" that might finally realize "mankind's most cherished dreams—the harnessing of the almost limitless energy of the sun for the uses of civilization."[21]

Yet despite the initial fanfare, the first solar cells were impractical for daily use. If you tried to use these earliest models to heat and light your home tomorrow, it would cost you about $1 million a day. Despite little utility on earth, solar technology found early promise in orbit. The first American satellite, Explorer 1, which had relied on heavy mercury batteries, lasted less than four months.[22] In a bold move, the US Navy turned to solar cells for its Vanguard 1 satellite, launched in March 1958. The gamble paid off: Vanguard 1's six solar cells powered its radio transmitter for six years.[23]

This success triggered a decade of intensive development. From 1958 to 1969, the US space program poured tens of millions of dollars into solar cells for its satellites.[24] Just as the environmental movement gained momentum, the 1973 oil crisis sent shock waves through the American economy and exposed the nation's vulnerability to foreign energy suppliers. In response, the US government launched a strong push to develop alternative energy sources. Solar power became a centerpiece of these efforts. Federal funding for its research and development took off. New agencies like the Energy Research and Development Administration and the Solar Energy Research Institute were established to coordinate and accelerate its progress.[25] The results were undeniable. Over the course of the decade, solar cell efficiencies tripled while costs plummeted by a factor of five, according to Gregory Nemet, a professor at the University of Wisconsin and the author of the book *How Solar Energy Became Cheap*. Thousands of scientists, engineers, and entrepreneurs flocked to the field, sensing the dawn of an energy revolution.

The election of Ronald Reagan in 1980, however, decimated the solar revolution in America. Driven by a conservative ideology that favored free markets and limited government intervention, Reagan dismantled much of the solar infrastructure built up over the previous decade. For secretary of energy, he appointed James Edwards, a dentist with no expertise or interest in developing nascent energy technology.[26] Solar R&D spending under Reagan fell by over 60 percent his first year in office.[27] Some of the dismantling was painfully literal: in 1986, Reagan removed the solar hot-water panels installed on the White House roof by Jimmy Carter.

Reagan's election was the most important factor in the slowdown of US solar development, according to Nemet.[28] His conservative revolution coincided with a huge drop in gasoline prices, as Saudi Arabia flooded the market with cheap oil in the 1980s. Consumers embraced gas-guzzling SUVs, and alternative energy fell out of favor. The spirit of imagining life after oil seemed to shrivel up and die. As late as the early 2000s, federal energy R&D spending was still 80 percent below its level in the 1970s.[29] The US solar industry gradually withered. Many companies couldn't survive without government support. By 2001, renewable energy accounted for 5 percent to 6 percent of total energy consumption—the lowest share since at least 1989.[30]

As American firms pulled back from solar power, other countries picked up the slack. In the 1990s, Germany subsidized solar technology from both sides—paying companies to make panels and paying consumers to buy them.[31] The solar market took off. Between 2001 and 2011, German employment in the industry surged alongside rooftop solar installations.[32]

If the US invented solar energy in the 1950s, and Germany made it a market in the 1990s, China made solar energy cheap in the

2000s.[33] Without sufficient oil and gas resources to power a billion-person economy, China has had existential motivation to develop its own domestic energy technology. In the 2010s, Beijing got serious about building out a solar energy business, lavishing subsidies, loans, and free land to upstart solar-panel makers. Recognizing this lasting commitment, Chinese solar companies invested for the long run. Whereas America whiplashed between "boom and bust cycles" in solar policy that have "surely slowed down its progress," Nemet wrote that China's consistent policy has allowed its firms to build more, faster, and cheaper.[34]

There is an idea in manufacturing history known as Wright's law, which says that some things get cheaper as we learn to build more.[35] The theory is named after Theodore Wright, an American aeronautical engineer who served as vice chairman of NASA's predecessor, the National Advisory Committee for Aeronautics.[36] In the 1930s, Wright recognized that the cost of building airplanes had declined with an eerie consistency since World War I: for every quadrupling of total aircraft production, unit costs consistently fell by about one-third. In 1936, Wright proposed that some products enjoy a kind of virtuous cycle of building and learning.

Wright's law runs counter to the eureka myth. It says that innovation is not a two-stage process, where a loner genius conceives of a brilliant idea and then a bunch of thoughtless brutes manufacture it. Innovation is enmeshed in the act of making. Wright's law is the story of penicillin, whose costs declined as the government learned to cook larger batches of the medicine. It is the story of the Model T automobile, which became more affordable as Ford built larger and larger factories. It is also the story of the computer chip. In the 1960s, Gordon Moore, the founder of Intel, wrote that the number of transistors on a chip might double every two years.[37] His prediction became prophecy. Fifty years later, transistor costs declined by a factor of *one billion*.[38]

Wright's law echoes loudly in the history of China's solar energy revolution. Drawing from the country's expertise at making cheap textiles and shoes, Chinese firms gradually learned how to make solar panels more efficiently. In one case, a Chinese company bought a saw from a Swiss company that could cut thinner and thinner silicon wafers, which meant more panels from the same crystal ingot.[39] They built machines to automate production lines. As they figured out what worked, they scaled up their lessons to build more production lines and larger factories. In 2000, China had barely enough solar energy to power a small town. By 2020, the nation was making 70 percent of the world's photovoltaic panels.[40] As China ramped up manufacturing, the cost of solar panels in the last fifteen years has declined by about 90 percent.[41]

Seventy years ago, the *New York Times* had anticipated that America's solar energy revolution would lead to "limitless energy." But rather than treat limitless clean energy as a project of national urgency, the US treated solar panels as a trifling inessential, with no long-term plan to make or deploy them at scale. And we lost decades of progress because of it. In Germany, between 1990 and 2015, the share of electricity production that came from renewable energy like solar rose from about 3.5 percent to 30 percent.[42] But in the US over the same period, solar's share of electricity stagnated. These were wasted decades, which we are paying for in the form of more modern pollution, more dependency on fossil fuels, less total energy, and more expensive electricity bills.

All is not lost. After a long hiatus, solar energy has taken off again to become America's fastest-growing electricity source, partly thanks to subsidies passed in the Inflation Reduction Act of 2022.[43] But while today's solar progress deserves our celebration, the policy errors of the last forty years deserve our attention. The US led the world in solar energy development throughout the 1970s. In a parallel universe where we had continued to develop and deploy solar, we might today have the green energy paradise of our dreams: an economy fully fueled by the sun. With such abundance of electricity, we might untap businesses that today are science fiction given their high energy demands, like machines that suck carbon dioxide from the sky and factories that grow animal meat without animal suffering.

But for too long, America fell for the eureka myth and its attending faith in markets alone to solve the problem of scaling new technology. Progress is now, as it has always been, about the combination of invention and implementation. John Arnold, the cochair of Arnold Ventures philanthropy, put it pithily: "America has the ability to invent. China has the ability to build. The first country that can figure out how to do both will be the superpower."[44]

For the past few decades, the eureka myth has walked hand in hand with another attractive fable: that the US government is helpless as an investor in new technologies. One useful summary of this view came from a 2012 *Economist* essay, which claimed "governments have always been lousy at picking winners, and they are likely to become more so, as legions of entrepreneurs and tinkerers swap designs online [and] turn them into products."

This dual image—the state, as a lazy slowpoke, versus the market, as the self-sufficient[45] dynamo of innovation—bears little resemblance to history. As the economist Mariana Mazzucato pointed out in *The Entrepreneurial State*, it is strange that we still debate whether the government ought to pick winners when it is obviously that we live in a world that has amply "picked" for us.[46] When you use an iPhone, you are playing with a technology that bundles silicon chips, the internet, GPS, voice-recognition software, and multi-touch technology, which were in part funded by the Defense Department, NIH, the National Science Foundation, and other government entities.[47] If you heat and cool your home with power drawn from natural gas, you're tapping into an energy revolution that began with federal research into drilling shale formations. If you own a home in the suburbs, you drive down state-funded roads with federally subsidized mortgages. We live in a ripely picked world.

The smartest question, then, is not *if* the government should intervene in markets, but how to do so. Nearly one hundred years ago, the economist John Maynard Keynes offered an elegant answer in his 1926 book *The End of Laissez-Faire*. "The important thing for government is not to do things which individuals are doing already, and to do them a little better or a little worse; but to do those things which at present are not done at all," he wrote. If technological progress requires money or resources that are beyond the scope of any one company, and government does nothing, progress slows down. This is exactly what we saw after 1980 in the solar industry. As the private sector lacked the resources to scale solar production, Washington slashed its support, and the industry went cold. The highest purpose of a pro-invention government is to make possible what would otherwise be impossible. No private company could orchestrate the national production of penicillin in World War II, so OSRD did it. No private companies were close to putting a man on the moon in the 1960s, so NASA did it.[48]

Government should have a vision of the future, and within

that vision it can create space for companies to do what they otherwise cannot, to make possible what is otherwise impossible. The COVID pandemic was a crisis that required a first-of-its-kind invention that no company could solve on its own. It was inconceivable that a single firm might invent, test, approve, and manufacture a therapy in record-breaking time. In the case of mRNA technology, an ingenious invention wasn't enough. We needed an equally ingenious plan to bring that invention to life. And, just as the US government did for penicillin in World War II, the US succeeded by providing a model for how to turn invention into implementation.

Progress at "Warp Speed"

In the spring of 2020, the typical timeline for new vaccine development was thought to be a decade or longer. "The grim truth," the *New York Times* journalist Stuart A. Thompson wrote in April, "is that a vaccine probably won't arrive any time soon."[49] Many scientists agreed. When the MSNBC host Brian Williams asked Irwin Redlener, a public health expert at Columbia University, about the prospects of a vaccine by the end of 2020, the scientist said the mission was "impossible."

On May 15, 2020, with the COVID death count screaming toward 100,000, the White House announced, in a Rose Garden kickoff, a mission to end the pandemic. The goal of the new plan, Operation Warp Speed (OWS), was to create the fastest vaccine development and distribution program in history—a new vaccine built, not in ten years, but in ten months.[50]

To succeed, officials had to map out the entire journey of a new therapy—research, clinical trials, regulatory approval, distribution. The people in charge of OWS weren't students of Vannevar Bush. They weren't experts on the history of the Office of Scientific Research and Development. In conversations with its top officials, they said they'd never heard of OSRD. But whether by accident or by instinct, they retraced many of the steps that made penicillin a wartime reality.

First, they had to solve the problem of basic science. In May 2020, nobody knew what kind of vaccine technology would have the best chance at knocking out COVID. Officials decided to spread their bets. "We embraced a venture capital approach," said Paul Mango, then deputy chief of staff for policy at the Department of Health and Human Services and the author of *Warp Speed*, an insider's history of the program. Rather than put all their money behind one type of vaccine technology or one pharmaceutical company, they spread their investments across three vaccine platforms, or technologies: synthetic mRNA, replication-defective live-vector, and recombinant-subunit-adjuvanted protein.[51] "We wanted to spread out the risk, because we didn't know what technology would solve the problem," he said. "But we also didn't want to make too many bets, because it would have been a logistical nightmare to coordinate the development of dozens and dozens of vaccine candidates at once."[52] Notably, Warp Speed didn't force any company to make vaccines. Instead, firms were lured with up-front subsidies and promises of future payouts.

Second, OWS had to accelerate the approval and production pipeline, where many drugs wait years to go to market. To reduce barriers that could slow down vaccine approval, OWS helped to recruit populations for clinical trials and to accelerate the timeline for FDA review. To fast-track production, OWS set up or expanded twenty-seven manufacturing facilities.[53] "Science is the easy part of making a vaccine," Moncef Slaoui, the head of OWS, said often to his team. "The hard part will be manufacturing this stuff at scale. Just because you know how to make five liters of vaccine doesn't mean you can make one hundred liters of it."[54] A vaccine's journey from the production plant to tens of thousands of pharmacies created other challenges. For example, the Pfizer vaccine needed to be stored at around minus 70° Celsius, a temperature at which most glass vials shattered.[55] So, Warp Speed approached the materials science company Corning to produce, in quantity, a special glass they had developed a few years earlier.[56] The program ultimately granted $347 million to Corning and one other glass manufacturer to ensure ultracold transport.[57]

Third, OWS had to solve the distribution problem. "It doesn't do any good to have millions of vaccines sitting on the shelf," Mango said. "We had to get them to seventy thousand sites, working with sixty-four separate health jurisdictions, in all fifty states. We had to do it very quickly and all at once."[58] OWS brought a combat-operation focus to procuring vaccines and ensuring their speedy delivery. Warp Speed leaned on officials from the Defense Department's Army Materiel Command to help with logistics, and lessons from the battlefield were pulled into the vaccine program. For example, for every 100 doses of vaccines sent to pharmacies, the government sent 110 needles and 110 syringes. "The equivalent of a frontline soldier will sometimes drop a syringe or contaminate a needle, so you need redundancy," Mango said.[59]

OWS solved problems by enabling the private sector rather than commanding it. With few exceptions, such as the Veterans Administration, "no federal employee was directly involved in manufacturing, packaging, shipping, or injecting a single dose of any Warp

Speed COVID vaccine," Mango wrote in his book on the program. "We let one of the biggest pharmaceutical distributors in the world (McKesson) handle the vaccines, let the most successful delivery companies in the world (UPS and FedEx) deliver the vaccines, let those entities who knew best how to vaccinate millions of Americans (CVS and Walgreens) conduct vaccinations."[60]

Finally, the simplest part of OWS is perhaps the most important: the vaccines were free. The federal government bought out the vaccines from pharmaceutical companies, which allowed them to sell the shots to the public for any price they wanted. They chose the price of $0.00. For much of 2021, the most cutting-edge biotechnology in America was also the cheapest therapy in the world.

"The single most important thing that Operation Warp Speed did was to provide a whole-of-government urgency" to the goal of rapid deployment, Caleb Watney, cofounder of the Institute for Progress, said. "Getting everything right meant you needed to make a million correct decisions in the right order."[61] If the government had bet only on traditional vaccine technology, we would have had no mRNA therapies. If the government hadn't done extensive supply-chain mapping in the summer of 2020, the initial vaccine rollout might have taken months rather than weeks. And if the government hadn't bought out vaccines from the pharmaceutical companies, they wouldn't have been free to consumers. But because Operation Warp Speed did all this, the vaccines were expeditiously approved, manufactured, and distributed at no cost to the public.[62]

In all, the US government spent less than $40 billion to develop, produce, and buy mRNA COVID vaccines.[63] It might be one of the best bang-for-buck policies in US history. COVID vaccines prevented up to 20 million[64] excess deaths worldwide, with several million of those saved lives directly attributable to the acceleration of the Pfizer and Moderna vaccines. Tens of millions of hospitalizations were prevented by the further prevention of severe disease. One analysis by three US economists estimated that the lives saved in just the eight months of the vaccinations were worth $6.5 trillion.[65] Stacked up against more popular American programs, such as the Apollo program, Warp Speed's accomplishment shines even brighter. For all the wondrous drama and exploratory genius of touching a human foot to moon dust, the Apollo missions did not directly save any lives or unveil any new technologies, even as they accelerated the development of computer chips and related fields.

Americans love to take credit for their accomplishments. So one might expect that Warp Speed would receive universal adulation today. Quite the opposite, however: Warp Speed has been practically abandoned by both parties. In January 2021, the incoming White House announced it would rename the program.[66] Rather than officially rename it, they basically stopped talking about it. Democrats rarely credit or mention Operation Warp Speed, perhaps because they're reluctant to be caught lavishing praise on anything that bears the fingerprints of Donald Trump. Meanwhile, Republicans—including Trump himself—rarely celebrate the vaccines, because much of the party is populated by anti-vax conservatives who refused to take the shot and came up with wild conspiracy theories to discredit its effectiveness. When Trump won reelection in 2024, he named Robert F. Kennedy Jr., perhaps the nation's most famous vaccine skeptic, to lead the Department of Health and Human Services.

Operation Warp Speed is the oddest political orphan. A program named after *Star Trek* has disappeared into its own kind of black hole. A policy that stimulated the economy more than the Apollo program, and which may have saved more lives than the Manhattan Project, has almost no loud champions in politics. Even its scarce champions seem intent on taking the wrong lessons from its success. In an essay for the *Wall Street Journal*, the University of Chicago professor Casey B. Mulligan, who had served as chief economist for the Trump White House, claimed that "the urgent lesson" from Operation Warp Speed was that "too much government hinders private innovation."[67] But OWS increased government spending by billions of dollars. With an urgency typically reserved for war, the federal government directed the development of vaccines from their testing to the final transport. It's odd to claim that a program that expanded government powers succeeded by proving that one should never expand government powers.

The right lesson from World War II and Warp Speed is that the state is no enemy of invention or innovation. In fact, the government can accelerate both. In the 1940s, the Office of Scientific and Research Development mapped out the chemistry and production challenges for penicillin and turned an obstacle course into a glide path. In 2020, the US government similarly identified the bottlenecks to rapid vaccine development and removed them. In both cases, the government served as a chief national problem solver, molding its policies to fit the moment. It is a vision of a new kind of entrepreneurial state. It is the government as a bottleneck detective.

The Bottleneck Detective

The US faces complex challenges in housing, energy, science policy, invention, and innovation. Solving them must begin with the appreciation that these are different industries, with different constraints, enmeshed in different markets. Figuring out how to build more apartments in Los Angeles might not be relevant to the problem of adding solar energy in Massachusetts, which has nothing to do with the question of how to accelerate scientific discovery in cancer. To be a bottleneck detective is to recognize that wise policy begins with an investigation rather than an ideology that tries to force the same key into a variety of ill-fitting locks. Making progress in these industries requires first that we want to understand: How does this industry actually work? From that question can emerge an agenda for overcoming the barriers to growth.

Sometimes being a bottleneck detective is about removing restrictions that shouldn't exist. The US has fewer primary-care physicians as a share of its population than almost any other rich country, despite having the world's most expensive health-care system. This shortage is partly by design. In the early 1980s, a special committee established to review the state of American medicine reported to the US Department of Health and Human Services that the US was on the verge of a massive surplus of doctors. Physician groups backed up the finding. "The size of medical schools must be diminished," Charles Evarts, the president of the American Orthopaedic Association, said in a 1985 speech. "Certain programs need to reduce their numbers, others must consolidate, and others need to terminate voluntarily or be terminated."[68] Starting in the 1980s, the government cut its support for medical schools and medical students, and many universities agreed to freeze the number of new studies and stop construction on medical programs. Between 1980 and 2005, the number of medical-school matriculants essentially flatlined[69] as the US added 70 million people.[70]

This policy of deliberate scarcity succeeded, and the inevitable result was a scarcity of doctors—especially those, like primary-care physicians, who make the least money. Years later, the US is still digging out from under the moratorium. Fixing this problem is eminently within the powers of the federal government. "The first thing I would do is to expand the residency system so that more doctors can become residents after medical school," Robert Orr, a policy analyst who studies health-care policy at the Niskanen Center, said. "This might be the key bottleneck. The medical schools say they can't easily expand, because there aren't enough residency slots for their graduates to fill. But there aren't enough residency slots because Washington has purposefully limited federal residency financing."[71] The arithmetic is simple: more funding means more residents; accepting more residents allows medical schools to grow; more medical students today means more doctors in a decade.

Being a bottleneck detective isn't just about removing things that don't work. Sometimes it's about creating entirely new programs that don't exist but should. Imagine somebody is trying to build a new kind of rocket, and you're the czar of rocket innovation policy at the Department of Defense. You have $1 billion that you can use to accelerate the invention. There are several things you can do. You can give the company $1 billion as a simple grant ("here, have the money for nothing"). You can make it a loan ("pay me back later, plus interest"). You can create a so-called loan guarantee ("if you default on a $1 billion loan, I'll pay the lender in full"). These are all examples of *push funding* because the up-front money pushes forward innovation.

But there is another, very different way to use that $1 billion. You can dangle a reward if the rocket company meets some target— say, the construction of three new rockets. As opposed to push funding, this is called *pull funding*. If push funding pays for effort, pull funding pays for success.[72] Warp Speed used both. With push funding, it covered the early expenses of several vaccine makers. With pull funding, it promised to buy a certain number of vaccine doses, provided that the therapies received FDA authorization.

Pull funding is efficient because it only pays out if the technology pans out. It's effective, because it solves a common bottleneck in new technology: demand uncertainty. Some companies are rightly concerned that consumers cannot afford the early, expensive versions of a product. These companies need more certainty about future profits to invest in the final stages of invention. For example, pneumococcal disease has been the world's most common form of bacterial pneumonia and one of the leading causes of child mortality in low-income countries. But for years, pharmaceutical companies seemed reluctant to invest in a vaccine for African strains of the disease, in part because they assumed its countries couldn't afford the medicine at full price. In 2007, the Bill & Melinda Gates Foundation joined several nations to offer pharmaceutical companies a deal: make a pneumococcal vaccine for low-income countries, and we'll pay you $1.5 billion to produce it at volume. The promise of future funding proved astonishingly effective. By 2020, several companies had developed the vaccine, and hundreds of millions of doses were purchased and distributed around the world. By one estimate, the vaccines saved seven hundred thousand lives.[73]

This policy—a promise to buy a certain number of early products to accelerate their invention—is called an "advance market commitment," or AMC. An AMC is particularly effective when the world needs an abundance of a brand-new technology that is currently too expensive. For example, pharmaceutical firms assumed that African buyers wouldn't pay back their investment in vaccines. So the commitment to pay for millions of doses unlocked an invention that otherwise wouldn't exist.

This AMC model could unlock other inventions. One of the most devilish challenges in energy is how to efficiently remove CO_2 from the atmosphere. By 2050, the world will need to permanently remove 10 billion tons of carbon dioxide from the skies every year to avoid the most catastrophic effects of climate change.[74] But in all of history, only 10,000 tons of CO_2 have been technologically removed—one million times short of what we'll soon need to do every year.[75] In 2022, Nan Ransohoff, the head of climate policy at the payment company Stripe, launched Frontier, an AMC that raised $1 billion to pay any company that develops carbon-removal technology that meets a high level of efficiency. The initiative has already encouraged more carbon-removal companies to jump into the race. One survey found that of all the firms that have launched since Frontier began, 7 in 10 say Frontier's launch was key to their founding.[76] If we eventually hit big with carbon-vacuuming machines that save the world from climate change, it might very well be due to policies that guarantee a return for the best early technologies.

Looking forward, AMCs could be used for a range of futuristic ideas. Staying in the realm of climate technology, AMCs could accelerate the development of clean cement. The traditional manufacture of cement is a major contributor to climate change. Every year, the world produces about 4 billion tons of cement to make concrete and other binding agents.[77] By most estimates, cement is responsible for 8 percent of the world's CO_2 emissions.[78] If it were a country, cement would be the third-biggest carbon emitter on the planet, the *New York Times* journalist David Wallace-Wells wrote.[79]

Cement poses a unique challenge to decarbonization. Cleaning up electricity is conceptually simple: it's possible to power an electric car battery with wind, or to run air-conditioning with electricity from solar energy. But the cement-manufacturing process is different. Making cement requires converting limestone (calcium carbonate) into quicklime (calcium oxide) by heating it to about 1500° F. This is a double whammy for carbon dioxide emissions. Not only does that level of heat often require burning fossil fuels like coal, but also the chemical reaction automatically produces carbon dioxide as a byproduct. To make traditional cement without releasing an enormous amount of carbon dioxide simply isn't possible.

As billions of people transition to urban living in the coming decades, demand for cement will only grow. The problem cannot be simply wished away. It's not realistic to demand that the entire planet stop building things. The only truly global solution is invention.

There are several technological paths. We can build machines and systems to scrub up the carbon released from the chemical process that makes calcium oxide. These carbon-capture technologies would trap emissions at the source, preventing them from entering the atmosphere. Another possibility is to replace limestone as the rock source of cement with a new material. "Maybe we don't need to use limestone at all," says the climate policy author Hannah Ritchie. "If we use a source rock that doesn't emit carbon, then there's nothing to scrub up."[80] Several companies are innovating with alternate rocks to produce cement-like products, such as basalt (the most abundant surface rock on earth) and calcium silicate, which produces the key ingredient of cement, calcium oxide, without releasing carbon dioxide in the process.

The few companies that are working on lower-emission cement replacements face significant bottlenecks in terms of cost and scale. That could make them prime candidates for pull funding. "Cement could be perfect for an AMC, because the government already buys forty percent of US cement, and suppliers don't know who will pay high prices in the short run," Ransohoff said. "We need a policy to move it down the cost curve."[81] If the US pledged to buy several billions of dollars' worth of affordable green cement, it could encourage investors and entrepreneurs to pour more time and treasure into its development. The up-front funds could help green cement companies expand their production facilities. As Wright's law works its magic, the cost of producing low-carbon cement would decline over time. The result would optimistically be a win-win-win-win: the start-ups would get funding, the public would get cleaner infrastructure, the treasury would protect taxpayers by only paying for success, and the climate would get a reprieve from carbon-coughing cement.

The most important lesson of AMCs is that they make government a more active agent of invention, by identifying bottlenecks in public demand and filling them. "The US often makes financial commitments contingent on failure, like loan guarantees, which pay a lender in the event of a default," said Thomas Kalil, the former deputy director for technology and innovation in the White House Office of Science and Technology Policy. "But we don't make enough financial commitments contingent on success, like a prize, or advance purchase order. Operation Warp Speed did it very successfully."[82] We should be looking for many more opportunities to identify what's holding back the invention and implementation of the most important technologies of the future and dangle prizes and purchase orders to pull them closer to the present.

• • •

Artificial intelligence might be the most important technology of the decade. In the last few years, tech firms have spent hundreds of billions of dollars to build machines that can carry out a dizzying array of tasks: writing essays and code, reading thousands of pages in seconds, carrying on fluent conversations, and even producing animated movies. AI has not transformed the US economy in the hour that we're writing these words, but things are moving fast enough that it is impossible to predict what effect AI will have had by the time you read them.

For all the uncertainties about AI's larval potential, one thing is very certain: its development will require a gigantic amount of energy. The computational intensity of training artificial intelligence consumes significantly more power than other computer systems. Data centers that house AI hardware are projected to triple their share of total American energy use in the next decade, and AI is already "wreaking havoc" on US power systems, Bloomberg reported in 2024.

The biggest tech firms, like Microsoft and Alphabet, have pledged to run their data centers on low-carbon energy. But these promises are smashing up against America's inability to build clean energy fast enough. So tech companies are hunting for electricity in surprising places. In March 2024, Amazon agreed to buy energy from the Susquehanna nuclear power plant in Pennsylvania to power its data centers. In September, Microsoft made a deal to buy the entire electricity output of the last working reactor of the Three Mile Island nuclear plant, which suffered a partial meltdown in 1979. Buying power from existing power plants is a short-term stopgap. But it's not a long-term solution. New nuclear power plants can take years, even decades, to complete.

The AI revolution makes the cause of energy abundance even more urgent. In the last few decades, US energy infrastructure projects have been being slowed by all the challenges we've described: a lack of productivity in construction, permitting blockages, extended environmental reviews, and long interconnection queues. These bottlenecks are largely self-made, and if we don't make it easier for AI companies to build in America, we should expect them to build data centers abroad. Some AI executives have met with Gulf states leaders about siting data centers in the Middle East.

In the next few decades, *trillions* of dollars of AI infrastructure could be built somewhere in the world. The biggest question is where. If the US fails to add energy supply in the US, the results could be chaotic, at best, and catastrophic at worst. As new data centers demand more energy, electricity prices would rise for consumers, in the absence of supply growth. More troublingly, it's conceivable that AI researchers are years, not decades, away from building a superintelligent system with the ability to hack foreign government secrets, cripple their military software systems, and partly collapse the energy grids of adversaries. This would be a breakthrough akin to a kind of digital nuclear bomb. "Do we really want the infrastructure for the Manhattan Project to be controlled by some capricious Middle Eastern dictatorship?" the AI researcher Leopold Aschenbrenner wrote in his 2024 manifesto "Situational Awareness." It is paramount, he said, for the US to prioritize energy construction in the next decade. "America sorely regretted her energy dependence on the Middle East in the '70s, and we worked so hard to get out from under their thumbs. We cannot make the same mistake again."[83]

An abundance of cheap and clean electricity would provide broad benefits, even if AI didn't pan out. Abundant energy would reduce electricity bills for households. It would make other futuristic technologies that need ample power more feasible. For example, desalination facilities that turn saltwater into drinkable water might be necessary to sustain populations in the American Southwest in this century. This technology is extremely energy intensive. In Israel, one of the world leaders in desalination, desalination accounts for about 3 percent of the country's total energy consumption.[84] In this light, energy abundance is not strictly speaking a "data center policy" or an "AI policy." It is an all-purpose national affordability policy and an innovation policy. Simply put, energy abundance might be the single most important technological bottleneck of our time.

Twenty years from now, it is possible that we will consider the combination of clean energy growth and AI the most important technology story of the decade. In 2024, Sam Altman, the chief executive and cofounder of OpenAI, framed our ability to make artificial intelligence in dramatic terms. "After thousands of years of compounding scientific discovery and technological progress," he wrote, "we have figured out how to melt sand, add some impurities, arrange it with astonishing precision at extraordinarily tiny scale into computer chips, run energy through it, and end up with systems capable of creating increasingly capable artificial intelligence."[85] Our breakthroughs in energy are no less mythic. After thousands of years of scientific discovery and technological progress, we have figured out how to turn the most elemental functions of nature—the sun's light, the wind, the heat beneath the earth—into a swarm of electrons that can run our machines and power our lives. The direction of progress in the twenty-first century might depend on America's ability to merge these breakthroughs—AI and clean energy, melted sand and swarming electrons—to bring broad prosperity and peace, rather than the opposite. Doing so requires, at least, that US policy has a say in directing AI. And that means building AI and its energy source here, in America, where it was invented.

Focus Is a Choice

When we asked Paul Mango to name the single most important part of Operation Warp Speed, he said it was focus. "On the Warp Speed team, you could have asked anyone what the project's goal was, from the generals and leaders, down to the lowest-ranking officials, and they would all give the same answer: deliver at least one safe and effective vaccine, manufactured at scale, before the end of the year," he said. "Every decision we made was based on those constraints."[86] The health crisis served as a focusing mechanism—a way of taking the tangles of competing priorities and rightening them into a straight thread.

A regrettable feature of history is that progress often requires the focusing mechanism of disaster. Penicillin took a world war, and mRNA vaccines took a plague. The Federal Reserve was created only after a string of financial disasters, culminating in the Panic of 1907. The tragedy of the Great Depression allowed for the boldness of the New Deal. The Nazi domination of Europe galvanized the creation of the Office of Scientific Research and Development. The Soviet Union's successful launch of Sputnik in 1957 moved Washington to create the Advanced Projects Research Agency, later renamed DARPA, which contributed to the invention of the personal computer, GPS, and drone technology. It also pushed the US to expand NASA and eventually launch the Apollo program. Again and again in American history, we seem to be at our very best when things are at their very worst.

This is a depressing thought. One interpretation might be that we are doomed to sleepwalk through history until a catastrophe jolts us into action. But there is comfort in the connection between perceived crisis and urgency. If crisis is the ultimate push-and-pull mechanism—both galvanizing action and rewarding success—we must remember that it is always up to us to decide what counts as a crisis.

In an alternate history of the twentieth century, the launch of Sputnik might not have led the US to do anything. After all, there was no real existential danger posed to any American by a metal box floating in orbit. Surely, if France or Britain had, by some miracle, managed to launch the first object into space, it wouldn't have caused much geopolitical angst in America. But the US government determined that because Sputnik was a Soviet instrument, the achievement was a crisis that required a response. And in that crucible of insecurity and inspiration, the US created a set of institutions that ultimately put a man on the moon and the internet in our pockets.

The moon race is remembered today as a necessary and broadly popular response to the Soviet threat. But one of the most misunderstood aspects of the space race is that the Apollo program survived because of political persistence, not because of its popularity. In its brief history, the moon mission polled poorly. A 1965 Gallup survey found that "only 39 percent of Americans thought that the US should do everything possible, regardless of cost, to be the first nation on the moon."[87] A majority of Americans consistently told pollsters that the Apollo missions weren't worth the cost, with up to 60 percent saying the government was spending too much on space.[88] At one point, President John F. Kennedy—who famously said, "We choose to go to the moon in this decade and do the other things, not because they are easy, but because they are hard"—told NASA chief James Webb, "I'm not that interested in space."[89] A majority of Americans supported the lunar missions only once in the 1960s: in a poll taken just after Neil Armstrong's televised landing.

One lesson of Apollo's surprising unpopularity is that the program was sustained by leaders within NASA and the White House, which never pulled the plug on an audacious task that polled poorly among the public. Kennedy was right when he said, "We choose to go to the moon." So did we choose to pass the New Deal, just as we chose to build OSRD, just as we chose to invent the bones of the internet in a government lab, just as we chose to break the record for vaccine development during a pandemic. Yes, crisis is a focusing mechanism. But leaders define what counts as a crisis. And leaders are the ones who choose to focus.

The US could announce a Warp Speed for heart disease tomorrow, on the theory that the leading cause of death in America is a national crisis. We could announce a full emergency review of federal and local permitting rules for clean energy construction, with the rationale that climate change is a crisis. The US could decide that the major diseases afflicting developing countries, such as malaria, deserve a concerted global coalition to eradicate them within a decade. Even in times without world wars and pandemics, crises abound. Turning them into national priorities is, and has always been, a political choice.

In the last half century, we have made several choices about invention and implementation and science and technology. We have chosen to create a system that rewards caution and punishes outsider thinking and risk in scientific research. We have chosen to embrace a political economy that encourages offshoring the development of American inventions that are key to our national security and flourishing. None of this was inevitable. These policies are the fruits of human decisions. They are artifacts of our ripely picked world.

Breakthroughs often involve a flash of luck, even when they follow decades of painstaking labor. The historian James Phinney Baxter III called penicillin "the blue mold which blew in through Fleming's window on that happy breeze." Many scientific breakthroughs similarly shock their discoverers, blowing in sideways through proverbial windows. Few people expected synthetic mRNA, an idea that had languished in the wilderness of academia, to match up so perfectly with the spiky crowns of a novel coronavirus. The serendipity of science is one reason why it's so important to untether research from politics and allow scientists to seek the truth freely without spending half their time deluged by bureaucratic paperwork and paralyzed by fear that their ideas might diverge from the moment's conventional wisdom.

But the next stages of technology are not about luck. Building, deployment, and implementation are not the stuff of happy breezes. They require deliberate acts, laws, and policies. They require choices. For too long, the US has been enthralled by the eureka myth—the idea that flashes of individual genius are the most important moments in the history of technology. This mind-set governed our approach to economic growth in the last forty years. In the next generation, the US needs a plan to build what it invents.

Conclusion
Toward Abundance

POLITICS IS A WAY OF ORGANIZING CONFLICT, AND SO OUR ATTENTION is naturally drawn to divisions. That is particularly true now, when the divisions are so fundamental. The Democratic and Republican parties do not merely disagree over the details of tax policy. They disagree over the legitimacy of elections, of institutions, of the structure of American government. They are split in their views of speech and history and decency and truth. Distinguished scholars write books considering the nearness of another civil war and wondering whether fascism is resurgent on American soil. The polarization of the 1990s feels quaint against the chasmic conflict of the 2020s.

These divisions are real. They are dangerous. But behind them is the murky outline of something very different. Perhaps a path out of the morass we're in. A new political order.

The term "political order" is the coinage of Gary Gerstle, an American historian and a professor at Cambridge University. Many historians focus on how Republicans and Democrats have fought and disagreed over the years. Gerstle's work focuses instead on how hidden points of consensus between the parties create distinctive periods of history, which he calls political orders. He defines a political order as "a constellation of ideologies, policies, and constituencies that shape American politics in ways that endure beyond the two-, four-, and six-year election cycles."[1] Two such constellations have extended across the last hundred years of American history, according to Gerstle. The New Deal order rose in the 1930s and collapsed in the 1970s. The neoliberal order rose in the 1970s and declined in the 2010s.

The New Deal order brought the agreement that the federal government must take an active role in managing the American economy and protecting workers. Begun under Franklin Roosevelt, a Democrat, it continued under Dwight Eisenhower, a Republican, who endorsed its basic framework. Rather than rail against big government programs, Eisenhower signed legislation to create the Interstate Highway System. Rather than bemoan welfare, he celebrated its growth. "We want a broader and stronger system of unemployment insurance," Eisenhower said, sounding much more like a Democrat from the 2020s than a Republican of the 1980s.[2]

Why did Eisenhower and the GOP of his era acquiesce to the New Deal order? "It had far less to do with Eisenhower the man than with the geopolitical situation in which the new president and his party had been thrust," Gerstle writes. The Cold War wasn't just an arms race or a military conflict with the Soviet Union. It was a competition over whose philosophy of government would produce the best outcomes for people. Eisenhower needed to prove that "he could take better care of his ordinary citizens than the leaders of Soviet communism could provide for theirs."[3] That meant embracing the policies of Roosevelt and the Democrats, who had succeeded in raising America's living standards after the Great Depression.

In the 1970s, the New Deal order collapsed beneath the weight of crises it could not contain—stagflation and the Vietnam War, most notably. But there was more to it than that. Abroad, the horrors and absurdities of communism became clearer. At home, millions of oppressed Americans marched, sat-in, and organized for rights. A change in values took hold. The promise of collective action lost its luster. Nurturing the dignity and genius of the individual, in the face of regimes that seemed to squelch both, became the reigning ethos.

A new kind of individualism was ascendant, and not just on the right. The New Deal Democrats found themselves challenged by the New Left. "We seek the establishment of a democracy of individual participation, governed by two central aims," read the Port Huron Statement, a left-wing student activist manifesto written in 1962. "That the individual share in those social decisions determining the quality and direction of his life; that society be organized to encourage independence in men and provide the media for their common participation."[4]

Policy is downstream of values, and by the 1970s, Washington was a changed place. Jimmy Carter, a Democrat, deregulated large parts of the economy, including the trucking and airline industries.[5] In the 1980s, Ronald Reagan slashed the high tax rates that Harry Truman had imposed and that Dwight Eisenhower had kept.[6] Much of even the liberal legislation of the age—including the major environmental bills we've discussed throughout this book—worked by centering the individual, making it easier for Americans to slow the government by suing it. The Soviet Union collapsed, proving the supremacy of the American model. Bill

Clinton emerged as the Eisenhower to Reagan's FDR, cementing the principles of a once-radical presidency into a political order. Clinton said the era of big government was over, and he proved it: he did what Reagan had only promised to do and slashed the federal budget while deregulating the financial and IT sectors.

When the spell of a political order breaks, ideas once regarded as implausible and unacceptable become possible and even inevitable. This happened in the 1930s, when the Great Depression created space for the rise of Roosevelt's social-democratic collectivism. It happened in the 1970s, when an upswing of individualism changed the way people thought about taxing and spending, regulating the economy, and managing our relationship to the environment.

It may be happening again.

We are in a rare period in American history, when the decline of one political order makes space for another. The crack-up was decades in the making. It started with the Great Recession, which shattered a broad belief in deregulated markets. The climate crisis revealed how much the profit motive missed. The aftermath of normalizing trade with China proved that the prophets of free trade understood neither China nor America.

Throughout the 2010s, a slow economic recovery fueled public resentment of inequality, and an affordability crisis gathered steam. In 2020, the pandemic obliterated many Americans' trust in government, or what was left of it. And between 2021 and 2024, inflation brought national attention to our interlocking crises of scarcity, supply, and unaffordability. For years, the boundaries of American politics had felt fixed, even settled. But now they are falling.

"For a political order to triumph, it must have a narrative, a story it tells about the good life," Gerstle says. Today's politics are suffused with cynicism and pessimism about government because "a way of living sold to us as good and achievable is no longer good, or no longer achievable."[7] In 2016, the rise of Bernie Sanders on the left and the rise of Donald Trump on the right revealed how many Americans had stopped believing that the life they had been promised was achievable. What both the socialist left and the populist-authoritarian right understood was that the story that had been told by the establishments of both parties, the story that had kept their movements consigned to the margins, had come to its end.

Transitions between orders are provoked by crises that can feel like derangements. As the tectonic plates of American politics shift, once-settled questions reopen, and once-unthinkable answers vie to become a new consensus. One way of understanding the era we're in is as the messy interregnum between political orders; a molten moment when old institutions are failing, traditional elites are flailing, and the public is casting about for a politics that feels like it is of today rather than of yesterday.

A Fork in the Road: Scarcity or Abundance?

This may be the moment for a politics of abundance. But the arc of history does not always bend toward our beliefs. There is no guarantee that the next political order will align with our values. Its opposite is just as likely.

The politics of scarcity can be seductive. When there is not enough to go around, we look with suspicion on anyone who might take what we have. In the 2024 election, JD Vance spoke often of the inadequacy of housing supply, which he wielded as a cudgel against immigrants. "Illegal aliens competing with Americans for scarce homes is one of the most significant drivers of home prices in the country," he said in the vice presidential debate.[8] Donald Trump sounded the same themes. Voters "cannot ignore the impact that the flood of 21 million illegal aliens has had on driving up housing costs," he warned.[9]

Right-wing populism seeks power by closing doors, halting change, and venerating the businesses and dominance hierarchies of the past. Scarcity is its handmaiden. So too is the sense that governments today are weak and corrupt and, therefore, that strongmen are needed to see the world clearly and deliver on democracy's failed promises.

Liberals might detest the language that Trump and Vance use to demonize immigrants. But blue America practices its own version of scarcity politics. Zoning regulations in liberal states and cities that restrict housing supply have increased costs far more than the recent influx of immigrants. These restrictions exacerbated an affordability crisis that was harnessed by the right. Thus, the mistakes of liberals contributed to the rise of illiberalism. "The tendency to turn against outsiders in the face of critical shortages is not restricted to a basket of deplorables," Jerusalem Demsas wrote in the *Atlantic*. "It's in all of us. Most people see others as a threat to their resources, whether it's immigrants coming for your housing, yuppies pushing up rents, other students taking slots at all the good schools, or just more people on the road, adding to congestion."[10]

As the chronic housing shortage and affordability crisis destabilized the reigning political order internally, America's greatest external threat has been the rise of China, a superpower that many now fear and even envy. How could they build so much as we struggled to complete even simple projects? As sluggishness and process came to feel like the defining features of American governance, it became common, even at the heights of American power, to hear China's speed and capacity spoken of wistfully. "Sit and watch us for seven days—just watch the [Senate] floor," Senator Michael Bennet said in 2010. "You know what you'll see happening? Nothing. When I'm in the chair, I sit there thinking, I wonder what they're doing in China right now?"[11]

China has been the great shadow pressure on American politics over the past two decades. The confidence brought by the fall of the Soviet Union has been replaced by a fear that China has learned what we've forgotten. In Washington, a consensus began to crumble. Republicans and Democrats alike had been too complacent about what China's rise meant for American workers and too certain that a richer China would embrace American values. But the blindness was not just about what China was capable of. It was also about what America was losing the capacity to do.

It's no accident that the most forceful challenge to this miasma of complacency and fear came from Donald Trump—a "builder" whose economic appeal centered around an obsession with manufacturing jobs and a deep suspicion of trade. America's political and economic class had ceased to see the value in making things. Workers were told to learn how to code even as Washington kept proving that America had forgotten how to build. Trump didn't care whether you knew how to code, but he seemed viscerally disgusted that America couldn't build as it once could, and that it didn't value the people who'd once done that work.

"I have been talking about China for many years. And you know what? Nobody listened," Trump said in 2016. "But they are listening now. That, I can tell you."[12]

The temperament needed to shatter a consensus does not often coexist with the judiciousness and patience needed to build something better in its place. Trump slapped tariffs on China and called Covid the "Kung Flu,"[13] but he did little to solve the problems he ran on. He promised one "infrastructure week" after another without ever passing an infrastructure bill. Trump understood the dark side of competition, but he never understood the possibilities of cooperation.

To the surprise of many, Joe Biden, as thorough a creature of the Washington establishment as has ever held the presidency, accepted many of Trump's premises. He kept Trump's anti-China tariffs and added more.[14] He barred the export of key technologies to China.[15] He never sought to revise or revisit the Trans-Pacific Partnership trade deal that the Obama administration had negotiated, which would have reduced trade barriers between the US and several countries on either side of the Pacific Ocean.[16] Biden even seemed to accept the way that Trump saw China's manufacturing supremacy as an indictment of the American spirit. "Somewhere along the way, we stopped investing in ourselves," Biden said in 2021. "We stopped investing in our people. And we've risked losing our edge as a nation. I don't even think it was conscious, but that's just what's happened. And China and the rest of the world are moving to catch up and, in some cases, in certain areas, move ahead."[17]

Under Trump, "infrastructure week" was a meme. Under Biden, it became an ethos. In his four years in office, Biden put his name to several laws that broke with the anti-build trend of modern politics. With the bipartisan infrastructure bill, he signed the largest authorization of infrastructure spending since the

Interstate Highway program of the 1950s.[18] With the CHIPS and Science Act, he announced America's intention to invest billions of dollars in scientific discovery and invention—and tens of billions more to build advanced computer chips within our borders.[19] With the Inflation Reduction Act, the US passed the largest clean energy bill in its history, with record investments in electric vehicles, batteries, solar and wind manufacturing, and next-generation climate technology, such as carbon-removal plants.[20] The core of this agenda—subsidies for computer chips and clean energy, historic investments in infrastructure—used the spur of China to get America building and manufacturing at home again. As in the 1930s, and again in the 1970s, external threats and internal crises are converging and making possible a new kind of politics.

Abundance Emerging?

This book has offered a critique of the ways that liberals have governed and thought over the past fifty years. It also reflects an opportunity open to liberals now.

Donald Trump won the 2024 election in part because of the failures of present-day liberalism. But that is very different from saying that he won by offering a compelling vision for America's future. Trump could have run on bringing the Texas housing miracle to the nation. Instead he ran on closing the border. He could have run on the success of Operation Warp Speed. Instead, he has disowned it as his coalition has rebuilt itself around skepticism of scientists and vaccines. Elon Musk has led some of the most innovative companies of the modern era, but according to the earliest reports of his role in Trump's government, he is focused on slashing what government does rather than reimagining what it can do. The right is abandoning many of its successes to embrace a politics of scarcity.

That has left room for liberals to embrace what Republicans have abandoned: a politics of abundance. In fact, there are signs that they already are.

We see it in the rise of the Yes In My Back Yard (or YIMBY) movement, a motley collection of housing obsessives who went from haranguing officials at public hearings in San Francisco to wielding influence nationally. Democratic governors across the nation have passed bill after bill trying to make it easier to build homes. In the 2024 election, one of Kamala Harris's first policy proposals was to build 3 million new homes:[21] a supply-side policy that reflected a decade of persuasion and organizing by liberals who'd come to see the suffering that housing scarcity was causing in their cities.

We see it in the climate movement, which helped persuade the Biden administration to pass a slew of bills intended to expand the supply of clean energy and pull forward needed innovations like green hydrogen. Environmentalists realized that sacrifice and scarcity was a losing politics. They needed a strategy that married the life Americans want with the clean energy the planet could tolerate. Investments in solar and wind installation, in electric vehicle plants and factories to manufacture next-generation batteries, have rocketed upward since.

But none of this will be easy. In California broadly, and San Francisco specifically, dozens of pro-housing bills have not led to the construction of more homes, in part because those bills are layered with additional requirements and standards that builders must meet in order to take advantage of the newly streamlined processes. For developers we spoke to, the added costs of compliance weren't worth it, so the legislation hadn't led them to build any new homes at all, much less build them faster.

The breakneck deployment of wind and solar infrastructure and battery manufacturing has been slowed by outdated permitting and procurement rules that split the Democratic coalition. A difficulty that Biden and Harris had in trying to run on their record in 2024 was that few communities were yet seeing benefit from all this construction their policies were meant to spark. The infrastructure bill, for instance, included $7.5 billion to build a national network of 500,000 electric vehicle charging stations; by March 2024—more than two years after the bill passed—only seven new chargers were up and running.[22] The bitter irony is that Trump and the Republicans might benefit from legislation Biden and the Democrats passed simply because the government spends and builds so slowly, so the changes Biden promised will now happen on Trump's watch.

The word "abundance" speaks of a cornucopia, all good things for everybody. But the world of abundance has trade-offs, and trade-offs require choices. Liberals spent decades working, at every level of government and society, to make it harder to build recklessly. They got used to crafting coalitions and legislation that gave everyone a bit of what they wanted, even if it meant the final product was astonishingly expensive, or slow to construct, or perhaps never found its way to completion at all. To unmake this machine will be painful. It will require questioning treasured nostrums and splitting old alliances.

It will also require opposing visions of scarcity that are gaining adherents on the left. The values of the degrowther movement have gained momentum among Western intellectuals. The environmental devastation that has accompanied modernity seems like an equation with an obvious solution: If this is what progress has wrought, then regress is necessary. If this is the cost of going forward, then we must go backward. In its strongest versions, this philosophy is too politically impractical to gain many adherents or wield much power. But its weaker manifestations are everywhere and have been since "Small Is Beautiful" became a rallying cry in the '70s.

Comparatively, abundance is a return to an older tradition of leftist thought. In *The Communist Manifesto*, Karl Marx and Friedrich Engels acknowledged that capitalism was superior to its predecessor, feudalism, at producing goods and wealth. "The bourgeoisie, during its rule of scarce one hundred years, has created more massive and more colossal productive forces than have all preceding generations together," they wrote.[23] They did not want to end this revolution in production. They wanted to accelerate it.

Just as feudalism blocked production that only capitalism could unleash, so did capitalism constrain an abundance that a new paradigm might unleash. Core to this analysis of the economy was an idea that has come to be called the "fettering of production."[24] Marx observed that many companies' obsession with profit kept the entire economy from exploring ideas that threatened incumbent margins or failed to produce immediate returns. Among capitalism's many sins, Marx wrote, was that it prevented the most wondrous and useful technology from being invented and deployed in the first place. An economy run amok with useless fettering serves the rich few at the expense of the poorer many.

Marx's aim was not to turn the production machine off, but to direct its ends toward a shared abundance: to unburden the forces of production and make possible that which had been impossible to imagine. There is much he got wrong, but one need not be a communist to see the wisdom in this analysis.

A Lens, Not a List

We considered calling this book "The Abundance Agenda." We could have easily filled these pages with a long list of policy ideas to ease the blockages we fear.

On housing, for example, cities should reform their zoning laws to make it easier to build homes and apartments of all sizes, legalize the construction of accessory dwelling units, reduce parking requirements, and pass new laws to create maximum permitting wait times. Stopping individuals or developers from building places for people to live on land they own should require unusual cause. Building homes, at a time when housing is scarce, should not.

The political economy of those ideas is fraught. It requires passing law after law in city after city. Today's housing rules are exquisitely local, which would be appropriate if housing policy was bound by city limits. But the consequences of housing policy reverberate across states, and even across the nation. Gate the great cities of California and families flee to Texas and Arizona. When you allow housing to become scarce where the wages are highest, you shut down a powerful engine that long kept social mobility in America high. So what level of government—and of society—is appropriate for housing policy? Should it be run by states? By the federal government?

This is where the shortcomings of a list of policy proposals become clear. It is easy to unfurl a policy wish list. But what is ultimately at stake here are our values. How do we weigh the role that the current inhabitants of a community should have in who enters that community next? How do we balance the interests of a town against the interests of a country?

Changing the processes that make building and inventing so hard now requires confrontations with whether the systems liberals have built really reflect the ends they've sought. Much that was designed to foster grassroots participation has been captured by incumbents and special interests. It can be difficult, in a raucous town meeting, to look around and remember who is not there: the mother working two jobs, the young family who couldn't afford the apartment they so badly wanted to move into. "This is what democracy looks like" is a common chant at protests, but what democracy should look like is a devilishly hard question to answer.

What we are proposing is less a set of policy solutions than a new set of questions around which our politics should revolve. What is scarce that should be abundant? What is difficult to build that should be easy? What inventions do we need that we do not yet have?

In the 1960s and '70s, environmentalism wasn't just a legislative sea change, a legal revolution, or a cultural phenomenon. It was all of them at once. Americans developed new ideas about their relationship to land and their stewardship of nature. New ideas gave way to new laws, new arguments, and new customs. People working at all levels of society, inside and outside government, brought those ideas into their labors.

The environmentalist movement bequeathed both correction and overcorrection, but it transformed the country for decades—it is transforming the country even now—because it touched something weightier than the legislator's pen. More than a law, it was a lens. A US senator could look through it and see the bills that needed to be written. A judge could look through it and see new decisions that needed to be made. A family could look through it and see that they were wasting too much and recycling too little. A heady college student could look through it and see a cause.

A lens is what we have sought to offer here. What keeps an apartment building from being built in San Jose is not what keeps a new transmission line from being built in Oklahoma. What keeps the IRS from successfully updating its software is not what has kept a high-speed rail system from being completed in California. What keeps an ambitious young scientist from proposing his best ideas is not what keeps us from discovering and scaling new ways to make cement. There are rhymes that we have found across these challenges, echoes across these problems, but they are not unified enough to yield a single set of answers.

Abundance Versus Scarcity

In 1964, at the turning point between two orders, New York City hosted a World's Fair to show off the stuff of our national genius. The scene was Flushing, a three-mile stretch of natural marshlands in Queens. In the 1920s, the area had been so full of trash and vermin that F. Scott Fitzgerald described it in *The Great Gatsby* as "the valley of ashes."[25] But for the World's Fair, this grim meadow was transformed into a glistening global sensation, with 140 pavilions across almost 700 acres, celebrating US history and accomplishment.

More than 50 million people passed through the event gates,

strolling by inventions that would soon fill their department stores and homes. Bell Labs had an exhibition that introduced millions of Americans to their first "Picturephone."[26] Westinghouse showed off a new electric toothbrush and credit card, before placing both in a time capsule to be opened in several thousand years.[27] At the fair's most popular event, the General Motors "Futurama II" exhibition, tens of millions of people glided through elaborate dioramas that imagined life at the end of the twentieth century. "It is now tomorrow . . . on the moon," a voiceover began, as the audience rolled up to a model of astronaut farmers building their first lunar bridgehead.[28] At another station in the exhibition, the diorama of a cityscape imagined a new system of double-decker highways connecting downtowns, whose skyscrapers had taken on the shape of towering, elongated eggs.

At the fair's opening ceremony, President Johnson delivered a dramatic keynote address, with this remarkable passage:

> The abundance and the might represented here is far beyond the vision of those early settlers. America has been transformed from an outpost of the edge of wilderness to one of the great nations of the world. The number of people who will visit your fair will be seventy times the entire population of North America when New York was born.
>
> The last time New York had a World's fair, we also tried to predict the future. A daring exhibit proclaimed that in the 1960's it would really be possible to cross the country in less than 24 hours, flying as high as 10,000 feet; that an astounding 38 million cars would cross our highways. There was no mention of outer space, or atomic power, or wonder drugs that could destroy disease.

These were bold prophecies back there in 1939. But, again, the reality has far outstripped the vision.

Then Johnson issued a warning. "Our pride in accomplishment must not ignore the fact that our progress has had two faces," he said. "Its final direction—abundance or annihilation—development or desolation . . . is in your hands."[29]

Six decades later, our technological frontier gleams with greater possibilities than the 1964 World's Fair could imagine. Medicines that erase complex diseases. Factories that slurp pollution from the sky. Intelligent machines that assist in the great project of living longer, healthier, and happier lives. But just as Johnson saw his own age darkened by the possibility of catastrophic politics, so too do we face an existential binary for our own time: abundance or scarcity.

Abundance reorients politics around a fresh provocation: *Can we solve our problems with supply?* Many valuable questions bloom from this deceptively simple prompt. If there are not enough homes, can we make more? If not, why not? If there is not enough clean energy, can we make more? If not, why not? If the government is repeatedly failing to complete major projects on time and on budget, then what is going wrong and how do we fix it? If the rate of scientific progress is slowing, how can we help scientists do their best work? If we need new technologies to solve our important problems, how do we pull these inventions from the future and distribute them in the present?

To pursue abundance is to pursue institutional renewal. One of the most dangerous political pathologies is the tendency to defend whatever your enemies attack. Decades of attacks on the state have turned liberals into reflexive champions of government. But if you

219

believe in government, you must make it work. To make it work, you must be clear-eyed about when it fails and why it fails.

What has surprised us most in this project have been the blind spots—our own, as much as anyone else's. Stories we once saw as exceptions to the rule of well-functioning government—a public works project that went over budget and remained unfinished; an absurd price tag on a public toilet; the explosion of homelessness in blue cities; the profusion of lawsuits against even well-meaning in-frastructure projects; the loss of manufacturing leadership in core technologies; the absence of an agenda that harnesses invention to social purpose—now seem frighteningly close to the norm. The purpose of a system is what it does. If an outcome recurs again and again, across time and place, it is the result of choices that became rules. Which means it is the result of ideas and movements.

The ideas and movements of the last few decades are not our villains. They were the responses to the crises of another time. They succeeded, often brilliantly. That we have not matched our institutions to our moment is our failure, not theirs. If we succeed, then future generations will have to grapple with our excesses to meet their moment. Let us hope.

But before the future, the present. "Establishing a political order demands far more than winning an election or two," Gerstle writes.

It requires deep-pocketed donors (and political action com-mittees) to invest in promising candidates over the long term; the establishment of think tanks and policy networks to turn political ideas into actionable programs; a rising political party able to consistently win over multiple electoral constituencies; a capacity to shape political opinion both at the highest levels (the Supreme Court) and across popular print and broadcast media; and a moral perspective able to inspire voters with visions of the good life. Political orders, in other words, are complex projects that require advances across a broad front.[30]

Political movements succeed when they build a vision of the future that is imbued with the virtues of the past. In the 1930s, Franklin D. Roosevelt pitched his expansive view of government as a sentinel for American freedoms—of speech, of worship, from want, from fear. Five decades later, Reagan hailed the same virtues, this time by casting government as freedom's nemesis rather than its protector.

Just as freedom has historically loomed large in the American consciousness, so has abundance. The theme of plenty filled the journals and letters of the first European writers who took stock of the continent. "Take foure of the best kingdomes in Christendome and put them all together, they may no way compare with this countrie either for commodities or goodnesse of soil," Sir Thomas Dale, the deputy governor of Virginia, said of his colony in 1611. In the following centuries, visitors and residents gawked at America's wealth of land, food, and opportunities. In 1817, William Cobbett, a British writer, wrote of the American diet that "such an abundance is spread before you . . . that you instantly lose all restraint."[31]

It was this abundance, Potter argues in *People of Plenty*, that formed the American character. It was in the midst of not just actual plenitude, but the belief in plenitude, that our peculiar set of ideals and aspirations could form. The abundance of his day—to say nothing of the abundance of the first decades of the American experiment—would be absolute deprivation by our standards. That is a measure of our success, but it is also a reminder that both abundance and scarcity are stories we tell ourselves. Right now, we see an America that is turning toward a story of scarcity. That turn is changing not just our politics, but our national character.

We seek a politics of abundance that delivers real marvels in the real world. We want more homes and more energy, more cures and more construction. This is a story that must be built out of bricks and steel and solar panels and transmission lines, not just words. But it is a story, and we believe it is truer to the American character and experience, truer to both what we have done and what we will do, than the narrow narrative of scarcity that has taken hold.

Abundance contains within it a bigness that befits the American project. It is the promise of not just more, but more of what matters. It is a commitment to the endless work of institutional renewal. It is a recognition that technology is at the heart of progress, and always has been. It is a determination to align our collective genius with the needs of both the planet and each other. Abundance is liberalism, yes. But more than that, it is a liberalism that builds.

Acknowledgments

THE BOOK *ABUNDANCE* IS ONLY POSSIBLE BECAUSE OF THE abundance of support, partnership, and provocation in our professional and personal lives.

Let's begin with the professional. Gail Ross is a dream agent and the best kind of person to have in your corner. She was boundlessly supportive of the book—but also of us, the harried human beings who were often struggling to write it.

We couldn't have had a better editorial partner than Ben Loehnen, whose intelligent edits and pitch-perfect balance of cheer and urgency saw the project through completion. His team at Avid Reader Press is top-notch. Many thanks to Carolyn Kelly for guiding the book through production; to Alison Forner, for spearheading the design of our beautiful jacket; and to Meredith Vilarello and Alexandra Primiani, for coordinating the marketing and book tour with such grace. The fact-checking process was overseen with painstaking expertise by Janet Byrne. Alayna Kennedy provided essential research for the project while we were putting together the outlines and core arguments for the chapters.

Acknowledgments

Behind this book lurk more conversations with more people than we can thank here. But we've particularly benefited from a community of thinkers and writers who've been chiseling away at these ideas, including Alex Tabarrok, Brink Lindsey, Henry Farrell, Heidi Williams, Jennifer Pahlka, Jesse Jenkins, Jerusalem Demsas, Marc Dunkelson, Matthew Yglesias, Noah Smith, Patrick Collison, Rogé Karma, Saul Griffith, Steven Teles, Tyler Cowen, and the folks at the Institute for Progress. Special thanks go to Heidi, Jesse, and Jerusalem, for reading early chapters and offering generous comments; and to Steve, the Center for Economy and Society at Johns Hopkin's SNF Agora Institute, and the Center for Advanced Study in the Behavioral Sciences at Stanford for an early workshop that helped sharpen our ideas.

We are lucky to be employed by two institutions, the *New York Times* and the *Atlantic*, whose support for and commitment to high-quality journalism are unparalleled. Derek would like to thank Bob Cohn for hiring him when he didn't really know what he was doing, Jeffrey Goldberg for kindly maintaining his employment, Juliet Lapidos for her relentlessly wise and efficient edits, and Don Peck for his masterly ability to shape argument in longform. He would also like to thank the wonderful team at the Ringer for supporting his podcast, the conversations for which deepened much of the reporting for this book (and which is also just a lot of fun to do).

Ezra thanks A. G. Sulzberger, Sam Dolnick, and Kathleen Kingsbury for their remarkable support and counsel. Aaron Retica is a truly astonishing editor, mentor, and friend, and this book benefited enormously from his insight, wisdom, and esoteric historical references. And it is hard to know how to properly thank the entire *Ezra Klein Show* team—Aman Sahota, Annie Galvin, Claire Gordon,

Jack McCordick, Elias Isquith, Jeff Geld, Kristin Lin, Michelle Harris, and Rollin Hu—for their partnership and incisiveness.

As lucky as we are in employment, we are even more so in friends and family.

For Derek: Thanks first and forever to my parents, for their undying love. To my dad, in whose lap I first learned to care about politics and journalism, and to my mom, in whose arms I learned everything else. You are both so missed and so eternally present. To Momi, danke for your love and support. To Kira, my extraordinary sister, thank you for being the rock of the family and an inspiration to me. Thanks to my friends—the Potomac crew, the Northwestern crew, and the Cult—and to Drew, for a lifetime of friendship and true brotherhood.

Thanks to the ones I call home. Laura, thank god I found you. Your wisdom, your counsel, your softness and light: you are the most extraordinary partner and the one I want to come running to when the writing is done. And then there is Isla. When I started writing this book, I was just a husband. When I finished writing this book, I was a dad. Thanks to my little one, the gift of a lifetime.

For Ezra: This is the hardest part of the book to write. All words fall short. Thank you to my friends: to the kuddelmuddel; to Charlie and Bess and Theo and Harry, for all the Blobbing; to PJ, for long hangs and much-needed lightness; to Tristan, for decades of friendship and insights and arguments; to Teresa, for the meandering voice notes, for asking the right questions, and for so much care and kindness; to Grant, for seeing me so clearly, for continually bringing me back to the reasons for this work, and for always being there.

Thank you to my family: to my mother, for reading me those 400 books and keeping me at the table while she canvassed, and for always, always seeing the best in me; to my father, who was my first and best example of taking ideas and news seriously, and for modeling an insistence that sense could be made of this world; to my brother, whose social conscience sparked my own, and whose activism made me believe that politics was a realm you could simply choose to be part of; to my sister, who makes me laugh like no one else does and who understands what no one else does; to Linda and Sara, for their thoughtfulness and compassion; and to John and Celine Lowrey, for being such wonderful grandparents.

And then there's the family I have built. To Moses and Kieran, who light my world. I am so glad to have my weekends with them back. And to Annie. To Annie. To Annie. I have benefited so much from her brilliance—"the affordability crisis" is her coinage and concept, and so much else that lodges in my mind is rooted in the unending conversation that is our marriage. And I have benefited beyond measure from her support: When I didn't see a path to finishing this book, she cleared one for me. As with this book, so with my life. Every day, I wake up wanting to know what she'll say next. It is my great gift to be in partnership with her. She is my abundance.

Notes

Introduction: Beyond Scarcity

1. Laffer Curve Napkin, National Museum of American History, Smithsonian Institution, September 14, 1974, https://www.si.edu/object/laffer-curve-napkin%3Anmah_1439217; "Can Countries Lower Taxes and Raise Revenues?," *Economist*, June 18, 2019, https://www.economist.com/graphic-detail/2019/06/18/can-countries-lower-taxes-and-raise-revenues.

2. President Jimmy Carter, State of the Union Address Delivered Before a Joint Session of the Congress, January 19, 1978, https://www.presidency.ucsb.edu/documents/the-state-the-union-address-delivered-before-joint-session-the-congress-1.

3. President William Jefferson Clinton, State of the Union Address, US Capitol, January 23, 1996, https://clintonwhitehouse4.archives.gov/WH/New/other/sotu.html.

4. Steven Teles, Samuel Hammond, and Daniel Takash, "Cost Disease Socialism: How Subsidizing Costs While Restricting Supply Drives America's Fiscal Imbalance," Niskanen Center, September 9, 2021, https://www.niskanencenter.org/cost-disease-socialism-how-subsidizing-costs-while-restricting-supply-drives-americas-fiscal-imbalance/.

5. Derek Fidler and Hicham Sabir, "The Cost of Housing Is Tearing Our Society Apart," World Economic Forum, January 9, 2019, https://www.weforum.org/agenda/2019/01/why-housing-appreciation-is-killing-housing/; Alexander Hermann, "Housing Perspectives," Joint Center for Housing Studies of Harvard University, January 22, 2024, https://

www.jchs.harvard.edu/blog/home-price-income-ratio-reaches-record
-high-0.

6. KFF, "2023 Employer Health Benefits Survey," October 18, 2023, https://
www.kff.org/report-section/ehbs-2023-section-1-cost-of-health-insur
ance/#figure11.

7. Digest of Education Statistics, table 330.10: Average Undergraduate
Tuition and Fees and Room and Board Rates Charged for Full-Time
Students in Degree-Granting Postsecondary Institutions, by Level
and Control of Institution: Selected Years, 1963–64 Through 2018–19,
National Center for Education Statistics, https://nces.ed.gov/programs
/digest/d19/tables/dt19_330.10.asp; Melanie Hanson, "Average Cost of
College by Year," EducationData.org, September 9, 2024, https://educa
tiondata.org/average-cost-of-college-by-year; Melanie Hanson, "Average Cost of College by State," EducationData.org, September 16, 2024,
https://educationdata.org/average-cost-of-college-by-state; College
Board, "Trends in College Pricing: Highlights," 2023–24 school year,
date of report: 2024, https://research.collegeboard.org/trends/college
-pricing/highlights.

8. Eric Cutler, "True Cost of Child Care by State," January 23, 2024, https://
tootris.com/edu/blog/parents/cost-of-child-care-in-all-50-states
-for-2022/.

9. Annie Lowrey, "The Great Affordability Crisis Breaking America: In
One of the Best Decades the American Economy Has Ever Recorded,
Families Were Bled Dry," *Atlantic*, February 7, 2020, https://www.the
atlantic.com/ideas/archive/2020/02/great-affordability-crisis-break
ing-america/606046/.

10. "Remarks by President Biden on the December 2021 Jobs Report,"
January 7, 2022, https://www.whitehouse.gov/briefing-room/speeches
-remarks/2022/01/07/remarks-by-president-biden-on-the-december
-2021-jobs-report/.

11. Aaron Bastani, *Fully Automated Luxury Communism* (London: Verso,
2019), 150–52.

12. Bastani, *Fully Automated Luxury Communism*, 10.

13. Andriy Blokhin, "The 5 Countries That Produce the Most Carbon Dioxide (CO_2)," Investopedia, July 26, 2024, https://www.investopedia.com
/articles/investing/092915/5-countries-produce-most-carbon-dioxide
-co2.asp; Wolfgang Fengler, Indermit Gill, and Homi Kharas, "Making
Emissions Count in Country Classifications," Brookings Institution,
September 7, 2023, https://www.brookings.edu/articles/making-emis

sions-count-in-country-classifications/; UN Environment Programme, "Emissions Gap Report 2023," https://www.unep.org/interactives /emissions-gap-report/2023/#section_0; "Global Emissions," Center for Climate and Energy Solutions, https://www.c2es.org/content/interna tional-emissions/; Kamwoo Lee, Jia Li, and Divyanshi Wadhwa, "From Climate Scient to Global Action: Who Contributes Most to Global Green-house Gas Emissions?," October 11, 2023, World Bank Blogs, https:// blogs.worldbank.org/en/opendata/climate-science-global-action-who -contributes-most-global-greenhouse-gas-emissions.

14. "Renewables Competitiveness Accelerates, Despite Cost Inflation," In-ternational Renewable Energy Agency, press release, August 29, 2023, https://www.irena.org/News/pressreleases/2023/Aug/Renewables -Competitiveness-Accelerates-Despite-Cost-Inflation.

15. State of California Air Resources Board, Advanced Clean Cars II Regu-lations, Resolution 22-12, August 25, 2022, https://ww2.arb.ca.gov/sites /default/files/barcu/board/books/2022/082522/prores22-12.pdf.

16. US Energy Information Administration, "Most U.S. Nuclear Power Plants Were Built Between 1970 and 1990," April 27, 2017, https://www .eia.gov/todayinenergy/detail.php?id=30972; US Energy Information Administration, "How Old Are U.S. Nuclear Power Plants, and When Was the Newest One Built?," May 8, 2024, https://www.eia.gov/tools /faqs/faq.php?id=228&t=21; US Energy Information Administration, "U.S. Commercial Nuclear Capacity Comes from Reactors Built Primar-ily Between 1970 and 1990," June 30, 2011, https://www.eia.gov/today inenergy/detail.php?id=2030; World Nuclear Association, "Nuclear Power in the USA," August 27, 2024, https://world-nuclear.org/informa-tion-library/country-profiles/countries-t-z/usa-nuclear-power; Nuclear Energy Institute, "Decommissioning Status for Shutdown U.S. Nuclear Plants," US Nuclear Regulatory Commission, US Department of Energy, and the International Atomic Energy Agency, updated August 2022, https://www.nei.org/resources/statistics/decommissioning-status-for -shutdown-us-plants; Elesia Fasching, Tyler Hodge, and Slade John-son, "First New U.S. Nuclear Reactor Since 2016 Is Now in Operation," US Energy Information Administration, August 1, 2023, https://www.eia .gov/todayinenergy/detail.php?id=57280; Georgia Power, "Vogtle Unit 4 Enters Commercial Operation," press release, April 29, 2024, https:// www.georgiapower.com/company/news-hub/press-releases/vogtle -unit-4-enters-commercial-operation.html; Bechtel, "America's Next Nuclear Power Plant Begins Construction," press release, June 10, 2024,

https://www.bechtel.com/newsroom/press-releases/americas-next-nu
clear-power-plant-begins-construction/.

17. Neil Postman, *Amusing Ourselves to Death: Public Discourse in the Age of Show Business* (New York: Penguin Books, 2006), 157.

18. Tyler Cowen, "What Libertarianism Has Become and Will Become—State Capacity Libertarianism," *Marginal Revolution*, January 1, 2020, https://marginalrevolution.com/marginalrevolution/2020/01/what-lib ertarianism-has-become-and-will-become-state-capacity-libertarian ism.html.

19. "Party Affiliation of the Mayors of the 100 Largest Cities," Ballotpedia, https://ballotpedia.org/Party_affiliation_of_the_mayors_of_the_100 _largest_cities.

20. "California Elected Officials," 270toWin, https://www.270towin.com /elected-officials/california.

21. "Cost of Living Index by State 2024," World Population Review, https:// worldpopulationreview.com/state-rankings/cost-of-living-index-by -state.

22. Bruce E. Cain and Preeti Hehmeyer, "California's Population Drain," Stanford University Institute for Economic Policy Research, October 2023, https://siepr.stanford.edu/publications/policy-brief/californias -population-drain; Alix Martichoux, "Leaving California: These Were the Top Destinations for Californians Who Moved in 2022," KTLA 5, October 20, 2023, https://ktla.com/news/local-news/are-californians -still-taking-over-texas-new-census-data-reveals-where-people-are -moving-most/.

23. William G. Howell and Terry M. Moe, *Presidents, Populism, and the Crisis of Democracy* (Chicago: University of Chicago Press, 2020), Kin dle, 6.

24. Christine Leonard, "Map Shows Which California Demographic Shifted Most Toward Trump," *San Francisco Chronicle*, November 14, 2024, https://www.sfchronicle.com/election/article/trump-vote-california -county-19897935.php.

25. Kevin Schaul and Kati Perry, "How Counties Are Shifting in the 2024 Presidential Election," *Washington Post*, November 6, 2024, updated November 22, 2024, https://www.washingtonpost.com/elections/inter active/2024/11/05/compare-2020-2024-presidential-results/.

26. US Census Bureau, "State-to-State Migration Flows," https://www.cen sus.gov/data/tables/time-series/demo/geographic-mobility/state-to -state-migration.html.

27. Jerusalem Demsas, "The Democrats Are Committing Partycide," *Atlantic*, November 14, 2024, https://www.theatlantic.com/politics/archive/2024/11/democrat-states-population-stagnation/680641/.

28. Derek Thompson, "The Urban Family Exodus Is a Warning for Progressives," *Atlantic*, August 5, 2024, https://www.theatlantic.com/ideas/archive/2024/08/the-urban-family-exodus-is-a-warning-for-progressives/679350/.

29. David M. Potter, *People of Plenty: Economic Abundance and the American Character* (Chicago: University of Chicago Press, 1954), 164.

30. Potter, *People of Plenty*, 173.

31. From the title of her book: Lizabeth Cohen, *A Consumers' Republic: The Politics of Mass Consumption in Postwar America* (New York: Alfred A. Knopf, 2003).

1. Grow

1. Horace Greeley, *The Autobiography of Horace Greeley* (New York: E. B. Treat, 1872), 38, 50.

2. Potter, *People of Plenty*, 94.

3. Alan Brinkley, *The End of Reform: New Deal Liberalism in Recession and War* (New York: Vintage Books, 1996), 132.

4. Brinkley, *The End of Reform*, 133.

5. Housing and Home Finance Agency, Washington, DC, "The Housing Situation—1950: An Analysis of Preliminary Results of the 1950 Housing Census," February 1951, 3, https://www.huduser.gov/portal/sites/default/files/pdf/Housing-Situation-1951.pdf.

6. OECD, "Housing Stock and Construction," figure HM1.1.1, 2, https://www.oecd.org/content/dam/oecd/en/data/datasets/affordable-housing-database/hm1-1-housing-stock-and-construction.pdf.

7. Chamber of Commerce, "Cities with the Most House Poor Homeowners," https://www.chamberofcommerce.org/cities-with-the-most-house-poor-homeowners/.

8. Annie Lowrey, "The Wrong-Apartment Problem: Why a Good Economy Feels So Bad," *Atlantic*, July 22, 2023, https://www.theatlantic.com/ideas/archive/2023/07/us-economy-labor-market-inflation-housing/674790/.

9. Glaeser, *Triumph of the City: How Our Greatest Invention Makes Us Richer, Smarter, Greener, Healthier, and Happier* (New York: Penguin Press, 2011), Kindle, 131.

10. Diane Cardwell, "Mayor Says New York Is Worth the Cost," *New York*

Times, January 8, 2003, https://www.nytimes.com/2003/01/08/nyregion /mayor-says-new-york-is-worth-the-cost.html.

11. Glaeser, *Triumph of the City*, Kindle, 6.

12. David Stringer, "Inside Foxconn's Plan to Build EVs," Bloomberg, November 2, 2023, https://www.bloomberg.com/news/newsletters /2023-11-02/what-does-foxconn-make-iphones-now-but-evs-are-on -the-way-big-take?sref=VpNSse6l.

13. US Securities and Exchange Commission, Form 10-Q, Apple Inc, for the quarterly period ended April 1, 2023, https://d18rn0p25nwr6d.cloudfront .net/CIK-0000320193/52f2576b-2775-4676-b40c-a63e2b5d8e60.pdf; Matthew Johnston, "How Apple Makes Money," Investopedia, June 27, 2024, https://www.investopedia.com/how-apple-makes-money-4798689.

14. "Alphabet Announces Fourth Quarter and Fiscal Year 2023 Results," January 30, 2024, https://abc.xyz/assets/95/eb/9cef90184e09bac55379 6896c633/2023q4-alphabet-earnings-release.pdf.

15. US Securities and Exchange Commission, Form 10-K, Tesla, Inc., for the fiscal year ended December 31, 2023, https://ir.tesla.com/_flysystem/s3 /sec/000162828024002390/tsla-20231231-gen.pdf.

16. Glaeser, *Triumph of the City*, Kindle, 6.

17. Katie Deighton, "Goldman Sachs Embeds Software Developers Deeper into the Business," *Wall Street Journal*, October 19, 2022, https://www .wsj.com/articles/goldman-sachs-embeds-software-developers-deeper -into-the-business-11666218724.

18. Enrico Moretti, *The New Geography of Jobs* (New York: Mariner Books /Houghton Mifflin Harcourt, 2013), Kindle, loc. 1641.

19. Moretti, *The New Geography of Jobs*, Kindle, loc. 1673.

20. Jackson Walker, "Zoom CEO Advises Employees to Return to Office or Risk Losing 'Trust,' Report Says," CBS Austin, August 24, 2023, https:// cbsaustin.com/news/nation-world/zoom-ceo-advises-employees-to -return-to-office-or-risk-losing-trust-report-says-remote-work-tele work-conferencing-virtual-hybrid-economy-employee-face-to-face.

21. Glaeser, *Triumph of the City*, Kindle, 37.

22. Moretti, *The New Geography of Jobs*, Kindle, loc. 173.

23. Raj Chetty et al., "The Fading American Dream: Trends in Absolute Income Mobility Since 1940," NBER Working Paper 22910, December 2016, http://www.nber.org/papers/w22910 and DOI 10.3386/w22910.

24. Derek Thompson, "The Secret to Reclaiming the American Dream," *Atlantic*, August 26, 2022, https://www.theatlantic.com/newsletters/ar chive/2022/08/american-dream-raj-chetty-friendship/671235/.

25. Raj Chetty, Nathaniel Hendren, Patrick Kline, and Emmanuel Saez, "Where Is the Land of Opportunity? The Geography of Intergenerational Mobility in the United States," June 2014, https://scholar.harvard.edu/files/hendren/files/mobility_geo.pdf.

26. Alexander M. Bell, Raj Chetty, Xavier Jaravel, Neviana Petkova, and John Van Reenen, "Do Tax Cuts Produce More Einsteins? The Impacts of Financial Incentives vs. Exposure to Innovation on the Supply of Inventors," NBER Working Paper 25493, January 2019, http://www.nber.org/papers/w25493.

27. Peter Ganong and Daniel W. Shoag, "Why Has Regional Income Convergence in the U.S. Declined?," NBER Working Paper 23609, July 2017, 2, DOI 10.3386/w23609.

28. Ganong and Shoag, "Why Has Regional Income Convergence in the U.S. Declined?," 4–5.

29. Ganong and Shoag, "Why Has Regional Income Convergence in the U.S. Declined?," 3.

30. See Lloyd A. Free and Hadley Cantril, *The Political Beliefs of Americans: A Study of Public Opinion* (New Brunswick, NJ: Rutgers University Press, 1967).

31. Wendell Cox, "2022 Residential Building Permits by Housing Market," March 14, 2023, *NewGeography*, https://www.newgeography.com/content/007766-2022-residential-building-permits-housing-market.

32. William A. Fischel, *Zoning Rules!: The Economics of Land Use Regulation* (Cambridge, MA: Lincoln Institute of Land Policy, 2015), Kindle, 190.

33. Fischel, *Zoning Rules!*, Kindle, 195.

34. Fischel, *Zoning Rules!*, Kindle, 214.

35. Meghan McCarty Carino, "Life in This Iconic Mid-Century Suburb Shows How California Dreams Are Shrinking," *LAist*, July 2, 2018, https://laist.com/news/kpcc-archive/life-in-this-iconic-mid-century-suburb-shows-how-c.

36. "City of Tomorrow," The Lakewood Story, City of Lakewood, California, https://www.lakewoodcity.org/About/Our-History/The-Lakewood-Story/02-City-of-Tomorrow.

37. "Suburban Pioneers," The Lakewood Story, City of Lakewood, California, https://www.lakewoodcity.org/About/Our-History/The-Lakewood-Story/03-Suburban-Pioneers.

38. US Census Bureau, "New Privately-Owned Housing Units Authorized by Building Permits in Permit-Issuing Places," Annual History by State, https://www.census.gov/construction/bps/pdf/annualhistorybystate.pdf.

39. "California's Housing Future: Challenges and Opportunities, Final Statewide Housing Assessment 2025," p. 6, fig. 1.2, https://www.hcd.ca.gov/policy-research/plans-reports/docs/SHA_Final_Combined.pdf.

40. Jacob Anbinder, "Cities of Amber: Antigrowth Politics and the Making of Modern Liberalism, 1950–2008," PhD diss., Harvard University Graduate School of Arts and Sciences, 18–19. Regarding "more than fifteen thousand buildings": Anbinder's source, Ingrid Gould, Ellen Brian, J. McCabe, Eric Edward Stern, "Fifty Years of Historic Preservation in New York City," distinguishes between "lots" and "buildings." See Gould et al., pp. 2, 14 (incl. fig. 2.3) and p. 4, https://furmancenter.org/files/NYU FurmanCenter_50YearsHistoricPresNYC_7MAR2016.pdf.

41. Mac Taylor, Chas Alamo, and Brian Uhler, "California's High Housing Costs: Causes and Consequences," Legislative Analyst's Office, March 17, 2015, https://lao.ca.gov/reports/2015/finance/housing-costs/housing-costs.pdf.

42. "New Private Housing Units Authorized by Building Permits for California," Federal Reserve Bank of St. Louis, updated October 24, 2024, https://fred.stlouisfed.org/series/CABPPRIVSA. Also see Kenneth Schrupp, "Why Dallas Permits More Housing Than All of California," *Pacific Research* (blog), July 23, 2024, https://www.pacificresearch.org/why-dallas-permits-more-housing-than-all-of-california/.

43. Margot Kushel and Tiana Moore, "Toward a New Understanding: The California Statewide Study of People Experiencing Homelessness," University of California–San Francisco, Benioff Homelessness and Housing Initiative, June 2023, https://homelessness.ucsf.edu/our-impact/studies/california-statewide-study-people-experiencing-homelessness.

44. Heather Mac Donald, "San Francisco, Hostage to the Homeless," *City Journal*, Autumn 2019, https://www.city-journal.org/article/san-francisco-hostage-to-the-homeless.

45. Gregg Colburn and Clayton Page Aldern, *Homelessness Is a Housing Problem: How Structural Factors Explain U.S. Patterns* (Oakland: University of California Press, 2022), Kindle, loc. 1086.

46. Colburn and Aldern, *Homelessness Is a Housing Problem*, Kindle, loc. 1054–1071 and loc. 1166 and fig.8.

47. Colburn and Aldern, *Homelessness Is a Housing Problem*, Kindle, loc. 1238.

48. Matthew Yglesias, *The Rent Is Too Damn High* (New York: Simon & Schuster, 2012).

49. Matthew Yglesias, "Homelessness Is About Housing," *Slow Boring* (Substack), May 17, 2021, https://www.slowboring.com/p/homelessness -housing.

50. "Rooming Houses," American Planning Association, Report No. 105, December 1957, https://www.planning.org/pas/reports/report105.htm, citing the *St. Louis Post-Dispatch*, October 18, 1957, p. 20, https://www .newspapers.com/search/results/?keyword=If+rooming+houses+are +permitted+to+spread+to+the+city%27s+&publication-ids=4064.

51. Yglesias, "Homelessness Is About Housing," citing "Rooming Houses," American Planning Association, Report No. 105.

52. Yglesias, "Homelessness Is About Housing."

53. "How Long Does It Take to Save for a House?," WTF Happened in 1971?, https://wtfhappenedin1971.com/.

54. Jonathan Skinner, "Housing and Saving in the United States," NBER Working Paper 3874, October 1991, p. 1, https://www.nber.org/system /files/working_papers/w3874/w3874.pdf.

55. Fischel, *Zoning Rules!*, Kindle, 205.

56. Jerusalem Demsas, "The Homeownership Society Was a Mistake," *Atlantic*, December 20, 2022, https://www.theatlantic.com/newslet ters/archive/2022/12/homeownership-real-estate-investment-renting /672511/.

57. Anbinder, "Cities of Amber," 46.

58. Fischel, *Zoning Rules!*, Kindle, 225.

59. Lyndon B. Johnson, "Remarks at the University of Michigan," May 22, 1964, University of Virginia/Miller Center, https://millercenter.org/the -presidency/presidential-speeches/may-22-1964-remarks-university -michigan.

60. John Kenneth Galbraith, *The Affluent Society* (New York: New American Library, 1958), 200.

61. Anbinder, "Cities of Amber," 3.

62. Federal Highway Administration, "State Motor Vehicle Registrations, by Years, 1900–1995," https://www.fhwa.dot.gov/ohim/summary95 /mv200.pdf.

63. Jess McNally, "July 26, 1942: L.A. Gets Its First Big Smog," *Wired*, July 26, 2010, https://www.wired.com/2010/07/0726la-first-big-smog/.

64. Elizabeth T. Jacobs, Jefferey L. Burgess, and Mark B. Abbott, "The Donora Smog Revisited: 70 Years After the Event That Inspired the Clean Air Act," *American Journal of Public Health* 108, S2 (April 2018): S85–S88, https://www.ncbi.nlm.nih.gov/pmc/articles/PMC5922205/.

65. Devra Lee Davis, *When Smoke Ran Like Water: Tales of Environmental Deception and the Battle Against Pollution* (New York: Basic Books, 2002). Twenty people "died during the fog itself" (22); fifty more died later, "in the month after the smog lifted" (27).

66. Nell Porter-Brown, "Paddling the Merrimack in Lowell and Lawrence," *Harvard Magazine*, July–August 2017, https://www.harvardmagazine.com/2017/06/reflections-on-a-river.

67. Lorraine Boissoneault, "The Cuyahoga River Caught Fire at Least a Dozen Times, but No One Cared Until 1969," *Smithsonian Magazine*, June 19, 2019, https://www.smithsonianmag.com/history/cuyahoga-river-caught-fire-least-dozen-times-no-one-cared-until-1969-180972444/; "The 1969 Cuyahoga River Fire," National Park Service, https://www.nps.gov/articles/story-of-the-fire.htm; "Cuyahoga River Fire," *Encyclopedia of Cleveland History*, Case Western Reserve University, https://case.edu/ech/articles/c/cuyahoga-river-fire.

68. "Forgotten History: Dooker's Hollow," *The Historical Dilettante*, February 19, 2021, https://historicaldilettante.blogspot.com/2021/02/forgotten-history-dookers-hollow.html.

69. Ronald Reagan, "Radio Address to the Nation on Environmental Issues," July 14, 1984, Ronald Reagan Presidential Library & Museum, https://www.reaganlibrary.gov/archives/speech/radio-address-nation-environmental-issues.

70. *Friends of Mammoth v. Board of Supervisors*, 8 Cal.3d 247, September 21, 1972, Sac. No. 7924, Supreme Court of California, https://scocal.stanford.edu/opinion/friends-mammoth-v-board-supervisors-32943; also available at https://caselaw.findlaw.com/court/ca-supreme-court/1826825.html.

71. John Zierold, "Environmental Lobbyist in California's Capital, 1965–1984," *California Legal History Journal* 13 (2018): 330–331. An oral history conducted in 1984 by Ann Lage, Sierra Club History Series, Regional Oral History Office, the Bancroft Library, University of California, Berkeley, 1988, https://www.cschs.org/wp-content/uploads/2018/02/Legal-Hist-v.-13-Environ-Oral-History-Zierold.pdf.

72. *Sacramento Bee*, October 22, 1972, p. 109, https://www.newspapers.com.

73. Anbinder, "Cities of Amber," 363.

74. Anbinder, "Cities of Amber," 365–66; Anne Jackson, "Agonizing Reappraisal for the Environmental Quality Act," *California Journal* 7 (1976): 59; Gladwin Hill, "Environmental Impact Statements, Practically a Revolution," *New York Times*, December 5, 1976.

75. Lewis Mumford, "The Highway and the City," *Architectural Record*, April 1958, https://google.it.ao/books?id=DmcWAAAAIAAJ&pg=PA371&dq=editions:HARVARDHWNP7V&lr=&output=html_text; and see Lewis Mumford, *The Highway and the City* (New York: Harcourt, Brace & World, 1963), 234.

76. As measured in percentage change. See US Census Bureau, "Booming Cities Decade-to-Decade, 1830–2010," October 4, 2012, https://www.census.gov/dataviz/visualizations/017/508.php.

77. Anbinder, "Cities of Amber," 183.

78. "American Scene: The Great Wild Californicated West," *Time*, August 21, 1972, https://time.com/archive/6815691/american-scene-the-great-wild-californicated-west/.

79. Gilliam, *For Better or for Worse: The Ecology of an Urban Area* (San Francisco: Chronicle Books, 1972), cited by Anbinder, "Cities of Amber," 207.

2. Build

1. Bill Gates, *How to Avoid a Climate Disaster: The Solutions We Have and the Breakthroughs We Need* (New York: Vintage Books, 2021), 19, 24.

2. Jason Hickel, *Less Is More: How Degrowth Will Save the World* (London: Penguin Books, 2022), Kindle, 32.

3. Hickel, *Less Is More*, Kindle, 28, 203.

4. Hickel, *Less Is More*, Kindle, 217.

5. "Global emissions need to fall by 45 to 50 per cent by 2030 in order to ensure temperatures don't rise above 1.5°C by 2100": UN Environment Programme, "How Do Countries Measure Greenhouse Gas Emissions?," citing the Emissions Gap Report, September 13, 2022, https://www.unep.org/news-and-stories/story/how-do-countries-measure-greenhouse-gas-emissions; Chris Mooney, Naema Ahmed, and John Muyskens, "We Looked at 1,200 Possibilities for the Planet's Future. These Are Our Best Hope," *Washington Post*, December 1, 2022, updated May 22, 2023, https://www.washingtonpost.com/climate-environment/interactive/2022/global-warming-1-5-celsius-scenarios/.

6. Hickel, *Less Is More*, Kindle, 146.

7. The BBC went back to 2021 and tracked and compared the two years. Efrem Gebreab, Thomas Naadi, Ranga Sirilal, and Becky Dale, "Fuel Protests Gripping More Than 90 Countries," BBC, October 17, 2022, https://www.bbc.com/news/world-63185186.

8. Kevin Liptak, Phil Mattingly, Natasha Bertrand, M. J. Lee, and Kylie Atwood, "Biden Turns to Countries He Once Sought to Avoid to Find Help

Shutting Off Russia's Oil Money," CNN, March 8, 2022, https://www.cnn
.com/2022/03/08/politics/joe-biden-saudi-arabia-venezuela-iran-rus
sia-oil/index.html.

9. Erik Voeten, "Is There a Green Policy Backlash?," *Good Authority*, September 21, 2023, https://goodauthority.org/news/is-there-a-green-pol
icy-backlash/.

10. Charles C. Mann, *The Wizard and the Prophet: Two Remarkable Scientists and Their Dueling Visions to Shape Tomorrow's World* (New York:
Alfred A. Knopf, 2018), 254–55.

11. "At any given time, around 130 people were enslaved at Monticello":
Thomas Jefferson Foundation, https://www.monticello.org/slavery
/people-enslaved-at-monticello/; Jefferson "enslaved over 600 human
beings throughout the course of his life," four hundred at Monticello,
two hundred "on . . . other properties." See also Annette Gordon-Reed,
The Hemingses of Monticello: An American Family (New York: W. W.
Norton, 2008), and Lisa Mann, "The Enslaved Household of President
Thomas Jefferson," White House Historical Association, November 20,
2019, https://www.whitehousehistory.org/slavery-in-the-thomas-jeffer
son-white-house.

12. Thomas Jefferson to Thomas Mann Randolph, November 28, 1796,
Monticello, https://www.monticello.org/exhibits-events/blog/i-shudder
-at-the-approach-jefferson-on-winter/; Thomas Jefferson to "Mr. Vol-
ney," January 8, 1797, National Archives, https://founders.archives.gov
/documents/Jefferson/01-29-02-0202.

13. Hans Rosling, "The Magic Washing Machine," TEDWomen 2010, December 2010, https://www.ted.com/talks/hans_rosling_the_magic_wash
ing_machine/transcript?subtitle=en.

14. Hannah Ritchie, "What the History of London's Air Pollution Can Tell
Us About the Future of Today's Growing Megacities," Our World in
Data," June 20, 2017, https://ourworldindata.org/london-air-pollution.

15. Hannah Ritchie, *Not the End of the World: How to Be the First Generation
to Build a Sustainable Planet* (New York: Little, Brown Spark, 2024), 48.

16. "Renewables Competitiveness Accelerates, Despite Cost Inflation," International Renewable Energy Agency, press release, August 29, 2023,
https://www.irena.org/News/pressreleases/2023/Aug/Renewables
-Competitiveness-Accelerates-Despite-Cost-Inflation; Felix Creutzig,
Jérôme Hilaire, Gregory Nemet, Finn Müller-Hansen, and Jan C. Minx,
"Technological Innovation Enables Low Cost Climate Change Mitiga-
tion," *Energy Research & Social Science* 105 (November 2023): 103276,

https://www.sciencedirect.com/science/article/abs/pii/S221462962300
3365?dgcid=author.

17. David Wallace-Wells, "What Will We Do with Our Free Power?," *New York Times*, August 28, 2024, https://www.nytimes.com/2024/08/28
/opinion/solar-power-free-energy.html

18. Rupert Way, Matthew C. Ives, Penny Mealy, and J. Doyne Farmer, "Empirically Grounded Technology Forecasts and the Energy Transition," *Joule* 6 (September 2022): 2057–082, https://www.cell.com/action/show
Pdf?pii=S2542-4351%2822%2900410-X.

19. US Energy Information Administration, "Levelized Costs of New Generation Resources in the *Annual Energy Outlook* 2022," p. 3, table 1a; p. 8, table 1b; p. 9.

20. Bill McKibben, "In a World on Fire, Stop Burning Things," *New Yorker*, March 18, 2022, https://www.newyorker.com/news/essay/in
-a-world-on-fire-stop-burning-things?_sp=71841c1f-c05f-43bb-8cad
-c1176340938e.1727888742505.

21. "Per Capita CO_2 Emissions, 2022," Our World in Data, https://ourworld
indata.org/grapher/co-emissions-per-capita; "CO2 Emissions per Capita," 2022, Worldometer, https://www.worldometers.info/co2-emissions
/co2-emissions-per-capita/#google_vignette.

22. "Per Capita CO_2 Emissions, 1979," Our World in Data, https://ourworld
indata.org/grapher/co-emissions-per-capita?time=1979.

23. Hannah Ritchie, "How Do CO_2 Emissions Compare When We Adjust for Trade?," Our World in Data, October 7, 2019, https://ourworldindata.org
/consumption-based-co2.

24. "I Thought Most of Us Were Going to Die from the Climate Crisis. I Was Wrong," *Guardian*, excerpt from Ritchie, *Not the End of the World*, January 2, 2024, https://www.theguardian.com/environment/2024/jan/02
/hannah-ritchie-not-the-end-of-the-world-extract-climate-crisis.

25. Mark Poynting and Esme Stallard, "UK to Finish with Coal Power After 142 Years," BBC, September 30, 2024, https://www.bbc.com/news/arti
cles/c5y35qz73n8o.

26. "Lawrence Livermore National Laboratory Achieves Fusion Ignition," Lawrence Livermore National Laboratory, December 14, 2022, https://
www.llnl.gov/article/49306/lawrence-livermore-national-laboratory
-achieves-fusion-ignition.

27. Ezra Klein, "The Dystopia We Fear Is Keeping Us from the Utopia We Deserve," *New York Times*, January 8, 2023, https://www.nytimes.com
/2023/01/08/opinion/nuclear-fusion-flying-cars.html.

28. Saul Griffith and Sam Calisch, "One Billion Machines," *Rewiring America*, June 2021, https://www.rewiringamerica.org/research/one-billion-electric-machines-report.

29. "AI workloads require substantially more energy than traditional computing. Estimates suggest that using ChatGPT requires up to 10x more power than a traditional web search. Further, it seems likely that data centers will be the largest contributor to U.S. power demand growth through the end of this decade": JPMorgan, "A Strong Economy in a Fragile World," 2024, https://assets.jpmprivatebank.com/content/dam/jpm-pb-aem/global/en/documents/mid-year-outlook-2024.pdf.

30. US Energy Information Administration, "What Is U.S. Electricity Generation by Energy Source?," https://www.eia.gov/tools/faqs/faq.php?id=427&t=8.

31. Bart Pfankuch, "Solar Surge: South Dakota Sees New Interest in Solar Power," South Dakota News Watch, April 8, 2024, https://www.sdnewswatch.org/south-dakota-solar-power-wind-renewable-energy-electricity/.

32. Amanda Zhou, "How Clean Is WA's Electricity? We Lead the Country in One Way," *Seattle Times*, February 13, 2024, https://www.seattletimes.com/seattle-news/environment/how-clean-is-was-electricity-we-lead-the-country-in-one-way/.

33. Nevada Governor's Office of Energy, "Status of Energy Report 2023," https://energy.nv.gov/uploadedFiles/energynvgov/content/Home/Features/2023_Status_of_Energy_Report.pdf.

34. US Energy Information Administration, "Wyoming State Energy Profile," updated June 20, 2024, https://www.eia.gov/state/print.php?sid=WY.

35. US Department of Energy, Office of Energy Efficiency & Renewable Energy, "Quarterly Solar Industry Update," August 2024, https://www.energy.gov/eere/solar/quarterly-solar-industry-update; US Energy Information Administration, "Florida: Profile Analysis," 2024, https://www.eia.gov/state/analysis.php?sid=FL#:~:text=In%202022%2C%20Florida%20was%20third,of%20Florida's%20total%20net%20generation.&text=About%20four%2Dfifths%20of%20the,1%20megawatt%20or%20larger)%20facilities.

36. Ezra Klein, interview with Jesse Jenkins.

37. Eric Larson et al., "Net-Zero America: Potential Pathways, Infrastructure, and Impacts," Interim report, Princeton University, Princeton, NJ, December 15, 2020, https://netzeroamerica.princeton.edu/img/Princeton_NZA_Interim_Report_15_Dec_2020_FINAL.pdf, 172.

38. J. B. Ruhl and James E. Salzman, "The Greens' Dilemma: Building To-morrow's Climate Infrastructure Today," *Emory Law Journal* 73, no. 1 (May 2023): 15, https://ssrn.com/abstract=4443474.

39. US Department of Energy, "Queued Up . . . but in Need of Transmission," April 2022, fig. 2, 3, https://www.energy.gov/sites/default/files/2022-04/Queued%20Up%E2%80%A6But%20in%20Need%20of%20Transmission.pdf; Jeff St. John, "Biden's Got a Plan for Ramping Up Energy Transmission," Canary Media, May 17, 2023, https://www.canarymedia.com/articles/transmission/bidens-got-a-plan-for-ramping-up-energy-transmission.

40. Joseph H. Eto, "Building Electric Transmission Lines: A Review of Recent Transmission Projects," Lawrence Berkeley National Laboratory, Prepared for the Office of Electricity Delivery & Energy Reliability and the Office of Energy Policy and Systems Analysis, US Department of Energy, September 2016, LBNL-1006330, https://emp.lbl.gov/publications/building-electric-transmission-lines.

41. "Rahm Emanuel on the Opportunities of Crisis," *Wall Street Journal* (video), November 19, 2008, https://youtu.be/_mzcbXi1Tkk?t=9.

42. The White House, "Remarks by the President and the Vice President on High-Speed Rail," April 16, 2009, https://obamawhitehouse.archives.gov/the-press-office/remarks-president-and-vice-president-high-speed-rail.

43. Office of Governor Edmund G. Brown Jr., "Governor Brown Delivers 2018 State of the State Address: 'California Is Setting the Pace for America,'" January 25, 2018, https://archive.gov.ca.gov/archive/gov39/2018/01/25/governor-brown-delivers-2018-state-of-the-state-address-california-is-setting-the-pace-for-america/index.html.

44. Office of Governor Gavin Newsom, "Governor Newsom Delivers State of the State Address," February 12, 2019, https://www.gov.ca.gov/2019/02/12/state-of-the-state-address/.

45. "2022 Business Plan, California High-Speed Rail Authority," February 8, 2022, https://hsr.ca.gov/about/high-speed-rail-business-plans/2022-business-plan/; Ralph Vartabedian, "Costs of California's Troubled Bullet Train Rise Again, by an Estimated $5 Billion," *Los Angeles Times*, February 8, 2022, https://www.latimes.com/california/story/2022-02-08/california-bullet-train-costs-rise-roughly-5-billion.

46. Alia Shoaib, "California Train Line Gets a Boost," *Newsweek*, May 7, 2024, https://www.newsweek.com/california-train-line-boost-1897948.

47. Library of Congress, "The Westinghouse Air Brake Co.," n.d., https://

www.loc.gov/collections/films-of-westinghouse-works-1904/articles
-and-essays/the-westinghouse-world/the-westinghouse-air-brake-co
/#:~:text=The%20first%20air%20brake%20invented,forms%20of%20
the%20automatic%20brake.

48. Adam Rogers, "Make America Build Again," *Business Insider*, November 16, 2023, https://www.businessinsider.com/america-build-infrastruc
ture-transportation-housing-regulation-environment-2023-11.

49. Eight months later, the California High-Speed Rail Authority "approved a contractor to begin designing track and overhead contact systems (OCS) for the initial 171-mile passenger service connecting Merced to Bakersfield," press release, June 26, 2024, https://hsr.ca.gov/2024/06/26
/news-release-california-high-speed-rail-authority-approves-contrac
tor-moves-design-of-track-and-overhead-electrical-systems-forward/.

50. Here and below, Brian Kelly in conversation with Ezra Klein, October 2023.

51. Ezra Klein, "'What the Hell Happened to the California of the '50s and '60s?,'" *New York Times*, June 18, 2023, https://www.nytimes.com/2023
/06/18/opinion/newsom-california-building-permitting-procurement
.html.

52. Klein, "'What the Hell Happened?'"; The White House, "Remarks as Prepared for Delivery by Senior Advisor John Podesta on the Biden-Harris Administration's Priorities for Energy Infrastructure Permitting Reform," May 10, 2023, https://www.whitehouse.gov/briefing-room
/speeches-remarks/2023/05/10/remarks-as-prepared-for-delivery-by
-senior-advisor-john-podesta-on-the-biden-harris-administrations-pri
orities-for-energy-infrastructure-permitting-reform/.

53. The White House, "Remarks on a Modern American Industrial Strategy by NEC Director Brian Deese," April 20, 2022, https://www.whitehouse
.gov/briefing-room/speeches-remarks/2022/04/20/remarks-on-a-mod
ern-american-industrial-strategy-by-nec-director-brian-deese/.

54. Transit Costs Project, "What the Data Is Telling Us," under the heading "4. Average Cost/km per Country," updated February 27, 2024, https://
transitcosts.com/new-data/.

55. Austan Goolsbee and Chad Syverson, "The Strange and Awful Path of Productivity in the U.S. Construction Sector," NBER Working Paper 30845, January 2023, rev. February 2023, http://www.nber.org/papers
/w30845.

56. Ezra Klein, "The Story Construction Tells About America's Economy Is Disturbing," *New York Times*, February 5, 2023, https://www.nytimes

.com/2023/02/05/opinion/economy-construction-productivity-mys tery.html.

57. Klein, "The Story Construction Tells."

58. Klein, "The Story Construction Tells."

59. Mancur Olson, *The Rise and Decline of Nations: Economic Growth, Stagflation, and Social Rigidities* (1982; New Haven, CT: Veritas/Yale University Press, 2022), 3.

60. Olson, *The Rise and Decline of Nations*, 40.

61. Klein, "The Story Construction Tells."

62. Klein, "The Story Construction Tells."

63. Klein, "The Story Construction Tells."

64. Leonardo D'Amico et al., "Why Has Construction Productivity Stagnated? The Role of Land-Use Regulation," December 30, 2023, https:// papers.ssrn.com/sol3/papers.cfm?abstract_id=4679195 and https://dx .doi.org/10.2139/ssrn.4679195.

65. D'Amico et al., "Why Has Construction Productivity Stagnated?," 2.

66. D'Amico et al., "Why Has Construction Productivity Stagnated?," 17.

67. Olson, *The Rise and Decline of Nations*, 72.

68. Noah Smith, "Interview: Patrick Collison, Co-Founder and CEO of Stripe," *Noahopinion*, March 8, 2021, https://www.noahpinion.blog/p /interview-patrick-collison-co-founder.

69. "Title I—Motor Vehicle Safety Standards," 718, https://www.govinfo .gov/content/pkg/STATUTE-80/pdf/STATUTE-80-Pg718.pdf; "Title II— Administration and Reporting," 735, https://www.govinfo.gov/content /pkg/STATUTE-80/pdf/STATUTE-80-Pg731.pdf#page=5.

70. Julius Duscha, "Nader's Raiders Is Their Name, and Whistle-Blowing Is Their Game . . . ," *New York Times*, March 21, 1971, https://www.nytimes .com/1971/03/21/archives/stop-in-the-public-interest-stop-in-the-pub lic-interest.html.

71. *Christian Science Monitor* quoted in Anon., "Your Book Review: Public Citizens," *Astral Codex 10* (Substack), June 23, 2023, https://www .astralcodexten.com/p/your-book-review-public-citizens; reprinted in "Public Interest Law and the Paradox of Justice by Lawsuit," *Candy for Breakfast* (Substack), October 23, 2023, https://www.candyforbreakfast .email/p/public-interest-law-and-the-paradox.

72. Paul Sabin, *Public Citizens: The Attack on Big Government and the Remaking of American Liberalism* (New York: W. W. Norton, 2021), Kindle, xvi–xvii.

73. Sabin, *Public Citizens*, Kindle, 100–101.

74. Environmental Protection Agency, "Progress Cleaning the Air and Improving People's Health," updated April 30, 2024, https://www.epa.gov/clean-air-act-overview/progress-cleaning-air-and-improving-peoples-health.

75. Environmental Protection Agency, "Progress Cleaning the Air and Improving People's Health," chart: "Health Effect Reductions (PM2.5 & Ozone Only)," updated April 30, 2024; Natural Resources Defense Council, "The Clean Air Act at 40: A Clear Track Record of Success," March 2011, https://www.nrdc.org/sites/default/files/cleanairactsuccess.pdf.

76. "Annual Air Quality, Los Angeles County, Air Quality Days by Year, 1980–2023," Los Angeles Almanac, https://www.laalmanac.com/environment/ev01b.php.

77. The authors also thank the writer Max Nussbaum for his analysis of the rise of Nader's revolution and its legacy.

78. Jim Lehrer, interview with Ralph Nader, "Newsmaker: Ralph Nader," *PBS News Hour*, air date June 30, 2000, https://www.pbs.org/newshour/spc/bb/politics/jan-june00/nader_6-30.html.

79. Sabin, *Public Citizens*, Kindle, xvii.

80. H.R.5—Regulatory Accountability Act of 2017, 115th Congress (2017–2018), https://www.congress.gov/bill/115th-congress/house-bill/5/all-actions?overview=closed#tabs.

81. Nicholas Bagley, "The Procedure Fetish," Niskanen Center, December 7, 2021, https://www.niskanencenter.org/the-procedure-fetish/. All quotes are from this iteration of the paper.

82. Bagley, "The Procedure Fetish."

83. Bagley, "The Procedure Fetish."

84. Robert A. Kagan, *Adversarial Legalism: The American Way of Law*, 2d ed. (Cambridge, MA: Harvard University Press, 2019), Kindle, 19.

85. Kagan, *Adversarial Legalism*, 2d ed., Kindle, 19.

86. Alexis de Tocqueville, *Democracy in America*, vol. 1, ed. Phillips Bradley: the Henry Reeve Text as Revised by Francis Bowen Now Further Corrected and Edited with a Historical Essay, Editorial Notes, and Bibliographies by Bradley (New York: Alfred A. Knopf, 1945), 290 (the page number is to the Vintage Books paperback).

87. Sean Farhang, "Regulation, Litigation, and Reform," in Jeffrey A. Jenkins and Sidney M. Milkis, eds. *The Politics of Major Policy Reform in Postwar America* (Cambridge, UK: Cambridge University Press, 2014), 48–76.

88. Bagley, "The Procedure Fetish."

89. Bagley, "The Procedure Fetish."

90. Pew Research Center, "Public Trust in Government: 1958–2024," June 24, 2024, https://www.pewresearch.org/politics/2024/06/24/pub lic-trust-in-government-1958-2024/.

91. See Stephen B. Burbank and Sean Farhang, *Rights and Retrenchment: The Counterrevolution Against Federal Litigation* (Cambridge, UK: Cambridge University Press, 2017).

92. J. B. Ruhl and James Salzman, "What Happens When the Green New Deal Meets the Old Green Laws?," *Vermont Law Review* 44 (2020): 694, https://scholarship.law.vanderbilt.edu/faculty-publications/1168.

93. Ruhl and Salzman, "What Happens When the Green New Deal?," 713.

94. Ruhl and Salzman, "The Greens' Dilemma," 1 and throughout.

95. Ruhl and Salzman, "The Greens' Dilemma," 24–25.

96. Derek Thompson, interview with Larry Selzer.

97. Ruhl and Salzman, "The Greens' Dilemma," 28.

98. Zachary D. Liscow, "Getting Infrastructure Built: The Law and Economics of Permitting," April 2, 2024, 18, https://ssrn.com/abstract=4775481 and http://dx.doi.org/10.2139/ssrn.4775481.

99. Liscow, "Getting Infrastructure Built," 16.

100. Liscow, "Getting Infrastructure Built," 12, 15.

101. David Shepardson, "Biden Exempts Some Semiconductor Factories from Environmental Reviews," Reuters, October 2, 2024, https://www .reuters.com/sustainability/boards-policy-regulation/biden-signs -bill-exempting-some-semiconductor-factories-new-environmental -2024-10-02/.

3. Govern

1. Heather Knight, "A New S.F. Housing Complex for Homeless People Was Faster, Cheaper to Build. So Why Isn't It Being Replicated?" *San Francisco Chronicle*, February 10, 2022, https://www.sfchronicle.com/sf /bayarea/heatherknight/article/Here-s-how-to-build-affordable-hous ing-in-SF-16823736.php.

2. Nathaniel Decker, "Strategies to Lower Cost and Speed Housing Production: A Case Study of San Francisco's 833 Bryant Street Project," Turner Center for Housing Innovation, UC Berkeley, February 2021, 2, https:// ternercenter.berkeley.edu/wp-content/uploads/2021/02/833-Bryant -February-2021.pdf.

3. Senate Bill 35, September 2017, California Legislative Information, https://leginfo.legislature.ca.gov/faces/billNavClient.xhtml?bill _id=201720180SB35.

4. San Francisco Administrative Code Chapter 14B, City and County of San Francisco, effective July 1, 2022, https://www.sf.gov/sites/default /files/2022-09/14B%20Rules%20and%20Regulations%20v.2022_0.pdf; Chapter 14B: Local Business Enterprise Utilization and Nondiscrimination in Contracting Ordinance, https://www.sf.gov/sites/default/files /2022-09/Chapter%2014B%20Local%20Business%20Enterprise%20 07%2001%2022.pdf; "Sec. 14B.1. Purpose and Findings" notes that Ordinance No. 139-84 was passed on April 2, 1984.

5. Proposition 209: Text of Proposed Law, https://vigarchive.sos.ca.gov /1996/general/pamphlet/209text.htm. It went into effect August 28, 1997.

6. San Francisco Board of Supervisors, "Administrative Code—Local Business Enterprise Program," October 18, 2021, chart, p. 5, https://sfbos.org /sites/default/files/o0203-21.pdf.

7. Ezra Klein, "The Problem with Everything-Bagel Liberalism," *New York Times*, April 2, 2023, https://www.nytimes.com/2023/04/02/opinion /democrats-liberalism.html.

8. Tipping Point, "Charles and Helen Schwab Invest $65M in Groundbreaking Homelessness Solutions in SF," October 21, 2020, https:// tippingpoint.org/press/press-releases/charles-and-helen-schwab -invest-65m-in-groundbreaking-homelessness-solutions-in-sf/; Maria Di Mento, "Billionaire Charles Schwab Gives $65 Million to House the Homeless," *Chronicle of Philanthropy*, October 26, 2020, https://www .philanthropy.com/article/billionaire-charles-schwab-gives-65-mil lion-to-house-the-homeless; J. K. Dineen, "Schwabs Donate $65 Million to Build Housing for Homeless in S.F.," *San Francisco Chronicle*, October 22, 2020, https://www.sfchronicle.com/bayarea/article/Schwabs-do nate-65-million-to-build-housing-for-15665785.php.

9. Krutika Amin, Imani Telesford, Rakesh Singh, and Cynthia Cox, "How Do Prices of Drugs for Weight Loss in the U.S. Compare to Peer Nations' Prices?," Peterson-KFF Health System Tracker, August 17, 2023, https:// www.healthsystemtracker.org/brief/prices-of-drugs-for-weight-loss -in-the-us-and-peer-nations/.

10. City of Houston, Texas, Planning and Development, Development Regulations, 2024, https://www.houstontx.gov/planning/DevelopRegs /#:~:text=The%20City%20of%20Houston%20does,how%20prop erty%20can%20be%20subdivided.

11. Point2, "Residential Construction Trends," https://www.point2homes .com/news/residential-construction-data; New Jersey Department of Community Affairs, Housing Units Authorized by Building Permits,

December 2023, February 7, 2024, https://www.nj.gov/dca/codes/reporter /2023monthly/HOUSE_12_2023.pdf; New York City, Department of City Planning, press release, April 25, 2024, https://www.nyc.gov/site/plan ning/about/press-releases/pr-20240425.page#:~:text=27%2C980%20 new%20homes%20were%20constructed,has%20depressed%20 new%20housing%20development.; US Census Bureau, Building Permits Survey, https://www.census.gov/construction/bps/current.html. See also M. Nolan Gray, "A Bold Case Against Zoning," *Fast Company*, July 11, 2022, https://www.fastcompany.com/90766731/a-bold-case-against-zoning.

12. California YIMBY, Ned Resnikoff, director, "Housing Abundance as a Condition for Ending Homelessness: Lessons from Houston, Texas," California YIMBY Education Fund, n.d., https://cayimby.org /wp-content/uploads/2023/10/Housing-Abundance-as-a-Condition -for-Ending-Homelessness-FINAL.pdf.

13. Roy Kent, "Is Buying a Home Easier or Harder in Houston? Here's How It Compares to Other Texas Metros," Rice University Kinder In- stitute for Urban Research, December 13, 2023, https://kinder.rice.edu /urbanedge/home-buying-Houston-Texas-affordability; Maurice Back- man, "Houston Housing Market Forecast," *U.S. News & World Report*, March 20, 2023, https://realestate.usnews.com/real-estate/housing -market-index/articles/houston-housing-market-forecast.

14. "San Francisco Housing Policy and Practice Review 2023," California Department of Housing and Community Development, https://www .hcd.ca.gov/sites/default/files/docs/policy-and-research/plan-report/sf -housing-policy-and-practice-review.pdf.

15. Ezra Klein, "The Way Los Angeles Is Trying to Solve Homelessness Is 'Absolutely Insane,'" *New York Times*, October 23, 2022, https://www.ny times.com/2022/10/23/opinion/los-angeles-homelessness-affordable -housing.html.

16. Los Angeles Housing Department, "City of Los Angeles Prop HHH Progress Report," tracks the figures. By September 2024, 5,327 units had been built: https://housing2.lacity.org/housing/hhh-progress-dash board. Also see City of Los Angeles Inter-Governmental Correspon- dence, June 2024, with charts, https://cao.lacity.gov/Homeless/Prop HHHAOC-20240627c.pdf; Los Angeles Housing Department, "Support- ive Housing Update," https://housing2.lacity.org/hhh-progress.

17. Los Angeles Housing Department, "City of Los Angeles Prop HHH Progress Report."

18. Klein, "The Way Los Angeles Is Trying to Solve."

19. Klein, "The Way Los Angeles Is Trying to Solve."

20. Klein, "The Way Los Angeles Is Trying to Solve."

21. Klein, "The Way Los Angeles Is Trying to Solve," and communication from Tong.

22. Eric Owen Moss, Venice Dell Community, https://ericowenmoss.com/project-detail/reese-davidson-community-housing/; Steven Sharp, "Eric Owen Moss–Designed Supportive Housing Gains Approval in Venice," Urbanize Network, June 1, 2021, https://la.urbanize.city/post/venice-eric-owen-moss-reese-davidson-approval; Trevor Bach, "'Grandfather Would Be Appalled': Family Member Wants Name Off Venice Homeless Housing," *The Real Deal*, November 8, 2021, https://thereal deal.com/la/2021/11/08/grandfather-would-be-appalled-family-mem ber-wants-name-off-venice-homeless-housing/.

23. Klein, "The Way Los Angeles Is Trying to Solve."

24. Ezra Klein, interview with Heidi Marston.

25. Klein, "The Way Los Angeles Is Trying to Solve."

26. Michael B. Gerrard, "A Time for Triage," *The Environmental Forum* 38 (2022): 40, https://scholarship.law.columbia.edu/cgi/viewcontent.cgi?a rticle=4885&context=faculty_scholarship.

27. Klein, "The Problem with Everything-Bagel Liberalism."

28. Semiconductor Industry Association, "Turning the Tide for Semiconductor Manufacturing in the U.S.," SIA Summary of Boston Consulting Group Report, volume 4, October 1, 2020, https://www.semiconductors.org/wp -content/uploads/2020/10/SIA-SUMMARY-OF-BCG-REPORT.pdf.

29. Semiconductor Industry Association, "Study Finds Federal Incentives for Domestic Semiconductor Manufacturing Would Strengthen America's Chip Production, Economy, National Security, Supply Chains," press release, September 16, 2020, https://www.semiconductors.org /study-finds-federal-incentives-for-domestic-semiconductor-manu facturing-would-strengthen-americas-chip-production-economy-na tional-security-supply-chains/.

30. Notice of Funding Opportunity (NOFO), CHIPS Incentives Program—Commercial Fabrication Facilities, 2023, https://www.nist.gov/system /files/documents/2024/04/19/Amended%20CHIPS-Commercial%20 Fabrication%20Facilities%20NOFO%20Amendment.pdf.

31. Klein, "The Problem with Everything-Bagel Liberalism."

32. California High-Speed Rail Authority, "Central Valley," n.d., https://hsr .ca.gov/high-speed-rail-in-california/central-valley/.

33. John J. DiIulio Jr., *Bring Back the Bureaucrats: Why More Federal*

Workers Will Lead to Better (and Smaller!) Government (West Conshohocken, PA: Templeton Press, 2014), Kindle, loc. 231 and loc. 1460.

34. Ralph Vartabedian, "How California's Faltering High-Speed Rail Project Was 'Captured' by Costly Consultants," *Los Angeles Times*, April 26, 2019, https://www.latimes.com/local/california/la-me-california-high-speed-rail-consultants-20190426-story.html.

35. Ezra Klein, interview with Brian Kelly.

36. BART, "Best Scoring Bid to Build BART's Fleet of the Future," April 23, 2012, https://www.bart.gov/news/articles/2012/news20120423.

37. Darwin BondGraham and Jose Fermoso, "BART Says It's Saving $394M on New Train Cars," *The Oaklandside*, January 10, 2024, https://oaklandside.org/2024/01/10/bart-saving-millions-new-train-cars-fleet-of-the-future/.

38. Bob Lettenberger, "BART New Car Fleet Under Budget," *Trains*, January 17, 2024, https://www.trains.com/trn/news-reviews/news-wire/bart-new-car-fleet-under-budget/.

39. Zachary D. Liscow, "Getting Infrastructure Built: The Law and Economics of Permitting," 22.

40. "Report: EDD Delayed, Denied Benefits to Millions During Pandemic; Quick Response Not a Priority," CBS News, August 8, 2022, https://www.cbsnews.com/sanfrancisco/news/report-edd-delayed-denied-benefits-to-millions-during-pandemic-quick-response-not-a-priority/.

41. Jennifer Pahlka, *Recoding America* (New York: Metropolitan Books/Henry Holt and Company, 2023), Kindle, 25, 26.

42. Pahlka, *Recoding America*, Kindle, 28.

43. Yolanda Richardson and Jennifer Pahlka, "Employment Development Department Strike Team Detailed Assessment and Recommendations," September 16, 2020, https://www.govops.ca.gov/wp-content/uploads/sites/11/2020/09/Assessment.pdf.

44. Michael Krigsman, "California Abandons $2 Billion Court Management System," *ZDNET*, April 1, 2012, https://www.zdnet.com/article/california-abandons-2-billion-court-management-system/; Maura Dolan, "Cutbacks in California Court System Produce Long Lines, Short Tempers," *Los Angeles Times*, May 10, 2014, https://www.latimes.com/local/la-me-court-cuts-20140511-story.html.

45. Office of the Inspector General, US Department of State, "Review of the Bureau of Consular Affairs' [CA] ConsularOne Modernization Program—Significant Deployment Delays Continue," November 2021, https://www.stateoig.gov/uploads/report/report_pdf_file/isp-i-22-03_7

.pdf; Tom Temin, "This State Department IT Project Started in 2009 and It's Nowhere Near Finished," *Federal News Network*, January 3, 2022, https://federalnewsnetwork.com/agency-oversight/2022/01/this-state-department-it-project-started-in-2009-and-its-nowhere-near-finished/.

46. US Government Accountability Office, "IRS's Efforts to Modernize 60-Year-Old Tax Processing System Is Almost a Decade Away," November 4, 2021, https://www.gao.gov/blog/irss-efforts-modernize-60-year-old-tax-processing-system-almost-decade-away; Tax Policy Center, "What Technology Does the IRS Use?," updated January 2024, https://taxpolicycenter.org/briefing-book/what-technology-does-irs-use.

47. Pahlka, *Recoding America*, Kindle, 34–35.

48. Pahlka, *Recoding America*, Kindle, 58.

49. Pahlka, *Recoding America*, Kindle, 69–70.

50. Pahlka, *Recoding America*, Kindle, 68.

51. Pahlka, *Recoding America*, Kindle, 50.

52. Ezra Klein, interview with Mike Carroll. All further quotes are from this source.

53. Commonwealth of Pennsylvania, Proclamation of Disaster Emergency, June 12, 2023, https://www.pa.gov/content/dam/copapwp-pagov/en/governor/documents/2023.6.12-Disaster-Emergency-Proclamation-I-95-PDF.pdf.

54. United Union of Roofers, Waterproofers & Allied Workers, July 5, 2023, https://unionroofers.com/philadelphia-building-trades-work-24-7-to-rebuild-i-95-collapse/.

55. Gregory Korte, Mark Niquette, and Skylar Woodhouse, "How the I-95 Bridge Reopened Just 12 Days After Fiery Collapse," *Bloomberg*, June 28, 2023, https://www.bloomberg.com/news/articles/2023-06-28/resurrection-of-i-95-in-just-two-weeks-is-dubbed-small-miracle; Heavy Construction Systems Specialists, "Getting a City Back to Work When Every Minute Counts," September 2023, blog post, https://www.hcss.com/blog/construction-of-i-95-bridge-after-collapse/.

56. Julia Terrero, "From TikToks to a 24/7 Live Stream, Gov. Josh Shapiro's I-95 Response Grows His National Profile," *Philadelphia Inquirer*, June 17, 2023, https://www.inquirer.com/politics/pennsylvania/pennsylvania-governor-response-i95-repairs-national-profile-20230616.html.

57. Josh Shapiro, "We Fixed I-95 in 12 Days. Here Are Our Lessons for U.S. Infrastructure," *Washington Post*, July 16, 2023, https://www.washing

tonpost.com/opinions/2023/07/17/interstate-95-repair-infrastructure
-shapiro-pennsylvania/.

58. Brink Lindsey, "State Capacity: What Is It, How We Lost It, and How
to Get It Back," Niskanen Center, November 2021, p. 8, https://www.nis
kanencenter.org/wp-content/uploads/2021/11/brinkpaper.pdf.

4. Invent

1. Katalin Karikó, with Ali Benjamin, *Breaking Through: My Life in Science*
(New York: Crown, 2023), Kindle, 4, 8.

2. Karikó, *Breaking Through*, Kindle, 10.

3. Biological Research Center, Szeged, SZTE Klebelsberg Library Gallery
and Media Gallery, https://mediateka.ek.szte.hu/exhibits/show/kata
lin_kariko_eng/brc_szeged; and https://www.brc.hu/en.

4. Derek Thompson, interview with Katalin Karikó.

5. Derek Thompson, interview with Katalin Karikó.

6. Chiara Franzoni, Paula Stephan, and Reinhilde Veugelers, "Funding
Risky Research," NBER Working Paper 28905, June 2021, 4–5, http://
www.nber.org/papers/w28905 and https://www.nber.org/system/files
/working_papers/w28905/w28905.pdf.

7. Karikó, *Breaking Through*, Kindle, 178. A variation on "Experience
never errs; it is only your judgments that err by promising themselves
effects such as are not caused by your experiments," *The Notebooks of
Leonardo da Vinci*, trans. Jean Paul Richter, vol. 1, 1888, Project Guten-
berg, https://archive.org/stream/thenotebooksofle05000gut/7ldvc09
.txt; and "Experience is never at fault; it is only your judgment that is in
error in promising itself such results from experience as are not caused
by our experiments," *The Notebooks of Leonardo da Vinci*, Arranged,
Rendered into English and Introduced by Edward MacCurd (New York:
George Braziller, 1955), 64.

8. Karikó, *Breaking Through*, Kindle, 183.

9. Andy Markowitz and Jenny Rough, "List of Coronavirus-Related Restrictions in Every State," March 17, 2020, updated May 1, 2024, https://
www.aarp.org/politics-society/government-elections/info-2020/coro
navirus-state-restrictions.html; Victor Fiorillo, "Yes, Even Your Out-
door Socially Distanced Thanksgiving Party Is Banned," *Philadelphia*,
November 17, 2020, https://www.phillymag.com/news/2020/11/17/out
door-thanksgiving-philadelphia-covid/; Gabrielle Connor, Vaishnavi
Vaidya, Jennifer Kolker, and Ran Li, "Indoor Dining and COVID-19: Im-
plications for Reopening in 30 U.S. Cities," Urban Health Collaborative,

Drexel University, September 2020, https://drexel.edu/~/media/Files /uhc/Additional%20Project%20Documents/IndoorDiningCOVID19 .ashx?la=en; "State Alcohol-Related Laws During the COVID-19 Emergency for On-Premise and Off-Premise Establishments as of June 15, 2020," National Institute on Alcohol Abuse and Alcoholism/National Institutes of Health, June 15, 2020, https://alcoholpolicy.niaaa.nih.gov /sites/default/files/file-page/apis_-_covid-19_memo_6.15.20_508c.pdf.

10. Jason Abaluck et al., "The Impact of Community Masking on COVID-19: A Cluster-Randomized Trial in Bangladesh," August 31, 2021, https://poverty-action.org/sites/default/files/publications/Mask _RCT___Symptomatic_Seropositivity_083121.pdf.

11. So, did mask mandates work, or didn't they? The frustrating answer is it depends. Jason Abaluck, a Yale professor who helped run the Bangladesh study, offered a sobering synthesis. The success of mask mandates—like the success of most behavioral interventions—hinges on many factors, including public trust in government, civilian adherence to the mask rules, and state capacity to enforce them. In places where a well-informed and motivated public conscientiously wore high-quality masks almost all the time, mask mandates probably worked, he said. "But if Alabama tomorrow mandated mask-wearing, it would do nothing." Derek Thompson, interview with Jason Abaluck.

12. Sandy Cohen, "The Fastest Vaccine in History," December 10, 2020, UCLA Health, https://www.uclahealth.org/news/article/the-fastest -vaccine-in-history; Maya Prabhu, "Mumps: The Story of the Second Fastest Vaccine Ever Developed," VaccinesWork/Gavi, April 22, 2022, https://www.gavi.org/vaccineswork/mumps-story-second-fastest-vac cine-ever-developed.

13. Colin Dwyer, "Moderna's COVID-19 Vaccine Becomes 2nd to Earn FDA Authorization," NPR, December 18, 2020, https://www.npr.org /sections/coronavirus-live-updates/2020/12/18/947948227/modernas -covid-19-vaccine-becomes-2nd-to-earn-fda-authorization; "Moderna Announces FDA Authorization of Moderna COVID-19 Vaccine in U.S.," Moderna, press release, December 18, 2020, https://investors.moder natx.com/news/news-details/2020/Moderna-Announces-FDA-Autho rization-of-Moderna-COVID-19-Vaccine-in-U.S/default.aspx.

14. Sarah Zhang, "The COVID Strategy America Hasn't Really Tried," *Atlantic*, February 14, 2022, https://www.theatlantic.com/health/archive /2022/02/vaccinate-old/622080/.

15. Emily Head and Dr. Sabine L. van Elsland, "Vaccinations May Have

Prevented Almost 20 Million COVID-19 Deaths Worldwide," Imperial College London, June 24, 2022, https://www.imperial.ac.uk/news/237591 /vaccinations-have-prevented-almost-20-million/.

16. Ezra Klein, "The Economic Mistake the Left Is Finally Confronting," *New York Times*, September 19, 2021, https://www.nytimes.com/2021/09 /19/opinion/supply-side-progressivism.html.

17. Steven Overly, "This Government Loan Program Helped Tesla at a Critical Time. Trump Wants to Cut It," *Washington Post*, March 16, 2017, https://www.washingtonpost.com/news/innovations/wp/2017/03 /16/this-government-loan-program-helped-tesla-at-a-critical-time -trump-wants-to-cut-it/; US Department of Energy Loan Programs Office, "Tesla," https://www.energy.gov/lpo/tesla; Maddow Blog and Steve Benen, "Tesla Repaying Obama Admin Loan 5 Years Early," NBC News, March 12, 2013, https://www.nbcnews.com/news/world/tesla-repaying -obama-admin-loan-5-years-early-flna1c8823565.

18. Andrew J. Fieldhouse and Karel Mertens, "Government-Funded R&D Produces Long-Term Productivity Gains," Federal Reserve Bank of Dallas, February 13, 2024, https://www.dallasfed.org/research/economics /2024/0213.

19. Derek Thompson, interview with Heidi Williams.

20. Meagan C. Fitzpatrick, Seyed M. Moghadas, Abhishek Pandey, and Alison P. Galvani, "Two Years of U.S. COVID-19 Vaccines Have Prevented Millions of Hospitalizations and Deaths," *The Commonwealth Fund* (blog), December 13, 2022, https://www.commonwealthfund.org/blog/2022/two -years-covid-vaccines-prevented-millions-deaths-hospitalizations.

21. Derek Thompson, interview with Katalin Karikó; Ting Yu, "How Scientists Drew Weissman (MED'87, GRS'87) and Katalin Karikó Developed the Revolutionary mRNA Technology Inside COVID Vaccines," *Bostonia*, November 18, 2021, https://www.bu.edu/articles/2021/how -drew-weissman-and-katalin-kariko-developed-mrna-technology -inside-covid-vaccines/.

22. Karikó, *Breaking Through*, Kindle, 223.

23. Karikó, *Breaking Through*, Kindle, 227.

24. Gina Kolata, "Long Overlooked, Kati Kariko Helped Shield the World from the Coronavirus," *New York Times*, April 8, 2021, updated October 2, 2023, https://www.nytimes.com/2021/04/08/health/coronavirus -mrna-kariko.html.

25. Karikó, *Breaking Through*, Kindle, 262.

26. Karikó, *Breaking Through*, Kindle, 263.

27. Derek Thompson, interview with Katalin Karikó.

28. Derek Thompson, "How mRNA Technology Could Change the World," *Atlantic*, March 29, 2021, https://www.theatlantic.com/ideas/archive/2021/03/how-mrna-technology-could-change-world/618431/.

29. John Holder, "Tracking Coronavirus Vaccinations Around the World," *New York Times*, updated March 13, 2023, https://www.nytimes.com/interactive/2021/world/covid-vaccinations-tracker.html; Pfizer, map of Pfizer-BioNTech COVID-19 vaccine shipments, n.d., https://www.pfizer.com/science/coronavirus/vaccine/working-to-reach-everyone-everywhere; Moderna, "U.S. Government Purchases Additional 100 Million Doses of Moderna's COVID-19 Vaccine," February 11, 2021, https://investors.modernatx.com/news/news-details/2021/U.S.-Government-Purchases-Additional-100-Million-Doses-of-Modernas-COVID-19-Vaccine/default.aspx.

30. Karikó, *Breaking Through*, Kindle, 195.

31. Derek Thompson, interview with Katalin Karikó.

32. Richard Harris, "Scientists Win Nobel for Work on How Cells Communicate," NPR, October 7, 2013, https://www.npr.org/2013/10/07/230192033/scientists-win-nobel-for-work-on-how-cells-communicate.

33. Derek Thompson, interview with Pierre Azoulay.

34. Thomas D. Snyder, ed., "120 Years of American Education: A Statistical Portrait," US Department of Education, Office of Educational Research and Improvement, Center for Education Statistics, January 1993, p. 75, table 23, https://nces.ed.gov/pubs93/93442.pdf.

35. According to IES/National Center for Education Statistics, "Between fall 2011 and fall 2022, the total annual number of faculty at degree-granting postsecondary institutions ranged from 1.5 to 1.6 million. There were 1.5 million faculty in both 2011 and 2022, with a peak at 1.6 million in 2015," https://nces.ed.gov/fastfacts/display.asp?id=61#fn1.

36. Nicholas Bloom, Charles I. Jones, John Van Reenen, and Michael Webb, "Are Ideas Getting Harder to Find?," *American Economic Review* 110, no. 4 (2020): 1104–144, https://web.stanford.edu/~chadj/IdeaPF.pdf and https://www.aeaweb.org/articles?id=10.1257/aer.20180338.

37. Derek Thompson, interview with Nicholas Bloom. Medical research productivity is hard to measure, and Bloom's conclusions are not universally supported. Some scholars have published persuasive work suggesting that medical research productivity is more likely stable. See "Distilling Data from Large Language Models," by Maya M. Durvasula, Sabri Eyuboglu, and David M. Ritzwoller. But whether productivity in

this all-important sector is flat or declining, the most important thing is that it is not obviously rising. Just as we should hope for rising productivity in any industry, we should hope for it in science.

38. Andrew von Eschenbach, "NCI Sets Goal of Eliminating Suffering and Death Due to Cancer by 2015," *Journal of the National Medical Association* 95, no. 7 (July 2003): 637–39, https://www.ncbi.nlm.nih.gov/pmc /articles/PMC2594648/?page=1.

39. The White House, "Remarks of President Barack Obama—Address to Joint Session of Congress," February 24, 2009, https://obamawhite house.archives.gov/the-press-office/remarks-president-barack -obama-address-joint-session-congress.

40. The White House, "President Biden Reignites Cancer Moonshot to End Cancer as We Know It," February 2, 2022, https://www.whitehouse.gov /briefing-room/statements-releases/2022/02/02/fact-sheet-president -biden-reignites-cancer-moonshot-to-end-cancer-as-we-know-it/.

41. Some research finds that the age-adjusted cancer mortality rate has declined meaningfully in the last few decades. This is welcome news, but it is not quite right to associate this entire decline with medical breakthroughs. For example, despite some advancements in the treatment of late-stage lung cancers, the rate of lung cancer has declined in the last few decades mostly because of the long-term decline of smoking in the United States.

42. Derek Thompson, interview with Eric Topol.

43. Benjamin F. Jones, "The Burden of Knowledge and the 'Death of the Renaissance Man': Is Innovation Getting Harder?," April 2008, https:// www.kellogg.northwestern.edu/faculty/jones-ben/htm/burden ofknowledge.pdf.

44. Periodic Table, Phosphorus, "History," https://www.rsc.org/periodic -table/element/15/phosphorus.

45. Oak Ridge National Laboratory, "Big Science: The Discovery of Tennessine," January 27, 2017, https://www.ornl.gov/sites/default/files /Ts_Program%20Final%20sm.pdf; Periodic Table, Tennessine, Element Summary, 3. History, National Institutes of Health, https://pubchem. ncbi.nlm.nih.gov/element/Tennessine#section=Estimated-Oceanic -Abundance; Scott Alexander, "Is Science Slowing Down?," *Slate Star Codex* (blog), November 26, 2018, https://slatestarcodex.com/2018/11/26 /is-science-slowing-down-2/.

46. Gregor Mendel, "Versuche über Plflanzenhybriden," *Verhandlungen des Naturforschenden Vereines in Brünn* 5 (1865): 3–47. Presented orally

at the February 8 and March 8, 1865, meetings of the Brünn Natural History Society. Published in 1866, Brünn, Czechoslovakia, by Verlag des Vereines. Biodiversity Heritage Library, https://www.biodiversityli brary.org/item/124139#page/5/mode/1up. Published in English in 1901: "Experiments in Plant Hybridization," trans. William Bateson, http://www.esp.org/foundations/genetics/classical/gm-65.pdf.

47. Derek Thompson, interview with Heidi Williams.

48. Derek Thompson, interview with Jeremy Neufeld.

49. Shai Bernstein, Rebecca Diamond, Abhisit Jiranaphawiboon, Timothy McQuade, and Beatriz Pousada, "The Contribution of High-Skilled Immigrants to Innovation in the United States," NBER Working Paper 30797, December 2022, DOI 10.3386/w30797, summary here: https://www.nber.org/digest/20233/outsize-role-immigrants-us-innovation; Katia Savchuk, "A New Look at Immigrants' Outsize Contribution to Innovation in the US," Stanford University, Institute for Economic Policy Research, April 14, 2023, https://siepr.stanford.edu/news/new-look -immigrants-outsize-contribution-innovation-us; Stuart Anderson, "Immigrants Keep Winning Nobel Prizes," *Forbes*, October 7, 2021, up- dated April 21, 2022, https://www.forbes.com/sites/stuartanderson/2021 /10/07/immigrants-keep-winning-nobel-prizes/.

50. Derek Thompson, interview with Jeremy Neufeld.

51. American Immigration Council, "The H-1B Visa Program and Its Impact on the U.S. Economy," October 8, 2024, https://www.americanimmigra tioncouncil.org/research/h1b-visa-program-fact-sheet; US Citizenship and Immigration Services, "USCIS Reaches Fiscal Year 2024 H-1B Cap," December 13, 2023, https://www.uscis.gov/newsroom/alerts/uscis -reaches-fiscal-year-2024-h-1b-cap.

52. The H-1B visa program is politically controversial, even among those who claim to support high-skilled immigration. One common criticism is that these foreign-born workers take jobs from Americans for less pay. The fear may be overstated. Several studies (see William R. Kerr and William F. Lincoln, "The Supply Side of Innovation: H-1B Visa Reforms and US Ethnic Invention," 2010, and John Bound, Nicolas Morales, and Gaurav Kahnna, "Understanding the Impact of H-1B Visas on the U.S. Economy," 2017) have found that increases in H-1B admissions are associated with more patents and higher growth at firms, while the effect on native-born employment is not significantly negative.

53. Derek Thompson, interview with Jeremy Neufeld.

54. Sally Rockey, "More Data on Age and the Workforce," National Institutes of Health Office of Extramural Research, March 25, 2015, https://nexus.od.nih.gov/all/2015/03/25/age-of-investigator/.

55. Michael Park, Erin Leahey, and Russell J. Funk, "Papers and Patents Are Becoming Less Disruptive Over Time, *Nature* 613 (2023): 138–44, https://www.nature.com/articles/s41586-022-05543-x.

56. Derek Thompson, interview with James Evans.

57. Derek Thompson, interview with Pierre Azoulay.

58. Gregory A. Petsko, "Goodbye, Columbus," *Genome Biology* 13 (2012): Article no. 155, https://genomebiology.biomedcentral.com/articles/10.1186/gb-2012-13-5-155.

59. Sources differ on the date of the White House meeting. See Robert Reinhold, "Dr. Vannevar Bush Is Dead at 84," *New York Times*, June 30, 1974, https://www.nytimes.com/1974/06/30/archives/dr-vannevar-bush-is-dead-at-84-dr-vannevar-bush-who-marshaled.html; photocopy of June 15, 1940, letter to Vannevar Bush from Roosevelt, creating the NDRC, http://www.fdrlibrary.marist.edu/_resources/images/atomic/atomic_02.pdf; Internet Pioneers, "Vannevar Bush," https://www.ibiblio.org/pioneers/bush.html; "Vannevar Bush: The Memex," Lemelson–MIT Program, https://lemelson.mit.edu/resources/vannevar-bush; Robert E. Sherwood, *Roosevelt and Hopkins: An Intimate History* (New York: Harper, 1948), 153–55; Bush to Seitz, September 16, 1968 (NAS Archives). Per draft notes for Bush's "Science, the Endless Frontier": "Summoned by President Roosevelt, in the spring of 1940, the President of the National Academy and others associated with him recommended the creation of a single central agency within the executive establishment . . . for the purpose of mobilizing . . . scientific personnel and the facilities of the nation": "Frank Baldwin Jewett (1939–1947)," in *The National Academy of Sciences: The First Hundred Years 1863–1963*, National Library of Medicine, National Center for Biotechnology Information, National Institutes of Health, https://www.ncbi.nlm.nih.gov/books/NBK217891/.

60. Vannevar Bush, *Science, the Endless Frontier*, A Report to the President by Vannevar Bush, Director of the Office of Scientific Research and Development, July 1945 (Washington, DC: United States Government Printing Office, 1945), 17, 75th anniversary edition (here and elsewhere, we refer to the report in its published book form; page numbers

are from this searchable edition): https://www.nsf.gov/about/history/EndlessFrontier_w.pdf.

61. Eva Åhrén, "Joseph Kinyoun, the Hygienic Laboratory, and the Origins of the NIH," *NIH Catalyst* 20, no. 6 (November–December 2012), National Institutes of Health, https://irp.nih.gov/catalyst/20/6/nih-in-history.

62. Bhaven N. Sampat, "Doubling Down: Will Large Increases in the NIH Budget Promote More Meaningful Medical Innovation?," *Journal of Law, Medicine & Ethics* 51, S2 (2023): 21–23, https://www.ncbi.nlm.nih.gov/pmc/articles/PMC10911986/.

63. Matt Faherty, "New Science's Report on the NIH," *New Science*, April 2022, https://newscience.org/nih/#how-are-indirect-cost-rates-calculated.

64. "Cassius James Van Slyke, M.D.," NIH Almanac, National Institutes of Health, https://www.nih.gov/about-nih/what-we-do/nih-almanac/cassius-james-van-slyke-md.

65. Cassius Van Slyke, "New Horizons in Medical Research," *Science* 104, no. 2711 (December 1946): 559–67, https://pubmed.ncbi.nlm.nih.gov/17772322/.

66. "James A. Shannon, M.D.," NIH Almanac, National Institutes of Health, https://www.nih.gov/about-nih/what-we-do/nih-almanac/james-shannon-md.

67. James A. Shannon and Charles V. Kidd, "Medical Research in Perspective," *Science* (New Series) 124, no. 3233 (December 1956): 1185–190, https://www.jstor.org/stable/1752817.

68. Bhaven N. Sampat, "The History and Political Economy of NIH Peer Review," Brookings Institution and the Institute for Progress, May 2023, https://www.brookings.edu/wp-content/uploads/2023/05/SampatFinal-3.pdf.

69. "Proxmire, William. Golden Fleece Awards, 1975–1987," press release, March 11, 1975, Wisconsin Historical Society, https://content.wisconsinhistory.org/digital/collection/proxmire/id/84/; Etienne S. Benson, "All That's Gold Does Not Glitter," Association for Psychological Science, June 1, 2006, https://www.psychologicalscience.org/observer/all-thats-gold-does-not-glitter.

70. Sampat, "The History and Political Economy of NIH Peer Review," 16.

71. Sampat, "The History and Political Economy of NIH Peer Review," 16; Philip H. Abelson, "More Paper Work, Less Research," *Science* 139, no. 3556 (February 22, 1963), https://www.science.org/doi/10.1126/science.139.3556.725.

72. The Editors, "Dr. No Money: The Broken Science Funding System," *Scientific American*, May 2011, https://www.scientificamerican.com/article/dr-no-money/.

73. National Institute of Allergy and Infectious Diseases, National Institutes of Health, "Timeline for Assignment, Review, and Council," n.d., https://www.niaid.nih.gov/grants-contracts/timelines-assignment-review.

74. "John Doench, Ph.D.," Broad Institute, October 2023, https://www.broadinstitute.org/bios/john-doench.

75. Derek Thompson, interview with John Doench.

76. Karikó, *Breaking Through*, Kindle, 183.

77. As Azoulay and Danielle Li note in "Scientific Grant Funding," NBER Working Paper 26889, June 2021, https://www.nber.org/system/files/working_papers/w26889/w26889.pdf), the term originated with Lawrence: Peter A. Lawrence, "Real Lives and White Lies in the Funding of Scientific Research," *PLoS Biology* 7, no. 9 (2009): e1000197, https://doi.org/10.1371/journal.pbio.1000197.

78. Derek Thompson, interview with Pierre Azoulay.

79. Derek Thompson, interview with Pierre Azoulay.

80. Kevin J. Boudreau, Eva C. Guinan, Karim R. Lakhani, and Christoph Riedl, "The Novelty Paradox & Bias for Normal Science: Evidence from Randomized Medical Grant Proposal Evaluations," Harvard Business School Working Paper 13–053, December 2012, https://dash.harvard.edu/bitstream/handle/1/10001229/13-053.pdf?sequence=1&isAllowed=y.

81. Jay Bhattacharya and Mikko Packalen, "Stagnation and Scientific Incentives," NBER Working Paper 26752, February 2020, https://www.nber.org/system/files/working_papers/w26752/w26752.pdf.

82. Mikko Packalen and Jay Bhattacharya, "NIH Funding and the Pursuit of Edge Science," *Proceedings of the National Academy of Sciences* 117, no. 22 (May 2020): 12011–016, https://www.pnas.org/doi/10.1073/pnas.1910160117.

83. Derek Thompson, interview with James Evans.

84. Adam M. Deane, Marianne J. Chapman, and Michael Horowitz, "The Therapeutic Potential of a Venomous Lizard: The Use of Glucagon-Like Peptide-1 Analogues in the Critically Ill," *Critical Care* 14, no. 5 (2010): 1004, https://www.ncbi.nlm.nih.gov/pmc/articles/PMC3219279/.

85. Marybeth Shea, "Discovering Life in Yellowstone Where Nobody Thought It Could Exist," National Park Service, n.d., https://www.nps.gov/articles/thermophile-yell.htm.

86. Yoshizumi Ishino et al., "Nucleotide Sequence of the IAP Gene,

Responsible for Alkaline Phosphatase Isoenzyme Conversion in *Escherichia coli*, and Identification of the Gene Product," *Journal of Bacteriology* 169 (1987): 5429–433, doi: 10.1128/jb.169.12.5429-5433.1987; Francisco J. M. Mojica, G. Juez, and F. Rodríguez-Valera, "Transcription at Different Salinities of *Haloferax mediterranei* Sequences Adjacent to Partially Modified PstI Sites," *Molecular Microbiology* 9 (1993): 613–21, doi: 10.1111/j.1365-2958.1993.tb01721.x.

87. Derek Thompson, interview with James Evans.

88. Email from Francis Collins to Peter Thiel, January 12, 2017, https://s3.documentcloud.org/documents/7203720/NIH-Thiel-Communications.pdf.

89. "NIH Director's Pioneer Award" and "NIH Director's New Innovator Award," Office of Strategic Coordination—The Common Fund, National Institutes of Health, 2024, https://commonfund.nih.gov/pioneer.

90. Derek Thompson, interview with Patricia Labosky.

91. James M. Anderson, "Evaluation of the NIH Director's Pioneer Award Program-DP1," Division of Program Coordination, Planning, and Strategic Initiatives, National Institutes of Health, May 14, 2013, https://dpcpsi.nih.gov/sites/default/files/CoC-051413-Pioneer-Award-Program-DP1.pdf.

92. Moderna, "DARPA Awards Moderna Therapeutics a Grant for Up to $25 Million to Develop Messenger RNA Therapeutics," press release, October 2, 2013, https://investors.modernatx.com/news/news-details/2013/DARPA-Awards-Moderna-Therapeutics-a-Grant-for-up-to-25-Million-to-Develop-Messenger-RNA-Therapeutics/default.aspx.

93. In fact, DARPA has inspired several offshoots, including ARPA-E and ARPA-H, for high-risk research in energy and health, respectively.

94. Office of Space Commerce, National Oceanic and Atmospheric Administration, Department of Commerce, https://www.space.commerce.gov/links/resources-for-space-entrepreneurs/opportunities-department-of-defense-national-security-agencies/#:~:text=Defense%20Advanced%20Research%20Projects%20Agency%20(DARPA)&text=Its%20mission%20is%20to%20make,have%20a%20dedicated%20space%20division.

95. Derek Thompson, interview with Erica R. H. Fuchs. All subsequent Fuchs quotes are from this interview.

96. Fuchs promised not to reveal the identity of the manager, given the sensitivity of his military work.

97. Don Clark, "IBM Reports Advance in Shrinking Chip Circuitry," *Wall Street Journal*, July 9, 2015, https://www.wsj.com/articles/ibm-reports -advances-in-shrinking-future-chips-1436414814.

98. Derek Thompson, interview with Jon Gertner.

99. Derek Thompson, interview with Jon Gertner.

100. Derek Thompson, interview with Jon Gertner.

101. Derek Thompson, interview with Heidi Williams.

102. "Metascience," Institute for Progress, https://ifp.org/category/metasci ence/.

103. Pierre Azoulay, Joshua S. Graff Zivin, and Gustavo Manso, "Incentives and Creativity: Evidence from the Academic Life Sciences," NBER Working Paper 15466, October 2009, https://www.nber.org/system/files /working_papers/w15466/w15466.pdf.

104. Matt Clancy et al., "To Speed Up Scientific Progress, We Need to Understand Science Policy," Metascience, September 11, 2023, https://ifp .org/to-speed-up-scientific-progress-we-need-to-understand-science -policy/.

105. Derek Thompson, interview with Pierre Azoulay.

5. Deploy

1. James Phinney Baxter III, *Scientists Against Time* (Cambridge, MA: MIT Press, 1968 [and previous publishers]), Kindle, 517.

2. Alexander Fleming, "On the Antibacterial Action of Cultures of a Penicillium, with Special Reference to Their Use in the Isolation of B. influenzæ," *British Journal of Experimental Pathology* 10, no. 3 (1929): 226–36, https://pmc.ncbi.nlm.nih.gov/articles/PMC2048009/?page=1. Fleming called it *Penicillium rubrum* in his landmark 1929 paper. It was subsequently identified as *Penicillium notatum* and *Penicillium chrysogenum*. Today it is recognized as *Penicillium rubens*: Jos Houbraken, Jens C. Frisvad, and Robert A. Samson, "Fleming's Penicillin Producing Strain Is Not *Penicillium chrysogenum* but *P. rubens*," *IMA Fungus* 2, no. 1 (June 2011): 87–95, https://pmc.ncbi.nlm.nih.gov/articles/PMC3317369/.

3. Baxter, *Scientists Against Time*, Kindle, loc. 6605–621. Also see E. Chain and H. W. Florey et al., "Penillin as a Chemotherapeutic Agent," *Lancet*, August 24, 1940, 226–28, Experiment 2, 227, file://C:/Users/User/Down loads/19400824_florey_penicillinasachemotherapeuticagent_lancet .pdf. The original sample size was eight mice only. See Eric Lax, *The Mold in Dr. Florey's Coat: The Story of the Penicillin Miracle* (New York:

Henry Holt and Company, 2015), Kindle, loc. 1940. Increasingly, over time, Florey and Chain used more mice, building up to Experiment 2—with its division into three groups of mice given three different bacteria, https://www.sciencedirect.com/sdfe/pdf/download/eid/1-s2.0 -S0140673601087281/first-page-pdf.

4. Baxter, *Scientists Against Time*, Kindle, loc. 704.

5. Derek Thompson, "Thomas Edison's Greatest Invention," *Atlantic*, November 2019, https://www.theatlantic.com/magazine/archive/2019/11 /edmund-morris-edison/598357/.

6. Derek Thompson, "Why the Age of American Progress Ended," *Atlantic*, December 12, 2022, https://www.theatlantic.com/magazine/archive /2023/01/science-technology-vaccine-invention-history/672227/.

7. Brink Lindsey, "Eli Dourado on Abundance and Collapse," a conversation with Dourado, *The Permanent Problem* (Substack), July 16, 2024, https://brinklindsey.substack.com/p/eli-dourado-on-abundance-and -collapse.

8. Robinson Meyer, "Why America Doesn't Really Make Solar Panels Anymore," *Atlantic*, June 15, 2021, https://www.theatlantic.com/science /archive/2021/06/why-the-us-doesnt-really-make-solar-panels-any more-industrial-policy/619213/.

9. "Our History: A Story of Innovation and Progress," Otis, https://www .otis.com/en/us/our-company/history.

10. Stephen Jacob Smith, "The American Elevator Explains Why Housing Costs Have Skyrocketed," *New York Times*, July 8, 2024, https://www .nytimes.com/2024/07/08/opinion/elevator-construction-regulation -labor-immigration.html.

11. David E. Sanger, "China Has Leapfrogged the U.S. in Key Technologies. Can a New Law Help?," *New York Times*, July 28, 2022, https:// www.nytimes.com/2022/07/28/us/politics/us-china-semiconductors .html.

12. Shoya Okinaga, "Japan Battery Material Producers Lose Spark as China Races Ahead," *Nikkei Asia*, April 4, 2022, https://asia.nikkei.com /Business/Materials/Japan-battery-material-producers-lose-spark-as -China-races-ahead2#_blank.

13. Bush, *Science, the Endless Frontier*. For the Committee on Medical Research, see 58–59 and elsewhere throughout; for malaria, see 53, https:// www.nsf.gov/about/history/EndlessFrontier_w.pdf.

14. Baxter, *Scientists Against Time*, Kindle, 528, and see 522–27.

15. Baxter, *Scientists Against Time*, Kindle, 530–32.

16. Christen Rayner, "How the Discovery of Penicillin Has Influenced Modern Medicine," *Oxford Scientist*, June 1, 2020, https://oxsci.org/how -penicillin-has-influenced-modern-medicine/.

17. Derek Thompson, "Why the Age of American Progress Ended," *Atlantic*, December 12, 2022, https://www.theatlantic.com/magazine/archive /2023/01/science-technology-vaccine-invention-history/672227/.

18. "Alessandro Volta," American Physical Society, n.d., https://www.aps .org/archives/publications/apsnews/201012/physicshistory.cfm.

19. "December 20, 1900: Nature Reports on William Duddell's 'Musical Arcs,'" American Physical Society, n.d., https://www.aps.org/archives /publications/apsnews/201012/physicshistory.cfm.

20. "The Incandescent Lamp Patent," (*The Consolidated Electric Light Company, Appellant, v. The McKeesport Light Company*), 159 U.S. 465 (1895), Appeal from the Circuit Court of the United States for the Western District of Pennsylvania, No. 10, argued October 29, 30, 1894; decided November 11, 1815, https://tile.loc.gov/storage-services/service/ll /usrep/usrep159/usrep159465/usrep159465.pdf, 476–477.

21. "Vast Power of the Sun Is Tapped by Battery Using Sand Ingredient," *New York Times*, April 26, 1954, https://timesmachine.nytimes.com /timesmachine/1954/04/26/issue.html.

22. "About Explorer 1," NASA, Jet Propulsion Laboratory, California Institute of Technology, n.d., https://nssdc.gsfc.nasa.gov/nmc/spacecraft /display.action?id=1958-002B.

23. "Vanguard 1," NASA, https://nssdc.gsfc.nasa.gov/nmc/spacecraft/dis play.action?id=1958-002B.

24. "Every NASA Budget Request, from 1961 to Now," The Planetary Society, https://www.planetary.org/space-policy/every-nasa-budget-request.

25. Alice Buck, US Department of Energy, "A History of the Energy Research and Development Administration," March 1982, https://www.energy .gov/management/articles/history-energy-research-and-development -administration.

26. Robert SanGeorge, "Focus '83: Energy Department Has New Secretary and a Fresh Lease on Life for 1983," United Press International, December 16, 1982, https://www.upi.com/Archives/1982/12/16/Focus -83-Energy-Department-has-new-secretary-amd-a-fresh-lease-on-life -for-1983/8180408862800/.

27. *The MacNeil/Lehrer Report*, episode 7171, "Reagan's Solar Policy," July 7, 1981, American Archive of Public Broadcasting, https://america narchive.org/catalog/cpb-aacip_507-8c9r20sj5v; Gregory F. Nemet,

How Solar Energy Became Cheap: A Model for Low-Carbon Innovation (London: Routledge, 2019), Kindle, 71.

28. Email from Gregory Nemet to Derek Thompson.

29. Matt Hourihan and David Parkes, American Association for the Advancement of Science, "Federal R&D Budget Trends: A Short Summary," January 2019, p. 6, fig. 8, https://www.aaas.org/sites/default /files/2019-01/AAAS%20RD%20Primer%202019_2.pdf; Nat Bullard, @NatBullard, tweet, March 26, 2023, 12:37 p.m., https://x.com/NatBul lard/status/1640060360181817344.

30. Matthew L. Wald, "U.S. Use of Renewable Energy Took a Big Fall in 2001," *New York Times*, December 8, 2002, https://www.nytimes.com /2002/12/08/us/us-use-of-renewable-energy-took-a-big-fall-in-2001 .html. Also see US Energy Information Administration, "Renewables Share of U.S. Energy Consumption Highest Since 1930s," May 28, 2015, https://www.eia.gov/todayinenergy/detail.php?id=21412.

31. "Sunspots: Germany Proves Solar Energy Is No Mirage," Knowledge at Wharton, May 30, 2012, https://knowledge.wharton.upenn.edu/article /sunspots-germany-proves-solar-energy-is-no-mirage/.

32. Joern Hoppmann, Joern Huenteler, and Bastien Girod, "Compulsive Policy-Making—the Evolution of the German Feed-In Tariff System for Solar Photovoltaic Power," *Research Policy* 43 (2014): 1422–1441, https:// scholar.harvard.edu/files/jhuenteler/files/rp_germany_pv.pdf; see p. 1426, table 2.

33. Derek Thompson, email interview with Gregory Nemet.

34. Nemet, *How Solar Energy Became Cheap*, Kindle, 185.

35. Theodore P. Wright. "Factors Affecting the Cost of Airplanes," *Journal of the Aeronautical Sciences* 3 (February 1936): 122–28, https://pdodds .w3.uvm.edu/research/papers/others/1936/wright1936a.pdf.

36. "Theodore Paul Wright," Daniel Guggenheim Medal biography, American Institute of Aeronautics and Astronautics, 1945, https://www.aiaa .org/docs/default-source/uploadedfiles/aiaa-foundation/medalist -for-1945.pdf?sfvrsn=a86c5fcc_2; "National Advisory Committee for Aeronautics, 1943," December 17, 1943, MIT Museum, https://mitmu seum.mit.edu/collections/object/GCP-00003754.

37. "Moore's Law," Intel, September 18, 2023, https://www.intel.com/con tent/www/us/en/newsroom/resources/moores-law.html#gs.h6ovyc; Gordon E. Moore, "Cramming More Components onto Integrated Circuits," *Electronics* 38, no. 8 (April 19, 1965), https://download.intel.com /newsroom/2023/manufacturing/moores-law-electronics.pdf.

38. "The End of Moore's Law Will Not Slow the Pace of Change," *Economist*, September 16, 2024, https://www.economist.com/technology-quarterly/2024/09/16/the-end-of-moores-law-will-not-slow-the-pace-of-change; Rachel Courtland, "How Much Did Early Transistors Cost? About a Billion Times More Than They Do Now," *IEEE Spectrum*, April 16, 2015, https://spectrum.ieee.org/how-much-did-early-transistors-cost.

39. Nemet, *How Solar Energy Became Cheap*, Kindle, 78, 148.

40. Institute for Energy Research, "Chinese Solar Panel Production Issues Are Mounting," November 18, 2020, https://www.instituteforenergyresearch.org/renewable/solar/chinese-solar-panel-production-issues-are-mounting/.

41. International Renewable Energy Agency, "Solar Energy," n.d., https://www.irena.org/Energy-Transition/Technology/Solar-energy#:~:text=The%20cost%20of%20manufacturing%20solar,93%25%20between%202010%20and%202020.

42. Hannah Ritchie, Max Roser, and Pablo Rosado, "Renewable Energy," December 2020, rev. January 2024, https://ourworldindata.org/renewable-energy.

43. Myra Saefong, "Why Solar Is the Fastest-Growing Source of U.S. Electricity," *MarketWatch*, July 9, 2024, https://www.marketwatch.com/story/why-solar-is-the-fastest-growing-source-of-u-s-electricity-72e7d489?tesla=y.

44. John Arnold, @JohnArnoldFndtn, tweet, September 27, 2024, 10:40 a.m., https://x.com/JohnArnoldFndtn/status/1839706693145415989.

45. "The Third Industrial Revolution," *Economist*, April 21, 2012, https://www.economist.com/leaders/2012/04/21/the-third-industrial-revolution.

46. Mariana Mazzucato, *The Entrepreneurial State: Debunking Public vs. Private Sector Myths*, rev. ed. (New York: Penguin Books, 2023), Kindle, 8.

47. Phil Goldstein, "How the Government Helped Spur the Microchip Industry," *FedTech*, September 11, 2018, https://fedtechmagazine.com/article/2018/09/how-government-helped-spur-microchip-industry.

48. Mazzucato, *The Entrepreneurial State*, Kindle, 8.

49. Stuart A. Thompson, "How Long Will a Vaccine Really Take?," *New York Times*, April 30, 2020, https://www.nytimes.com/interactive/2020/04/30/opinion/coronavirus-covid-vaccine.html.

50. Jon Cohen, "Unveiling 'Warp Speed,' the White House's America-First Push for a Coronavirus Vaccine," *Science*, May 12, 2020, https://www.sci

ence.org/content/article/unveiling-warp-speed-white-house-s-amer
ica-first-push-coronavirus-vaccine.

51. David Adler, "Inside Operation Warp Speed: A New Model for Industrial Policy," *American Affairs* 5, no. 2 (Summer 2021), https://americana
ffairsjournal.org/2021/05/inside-operation-warp-speed-a-new-mode
l-for-industrial-policy/.

52. Derek Thompson, interview with Paul Mango.

53. Paul Mango, *Warp Speed: Inside the Operation That Beat COVID, the
Critics, and the Odds* (New York: Republic Book Publishers, 2022), Kindle, loc. 1187.

54. Derek Thompson, interview with Paul Mango.

55. Alice Park, "FDA: Pfizer-BioNTech Vaccine Doesn't Need Ultra-Cold
Freezer Storage," *Time*, February 26, 2021, https://time.com/5942452
/pfizer-biontech-vaccine-cold-storage-fda/; Deb Balzer, "Inside the
Ultracold Freezers That Will House COVID-19 Vaccines," Mayo Clinic,
December 10, 2020, https://newsnetwork.mayoclinic.org/discussion
/inside-the-ultracold-freezers-that-will-house-covid-19-vaccines/.

56. "Nonex to Valor® Glass: Corning's 100-Year History of Life-Saving Innovation for Vaccine Development," Corning, n.d., https://www.corning
.com/worldwide/en/innovation/materials-science/glass/vaccine-time
line.html; Jennifer Brant and Mark F. Schultz, "Unprecedented: The
Rapid Innovation Response to COVID-19 and the Role of Intellectual
Property," International Federation of Pharmaceutical Manufacturers
and Associations, November 2021, https://www.ifpma.org/wp-content
/uploads/2023/01/i2023_Unpacking-IP_2021_Final.pdf.

57. Megan Molteni, "Vaccine Makers Turn to Microchip Tech to Beat
Glass Shortages," *Wired*, June 26, 2020, https://www.wired.com/story
/vaccine-makers-turn-to-microchip-tech-to-beat-glass-shortages/;
Bill Bostock, "Inside the US Government's $347 Million Plan to Fight
the Global Glass Vial Shortage Ahead of a Coronavirus Vaccine Rollout," *Business Insider*, June 22, 2020, https://www.businessinsider.com
/coronavirus-vaccine-glass-shortage-operation-warp-speed-corning
-sio2-2020-6; Brant and Schultz, "Unprecedented."

58. Derek Thompson, interview with Paul Mango.

59. Derek Thompson, interview with Paul Mango.

60. Mango, *Warp Speed*, Kindle, loc. 2386 and loc. 2384.

61. Derek Thompson, interview with Caleb Watney.

62. The authors thank David Adler for his analysis of OWS as a model of industrial policy. See Adler, "Inside Operation Warp Speed: A New Model

for Industrial Policy," *American Affairs* V, no. 2 (Summer 2021): 3–32, https://americanaffairsjournal.org/2021/05/inside-operation-warp -speed-a-new-model-for-industrial-policy/.

63. Hussain S. Lalani et al., "US Public Investment in Development of mRNA COVID-19 Vaccines: Retrospective Cohort Study," *BMJ Open Science* 380, no. 1 (March 2023): e073747, https://pmc.ncbi.nlm.nih.gov /articles/PMC9975718/.

64. "Lives Saved by COVID-19 Vaccines," *Journal of Paediatrics and Child Health* 10 (September 2022): 1111/jpc.16213, https://www.ncbi.nlm.nih .gov/pmc/articles/PMC9537923/.

65. Virat Agrawal, Neeraj Sood, and Christopher M. Whaley, "The Impact of the Global COVID-19 Vaccination Campaign on All-Cause Mortality," NBER Working Paper 31812, October 2023, https://www.nber.org/papers /w31812.

66. Jen Psaki, @jrpsaki, tweet, January 15, 2021, 9:44 a.m., https://x.com /jrpsaki/status/1350121790148902912?s=20.

67. Casey B. Mulligan, "We Need More 'Warp Speed' Operations," *Wall Street Journal*, October 6, 2023, https://www.wsj.com/articles/we-need -more-operation-warp-speed-covid-cancer-diabetes-bureaucracy-fda -ace77028.

68. Robert Orr, "Unmatched: Repairing the U.S. Medical Residency Pipe-line," Niskanen Center, September 2021, https://www.niskanencenter .org/wp-content/uploads/2021/09/Unmatched-Repairing-the-US-Resi dency-Pipeline.pdf, 11.

69. Orr, "Unmatched," p. 12, fig. 4.

70. "Population Growth 1980–2005," *U.S. News & World Report*, January 9, 2006, https://www.usnews.com/opinion/blogs/barone/2006/01/09/pop ulation-growth-1980-2005#:~:text=The%20nation's%20population%20 rose%2031,%2C%20and%20Tennessee%20(30).

71. Derek Thompson, "Why America Has So Few Doctors," *Atlantic*, Febru-ary 14, 2022, https://www.theatlantic.com/ideas/archive/2022/02/why -does-the-us-make-it-so-hard-to-be-a-doctor/622065/.

72. Arielle D'Souza, Kendall Hoyt, Christopher M. Snyder, and Alec Stapp, "Can Operation Warp Speed Serve as a Model for Accelerating Innova-tions Beyond COVID Vaccines?," NBER Working Paper 32831, August 2024, https://www.nber.org/papers/w32831.

73. Susan Athey, Rachel Glennerster, Nan Ransohoff, and Christopher Sny-der, "Opinion: Advance Market Commitments Worked for Vaccines. They Could Work for Carbon Removal, Too," *Politico*, December 22,

2021, https://www.politico.com/news/agenda/2021/12/22/carbon-re
moval-advance-market-commitments-525988.

74. *IPCC Sixth Assessment Report*, 2022, https://www.ipcc.ch/report/ar6
/wg3/.

75. Nan Ransohoff, "How to Start an Advance Market Commitment," *Works
in Progress* (newsletter), May 31, 2024, https://worksinprogress.co/issue
/how-to-start-an-advance-market-commitment/.

76. Derek Thompson, interview with Nan Ransohoff.

77. Vaclav Smil, "The Modern World Can't Exist Without These Four Ingredients. They All Require Fossil Fuels," *Time*, May 12, 2022, https://time
.com/6175734/reliance-on-fossil-fuels/.

78. Ben Tracy and Analisa Novak, "Cement Industry Accounts for About
8% of CO_2 Emissions. One Startup Seeks to Change That," CBS News,
January 16, 2023, https://www.cbsnews.com/news/cement-industry
-co2-emissions-climate-change-brimstone/.

79. David Wallace-Wells, @dwallacewells, tweet, January 6, 2020, 11:04
p.m., https://x.com/dwallacewells/status/1221675214259605506.

80. Hannah Ritchie, "How to Decarbonise the World's Cement," *Sustainability by Numbers* (blog), June 30, 2024, https://www.sustainabilit
ybynumbers.com/p/low-carbon-cement.

81. Derek Thompson, interview with Ned Ransohoff.

82. Derek Thompson, interview with Thomas Kalil.

83. Leopold Aschenbrenner, "Situational Awareness: The Decade Ahead,"
June 2024, 87, https://situational-awareness.ai/wp-content/uploads
/2024/06/situationalawareness.pdf.

84. Iphigenie Bera, Destiny Lara, and Damien Koh Tze-In, "GET Israel:
Topic 9—Sorek and Overall Desalination Water Supply in Israel,"
Northwestern University, September 21, 2022, https://water.northwest
ern.edu/2022/09/21/get-israel-topic-9-sorek-and-overall-desalination
-water-supply-in-israel/.

85. Sam Altman, "The Intelligence Age."

86. Derek Thompson, interview with Paul Mango.

87. Frank Newport, "Landing a Man on the Moon: The Public's View,"
Gallup, July 20, 1999, https://news.gallup.com/poll/3712/landing-man
-moon-publics-view.aspx.

88. Roger D. Launius, "Public Opinion Polls and Perceptions of US Human
Spaceflight," *Space Policy* 19, no. 3 (August 2003): 163–75, https://www
.sciencedirect.com/science/article/abs/pii/S0265964603000390.

89. Mark Whitaker, "The Dreams and Dedication Behind Our Leap to the

Moon," *Washington Post*, review of Charles Fishman, *One Giant Leap* (New York: Simon & Schuster, 2019), July 11, 2019, https://www.washing tonpost.com/outlook/the-dreams-and-dedication-behind-our-leap-to-the -moon/2019/07/11/6ae625f4-9456-11e9-b570-6416efdc0803_story.html.

Conclusion: Toward Abundance

1. Gary Gerstle, *The Rise and Fall of the Neoliberal Order: America and the World in the Free Market Era* (New York: Oxford University Press, 2022), Kindle, 153–160.

2. Dwight D. Eisenhower, "Radio and Television Address to the American People on the Tax Program," March 15, 1954, https://www.presidency .ucsb.edu/documents/radio-and-television-address-the-american-peo ple-the-tax-program.

3. Gerstle, *The Rise and Fall of the Neoliberal Order*, Kindle, 615.

4. Tom Hayden, The Port Huron Statement, written for the Students for a Democratic Society, June 15, 1962. Courtesy Office of Sen. Tom Hayden, https://images2.americanprogress.org/campus/email/PortHuronState ment.pdf.

5. Motor Carrier Act, 94 Statute 793, Public Law 96-296, 96th Congress (1980) (enacted), https://www.govinfo.gov/content/pkg/STATUTE-94 /pdf/STATUTE-94-Pg793.pdf#page=1; Airline Deregulation Act, 92 Stat ute 1705, Public Law 95-504, 95th Congress (1978) (enacted), https:// www.govinfo.gov/content/pkg/STATUTE-92/pdf/STATUTE-92-Pg1705 .pdf.

6. Tax Foundation, "Historical US Federal Individual Income Tax Rates & Brackets, 1862–2021," August 24, 2021, https://taxfoundation.org/data/all /federal/historical-income-tax-rates-brackets/; Adam Carasso and Gene Steuerle, "A Brief History of the Top Tax Rate," Tax Policy Center, Novem ber 25, 2002, https://www.urban.org/sites/default/files/publication/59856 /1000459-A-Brief-History-of-the-Top-Tax-Rate.PDF; Josephine Nesbit, "5 Presidents Who Raised Taxes the Most, and 5 Who Lowered Them: Is Trump One of Them?," Yahoo! Finance, November 5, 2024, https:// finance.yahoo.com/news/5-presidents-raised-taxes-most-140035413 .html#:~:text=Harry%20Truman%2C%201945%2D1953&text=The%20 Revenue%20Act%20of%201950,pay%20for%20the%20Korean%20War.

7. Gary Gerstle, interview with Derek Thompson.

8. Stefan Becket, "Read the Full VP Debate Transcript from the Walz- Vance Showdown," October 2, 2024, https://www.cbsnews.com/news /full-vp-debate-transcript-walz-vance-2024/.

9. Donald Trump, The Economic Club of New York, September 5, 2024, transcript of speech, p. 27, https://www.econclubny.org/documents /10184/109144/20240905_Trump_Transcript.pdf.

10. Jerusalem Demsas, "Blue States Gave Trump and Vance an Opening," *Atlantic*, October 26, 2024, https://www.theatlantic.com/politics/a rchive/2024/10/trump-vance-malthusian-housing-views/680384/.

11. George Packer, "The Empty Chamber," *New Yorker*, August 2, 2010, https://www.newyorker.com/magazine/2010/08/09/the-empty-cham ber.

12. "Read Donald Trump's Speech on Trade," *Time*, June 28, 2016, https:// time.com/4386335/donald-trump-trade-speech-transcript/.

13. Donald Trump rallies in Phoenix, Arizona (June 23, 2020), and else-where, https://www.youtube.com/watch?v=UQjTCatM0Ww.

14. Erica York, "Tariff Tracker: Tracking the Economic Impact of the Trump-Biden Tariffs," Tax Foundation, June 26, 2024, https://taxfoun dation.org/research/all/federal/trump-tariffs-biden-tariffs/.

15. Ana Swanson, "Biden Administration Clamps Down on China's Access to Chip Technology," *New York Times*, October 7, 2022, https://www .nytimes.com/2022/10/07/business/economy/biden-chip-technology .html; Michelle Toh and Kayla Tausche, "US Escalates Tech Battle by Cutting China Off from AI Chips," CNN, October 18, 2023, https://www .cnn.com/2023/10/18/tech/us-china-chip-export-curbs-intl-hnk/index .html; Department of Commerce, Bureau of Industry and Security, 15 CFR Parts 736, 738, 740, 742, 743, 772, and 774 [Docket No. 240813-0217] RIN 0694-AJ60, "Commerce Control List Additions and Revisions; Im-plementation of Controls on Advanced Technologies Consistent with Controls Implemented by International Partners," September 6, 2024, https://public-inspection.federalregister.gov/2024-19633.pdf.

16. Ana Swanson, "Biden Administration Announces Indo-Pacific Deal, Clashing with Industry Groups," *New York Times*, May 27, 2023, https://www.nytimes.com/2023/05/27/business/economy/biden-indo -pacific-trade-deal.html.

17. Joe Biden, "Remarks on Signing the Infrastructure Investment and Jobs Act," November 6, 2021, transcript by Smith Dawson & Andrews, https://www.sda-inc.com/news/remarks-by-president-biden-on-pas sage-of-the-bipartisan-infrastructure-deal/.

18. Infrastructure Investment and Jobs Act, H.R. 3684, 117th Congress (2021–2022) (enacted), https://www.congress.gov/bill/117th-congress /house-bill/3684/text; The White House, "Fact Sheet: The Bipartisan

Infrastructure Deal," November 6, 2021, https://www.whitehouse.gov /briefing-room/statements-releases/2021/11/06/fact-sheet-the-biparti san-infrastructure-deal/.

19. CHIPS and Science Act, H.R. 434, 117th Congress (2021–2022) (enacted), https://www.congress.gov/bill/117th-congress/house-bill/4346.

20. Inflation Reduction Act of 2022, H.R. 5376, 117th Congress (2021–2022) (enacted), https://www.congress.gov/bill/117th-congress/house-bill/53 76/text.

21. Harris-Walz campaign, "A New Way Forward for the Middle Class," 2024, https://kamalaharris.com/issues/; Harris-Walz campaign, "Vice President Harris Lays Out Agenda to Lower Costs for American Families," press release, August 16, 2024, https://mailchi.mp/press.kamalaharris .com/vice-president-harris-lays-out-agenda-to-lower-costs-for-american -families; Josh Boak, "Harris Campaign Releases New Ad to Highlight Plans to Build 3 Million Homes and Reduce Inflation," AP, August 27, 2024, https://apnews.com/article/harris-trump-housing-home-inflation -build-construction-00ae665790649d3b25d77a6cc0d111d0.

22. Shannon Osaka, "Biden's $7.5 Billion Investment in EV Charging Has Only Produced 7 Stations in Two Years," *Washington Post*, March 28, 2024, https://www.washingtonpost.com/climate-solutions/2024/03/28 /ev-charging-stations-slow-rollout/.

23. Karl Marx and Friedrich Engels, *The Communist Manifesto*, edited and annotated by [Frederick] Engels (1848; Chicago: Charles H. Kerr & Company, 1888), available at https://oll.libertyfund.org/titles/manifesto-of -the-communist-party.

24. "The productive forces at the disposal of society no longer tend to further the development of the conditions of bourgeois property; on the contrary, they have become too powerful for these conditions, by which they are fettered": Marx and Engels, *The Communist Manifesto*.

25. F. Scott Fitzgerald, *The Great Gatsby* (New York: Charles Scribner's Sons, 1925; critical edition published by Cambridge University Press, 1991), 21, 54.

26. *Bell Telephone Magazine*, Spring 1964, https://www.worldsfairphotos .com/nywf64/articles/bell-telephone-magazine-spring-64.pdf; Damon Darlin, "How the Future Looked in 1964: The Picturephone," *New York Times*, June 26, 2014; Bell System Pavilion (photographs), The 1964–1965 New York World's Fair, worldsfairphotos.com, Bill Cotter, updated December 27, 2022, https://www.worldsfairphotos.com /nywf64/bell-system.htm.

27. "Westinghouse Time Capsule," Westland, Jeffrey Stanton, 1997, https://www.westland.net/ny64fair/map-docs/westinghouse.htm #:~:text=A%20window%20along%20one%20side,Robert%20Mil likan%20and%20Thomas%20Mann; Westinghouse (photographs), The 1964–1965 New York World's Fair, worldsfairphotos.com, Bill Cotter, updated December 27, 2022, https://www.worldsfairphotos.com/nywf64 /bell-system.htm.

28. Futurama II (photographs and audio recording), phrenicea.com, John Herman, 2000–2011, https://www.phrenicea.com/futurama_chip.htm.

29. Lyndon B. Johnson, "Remarks at the Opening of the New York World's Fair," April 22, 1964, https://www.presidency.ucsb.edu/documents /remarks-the-opening-the-new-york-worlds-fair.

30. Gerstle, *The Rise and Fall of the Neoliberal Order*, Kindle, 167.

31. David M. Potter, *People of Plenty: Economic Abundance and the American Character* (Chicago: University of Chicago Press, 1954), 78, 210. And see George Bancroft, History of the Colonization of the United States, Vol. 1, 17th ed. (Boston: Little, Brown, and Company, 1859–75), https:// www.perseus.tufts.edu/hopper/text?doc=Perseus%3Atext%3A2001.05 .0326%3Achapter%3D8#note-link69.

Index

About the Authors

EZRA KLEIN is an opinion columnist and host of the award-winning *Ezra Klein Show* podcast at the *New York Times*. He is the author of *Why We're Polarized*, an instant *New York Times* bestseller, named one of Barack Obama's top books of 2022. He lives in Brooklyn, New York.

DEREK THOMPSON is a staff writer at the *Atlantic* and the host of the podcast *Plain English*. He is the author of the national best-seller *Hit Makers* and *On Work*, an anthology of his writing on labor and technology. He lives in Chapel Hill, North Carolina.